The Path to Forgotten Freedom

Nature Blessings

The Path to Forgotten Freedom

HEALING UNRESOLVED ANCESTRAL TRAUMA

Nicola Smalley

BuzzardPress is part of The Way of the Buzzard Limited,
Anglezarke, Lancashire, UK

Copyright © 2022 Nicola Smalley

A catalogue version is available at the British Library

First paperback edition October 2022

Book cover design by Jason Conway

Printed and bound in Bulgaria by Pulsio Print

ISBN 978-1-7391669-0-8

www.thewayofthebuzzard.co.uk

For the forgotten ones: those ancestors
whose stories haven't been heard

A time there was, ere England's griefs began,
When every rood of ground maintained its man;
For him light labour spread her wholesome store,
Just gave what life required, but gave no more:
His best companions, innocence and health;
And his best riches, ignorance of wealth.

Oliver Goldsmith, *The Deserted Village, 1770*

Contents

INTRODUCTION

The home that I share with my husband, Jason, looks out across Anglezarke Moor, perched on the edge of the West Pennine Moors. This wild landscape has claimed me. Despite being only thirty minutes' drive from Manchester, it isn't widely known about. I can spend hours up there and not see anyone.

Anglezarke is rich in history. Dating back to prehistoric times, there are the remains of Bronze Age settlements and several burial mounds. My favourite places, however, aren't the places of the Neolithic people. They are the ruined homes of the farmers of the nineteenth and twentieth centuries. These twenty or so ruined farmsteads were once homes to families, cleared by the Water Board to create reservoirs to quench the thirst of Liverpool workers during the Industrial Revolution. It is known as the Anglezarke Clearances. Evicted from their homes many of these country dwellers moved into the surrounding towns to work the mills. Some people chose not to leave the moorland and, instead, took their own lives.

When I sit amongst these ruins, something awakens in me. The windows still exist in some of the buildings and I love to look through them across the moorland. I feel melancholy as my eyes fix upon the same windswept grassland that they would have looked upon as each season passed, summer to autumn, winter to spring. I can make out the rooms in some of the homes and barns, and still see the furrows where they ploughed the soil. These are the homes of Jason's distant relatives: his great-great-great-grandparents and beyond. Knowing this has made me wonder about the ruined homes of my ancestors.

Whilst researching my family tree, I found out that my ancestors were also cleared from their land. They too had to close the door on their homes for the final time to make their way to the engine houses of the Industrial Revolution and take their chances at a life in the slums of Victorian Britain.

The story in this book is about the life of one of my ancestors, my great-great-great-grandmother Catherine Riley. In the telling of this tale, I reflect on what it might have been like to be forced to leave everything: family, community, land, the ability to grow food. I explore what might happen when someone sets off to a foreign place to forge a life amongst hundreds of thousands of strangers. This would have been such a contrast to growing up in a close-knit community where you knew every person you met. It has made me wonder what effect this would have had on a person, and what impact there might be on future generations.

Two hundred years might seem like a long time ago: long enough that it bears no relevance today. However, Catherine was my great-grandad's grandmother. I feel that if I'd met my great-grandad, and he had known his grandmother, Catherine, he would've told me stories about her. In tribal life, this is the way. However, there were no stories passed down about Catherine. When I came to research my family tree, I found that she was the unknown ancestor: the person where the line stopped. With my other family lines, I know the names of all of my other great-great-great-grandparents, and in many cases one or two generations beyond them.

Why was this ancestor hidden from me? I kept on picking up and putting this down for almost a whole decade until at last, I found Catherine's records. Through researching my family tree, I have uncovered many stories about my ancestors, but hers is the most heart-wrenching of all. Catherine came to

London after fleeing Ireland at the time of the Great Famine. She experienced a lifetime of despair and destitution that is beyond most people's comprehension today.

What I have found through undertaking ancestral research is that such secrets, stories buried away, are far from quiet. In fact, they have the loudest voices of all. Catherine's story was waiting for me in amongst the dusty pages of archival records, waiting to come to light at the right time. Her story is an amplification of a scenario playing out in the world today: one of power and powerlessness, privilege and poverty. I can understand through her story the consequence of being born into a world where there are landowners and people without land, where people have lost their connection to the earth, where they are living in a world of oppression and control. Catherine's story also shows me the things people are driven to do because of shame. This is a shame that hides in dark corners.

THE STORY

I tell Catherine's story through this book and offer my interpretation on how the scenario of power and powerlessness impacted on my ancestors. I reflect on how this scenario is still playing out in our world and share how it impacts on me and the choices I make in my life. I also provide practical suggestions to overcome these impacts based on my experiences. There are some parts of her story that are based on fact, and other parts where I have used creative licence in order to fill in the gaps. It is important to me that I distinguish what is fact and what is fiction, so I will give an overview here and then go into more detail in the appendix.

Finding her story

Catherine left a greater paper trail behind her than my other ancestors because she was so poor. Yet, I could easily have never told her story because there are parts that remain hidden.

The part covering the second half of Catherine's life in London is based on facts. I've gathered information such as details about Catherine's children, where she lived and what she did for work at the time of each census. To turn this data into a story, I have had to delve into the depths of the imaginal realm. Where there is data missing, I have filled in the gaps through shamanic journeying, observing my dreams and my thoughts as I mused over various points and visited the places where my ancestors lived. I have drawn inspiration from novels, many written during the nineteenth century, and watching films about poverty in London and Ireland during the early Victorian period. I have undertaken historical research by studying books and watching documentaries, as well as visiting museums and having conversations with the staff who work there about what life was like for the people alive at that time.

Unfortunately, I don't have any records covering the period of the first half of Catherine's life when she lived in Ireland. I don't know which part of Ireland she was from. Frustratingly any records I have simply refer to her place of birth as 'Ireland'. I've made two trips to Belfast to search through the public record archives looking for birth or marriage records relating to her and her family, but with no success. Without her maiden name and place of birth, it's like looking for a needle in a haystack.

This is coupled with the reality that only half of parish records in Ireland have survived. There are barely any census records. This is one of the reasons it has taken me so long to write this story. Without knowledge of the exact location she was from, I struggled. However, in time I came to the conclusion that I could write her story without this knowledge. What I lack in information about her life in Ireland I make up for using the records I have from her time in London.

During my research phase, I had a dream one night of a location immediately to the east of Belfast in Ulster. So, I have based her story in County Down.

In order to tell this story, I've developed personalities for the characters of Catherine and her family. This has been combined with the historical facts about Catherine's life acquired through ancestral research. The sources and details can be found at the back of this book. Writing this story is a huge responsibility. I have had to use my imagination to fill in the gaps, create personalities and describe emotions about someone I do not know. I feel the weight of this.

I found it challenging to write about a period in history where there is so much complexity. This is the time of the Great Famine in Ireland that was preceded by almost seven hundred years of English rule. I am not able to cover historical details in depth. Also, I feel uneasy writing about Irish history as an English person. It was my country that inflicted atrocities on Ireland and I have had to find my way through this in order to complete the book.

HEALING THE LINES

This book is a practical guide for readers who are interested in ancestral healing and working with genealogical research to tell their ancestors' stories. In recent years I have noticed that more and more people are developing an interest in researching their family tree. I believe there is a reason, as these stories need to come up and out into the world. There is great healing to be achieved through this process.

Here I offer advice on researching a family tree and outline the healing practices that I've used to help heal ancestral wounds. As a shamanic practitioner, I offer examples of how to use the shamanic toolkit in the healing process. For example, practices such as shamanic journeying and ceremony, soul exchange and psycho-pomping. These terms are not widely known about or used in modern Western culture. They are about spiritual connection and healing practices of nature-based peoples of the world. These are indigenous communities who survive today and from whose ancient wisdom and practices there is so much to learn.

This book is for anyone who has an interest in bringing their hidden family stories into the light, to heal any resulting trauma that has been passed down the family line. It will also be of interest to people who are exploring the idea of there being a different narrative of our world: one which from my experience we weren't taught at school. There are some boundaries to this that I'd like to set out here in terms of what this book does not cover.

The methodology I discuss will be difficult to apply if the reader has been adopted and cannot research their birth parents. If you were adopted and want to connect with your ancestors, I'd recommend Daniel Foor's book *Ancestral Medicine: Rituals for Personal and Family Healing.*[1] Also, David Furlong's *Healing Your Ancestral Patterns: How to access the past to heal the present.*[2]

In this book, I share methods that can heal ancestral trauma, but I do not go into the specifics of the kinds of trauma that can be reconciled. If this is of interest, I recommend Mark Wolynn's book *It Didn't Start With You: How Inherited Family Trauma Shapes Who We Are and How to End the Cycle,*[3] and *Ancestral Continuum: Unlock the Secrets of Who You Really Are* by Natalia O'Sullivan and Nicola Graydon.[4]

Finally, I don't go into any detail as to how to determine whether an illness or condition a person is experiencing is ancestral. In my experience, when someone has explored a number of different avenues of healing without any ongoing success, they may find they have an intuitive feeling that it's ancestral. That gut feeling is rarely wrong.

REWRITING THE STORY

Catherine's story shines a light on so many of the issues humanity is facing today. It has not been possible to cover them all.

If I had felt that I needed to, I would never have started this book. For example, I am aware that the themes of the oppression of women and oppression by the Church running through Catherine's story have not been addressed. I have chosen to focus on the themes that are most present with me, knowing and trusting that someone else has and is writing about the other topics. I am in no doubt that more material will come up from my unconscious for me to work with over the coming years. What I have learnt about ancestral healing is that it's an ongoing process with many layers to work through over time.

I am also aware that I am writing this book from my position as a white privileged person. I find it very hard to imagine being poor and powerless. I have done my best. What I do know is that this book is about slavery in the widest sense. I know that there are many kinds of slavery. I would like to acknowledge here that people of colour and ethnic minorities have suffered greatly from oppression throughout history and up to the present day, and that while white people have more privilege in the world, the stories of oppression everywhere need to be told and heard.

Hope for the future

I have strong views about the injustice in the world that I've been born into, the ongoing high level of oppression and how this plays out in people's lives. I speak of this throughout the book, but here I'd like to state my hopes for the future. I would like to see wealth more evenly distributed and people's health and well-being put above profitable gain for the minority. I'd like to see our planet, the air, water, animals, plants and rocks all cared for with the respect they deserve. I'd like to see a government elected that puts the people before their own interests. I'd like to see the media give a fair and true account of facts rather than being used to manipulate the masses for the benefit of a few wealthy and corrupt individuals. I'd like to see a move away from the capitalist model, which if left unchecked for many more years will be the downfall of humanity.

I realise these are big asks and yet there is incredible work being undertaken in all of these areas. Fundamental system changes are required. I find it empowering that on an individual level I can start to live in this new world today, by taking steps that are within my own capability to move closer towards this vision I hold for the future.

New ground

Several years ago, I had a dream where I was watching a play acted out through mime. There was a pivotal moment where I wept and wept as I heard these words spoken: "Her skin marked with no scars, unblemished like the day she was born. So pure, please keep her. Such a joy to see and be in the presence of. Such a thing of beauty to behold."

This dream highlights to me how difficult the world is that I have been born into. I believe the spiritual work is to strip off all the layers of conditioning, delve beneath all the wounds and scars accumulated through life, to find that wild, pure, free spirit that lies deep within the core essence of us. This is the spiritual awakening process. As I stepped into my spiritual awakening, I had the feeling of straddling two worlds and each year this seems to become more pronounced. There is the old world, a paradigm that is falling away. This is a paradigm of slavery, of power and powerlessness, of disassociation from the land, of domestication and conditioning. Then there is the new world, a paradigm that is forming. This is a paradigm where people are free, wild, untainted and undamaged. This is the world I am helping to build and it feels like uncharted territory. I am forging a new path and there isn't much ground to stand on.

To do this work I need to stand firm in my position, moving into the new paradigm and yet with a foot in the old one. I am the bridge between the two worlds. It is a difficult place and I am living through a challenging time. Yet I am not here alone: there are many who stand on these burning coals alongside me. We support each other, and every year I am uplifted to see more and more people amassing together. One day I hope the balance will tip and we will at last live in a different world: one where each of us can see in the other their true beauty and not feel the need to have power or control over anybody.

I have come to realise I can't avoid being controversial in this space. As hard as this is, I need to keep on going and let the muscle get stronger. Through this book, I am standing in my truth and rewriting my own story: changing the core language that has played out in my life up until this point. This is the work. This is *my* work. I am delighted to be sharing this with you, and I am honoured that you are here with me, ready to embark on this journey. I believe that great things await us both in this place.

CHAPTER 1

SCENE SETTING

It was my fifth day without food and a new kind of exhaustion had set in. My body was weak, and I was struggling to concentrate on the simplest of tasks. Just standing up and walking a few paces was a struggle. I hadn't seen anybody or spoken a word for over one hundred hours. Yet I wasn't lonely. Far from it; I had grown to know every square inch of the woodland glade I'd made my home. I had found a new kind of intimacy with the wildlife, trees, insects, mosses and lichens who I now considered to be my friends. Every evening, I witnessed silver jewels form in cobwebs as the sun set. That particular night I saw stars move from the sky and rest in amongst the trees. I had come some way to learning the secret language of the forest.

This was the final morning of my wilderness vigil. I was coming to the end of this ancient tradition that still holds importance for indigenous communities across the world. For four days and nights, I had survived on my own in a spot in the forest, alone with just my thoughts, a few things to keep me warm and dry, some water and my journal.

Dawn finally arrived after the longest of nights. Instead of sleeping, I had leant against the ivy-covered trunk of an oak tree and stared into the thing I am most scared of above all else: looking into the heart of the dark forest. It had been a long dark night of the soul, and fear had presented itself, but I was spared the cold sweats. I had discovered it isn't possible to be terrified indefinitely. Once the terror has moved through, a calmness prevails – a submission to the unknown.

The sun rose up through the tree canopy and I left my ivy-covered back support and packed my tarp into my rucksack. I stepped out of that forest glade and traced my footsteps back to base camp. At the time, as I picked my way through holly bushes and climbed over fallen trees, I had no idea what the significance of that date was.

Ancestral ties

What I discovered a few months later was that the morning I left my wilderness vigil on 12 June 2018 was a significant date. This was exactly one hundred and forty-two years since my great-great-great-grandmother Catherine Riley drew her final breath to end the grimmest of lives. She died alone in one of the world's greatest horrors of civilisation, the workhouse. This was an institution built to house the destitute and designed to strip the very soul from a human being. In this book, I tell Catherine's extraordinary story where she survived against all odds. I have no idea how I would have coped in her situation. She was severed from her homeland as a young woman, survived famine and was plunged into the slums of Victorian London to carve out a life of destitution.

At the time of my wilderness vigil, I didn't know of the correlation between our lives. I had only recently discovered who she was after centuries of her story lying buried in basement archives as data on dusty pages. Catherine lived two centuries ago – in the nineteenth century. With my feet firmly in the twenty-first century, how could her life possibly be affecting me now? Yet, during those four days alone in a dark wood, with my stomach knotted with hunger and my energy waning with every sunset, she was very much in my thoughts. It has taken several years to unpick why.

In recent years I have learned that Catherine's life, her

experiences, what she endured, has everything to do with my life now. She is my determination and drive, my guilt and shame. She is my destructive work ethic and my disconnect from my land. She is my trauma and grief, my powerlessness and power. She is my inspiration and my compassion. She is my despair at the oppressive system that has been endured for generations. She is my longing for a different world. She is my hope. She is all of this and so much more.

In this book, I am going to take you on a journey to explain all. This work sits at the interface between socio-political history, genealogy, Shamanism, epigenetics, dreamwork and the therapeutic process. I stumbled upon this interface by chance, although nothing is ever by chance. I have been guided by an invisible hand along the way, the same invisible hand that has led me to write this book.

The forgotten ones

How much better do you feel when someone has sat down and really listened to you? When someone has taken the time to understand your life, the reasons you made certain decisions, and how the path has been woven into the place you are in now? I know in my life when someone has sat down and listened to me, it has made all the difference. What impact does it have on you when you hear someone's story spoken from the heart? There is great healing that takes place when we listen and are heard. When stories are shared, emotions are stirred within us. We can draw on each other's experiences to help make sense of our own. This is true now and it was true for our ancestors who stand behind us, listening and guiding us.

How do we go about finding their stories? We live in a culture where our ancestors aren't honoured, and their stories aren't passed on. We may know a few anecdotes from our parents and grandparents, but this rarely goes back more than three generations. Indigenous communities have rituals and practices that ensure the stories of their ancestors are kept alive. Yet, we have no such thing in our culture anymore. On the contrary, the opposite happens. History was written by the winners: those people who lived a privileged life and were able to read and write. Their narrative, from their perspective, is shared with the world. I grew up believing that their side of the story was 'the truth' and did not consider that there might be another version of events. Many people in Western culture don't know much about their families' lives from several generations ago because of the way history was told. They aren't necessarily aware of the conditions endured by our ancestors or the power that was taken from them. When I was taught about the Industrial Revolution and the Victorian era at school, it was used as an example of how far humanity has come and how civilisation is a 'marvellous' thing.

What are those untold stories? What about the stories of the 'marginalised', stories of the downtrodden; the casualties of a civilised world? Do these stories matter?

Stories that matter

From the work I have done in uncovering my ancestors' stories, my answer is yes. They matter, and more than we can possibly imagine. I will explain why through the words on these pages. This book is dedicated to the forgotten ones; the people who haven't been talked about. It will present one of these stories. The year I began writing this book, 2020, marks the 200th anniversary of Catherine's birth. There is no better time to bring her story to the world. Catherine's story has claimed me and has gone to work in the dark corners of my psyche. By sharing it with the world, I wonder how it will unfold within you as it has within me.

We will spend much of our time during this book exploring events that happened in the nineteenth century, and you may ask what relevance someone's life who was born two centuries ago has on us now. With the fallout of capitalism reaching an all-time high, climate change, political oppression, poverty and inequality, why should we look back to the past?

My response to this is that this is exactly the place we should look to, and I am not alone in that thinking. The Dalai Lama was asked his opinion on the most powerful meditation we can do to help heal the world. He replied:

> Critical thinking followed by action. Discern what your world is. Know the plot, the scenario of this human drama. Then figure out where your talents might fit into making a better world.[5]

In order to help me find my place in moving forward, my method of 'knowing the plot' has been to look back at what has happened throughout the history of Western civilisation. I would argue there is no better place to look than how our ancestors played a role in shaping the world we live in today. Their lives are relevant because the experiences they endured are passed down in our genes. Within our DNA, their trauma lies in the very cells that make up our being. To understand how this works, we need to dip into the science of epigenetics.

Epigenetics

I will give a brief overview here of relevant epigenetic theory. We humans inherit our physical characteristics from our parents through DNA, such as eye colour, hair type, facial expressions, and our mannerisms. During genetic studies, scientists were surprised to find that physical characteristics contributed to only 2 per cent of a person's DNA. It was assumed that the remaining 98 per cent was blank and it was labelled 'noncoding DNA', or 'junk DNA'.

Recent scientific evidence has revealed that this is not the case. The junk DNA is now known to hold genetic memory about inherited emotional, behavioural and personality traits.⁶ The types of things that affect this noncoding DNA are environmental conditions, such as exposure to toxins or poor nutrition, and stress. To me, this research makes sense as this is how animals can pass down information to help their offspring survive. Through this evolutionary process an animal can teach offspring what is dangerous and a threat to their survival.

With this in mind, if our ancestors experienced a traumatic incident and they hadn't the opportunity to process this trauma, it was coded into their genes and passed on. When I look at the stories of my ancestors, I can see there are all kinds of events that would have resulted in trauma. For example, the circumstances under which someone leaves behind a community and a way of life, the death of a child, the death of a husband leaving the family destitute, the withdrawal of a mother's attention, and forbidden love. All of these experiences would have had the effect of diminishing support and restricting the flow of love in a family, resulting in trauma. There is the potential that some of these traumas were left unresolved.

However, it stands to reason that if this noncoding DNA can be altered in one way, it can be modified the other way too. Through the science of epigenetics, we now know that these inherited emotional traits that are in our DNA can be changed. We can literally recode our DNA. This means that we are born with the ability to heal ourselves and rewrite that which we inherited. This is very empowering, as once we have the origin of these traumas in view, long-standing family patterns can finally be laid to rest.

Let me give you another example to help explain this. In his book *It Didn't Start with You*, Mark Wolynn shares the results of an experiment.⁷ It involves the testing on animals, something I don't necessarily find right or agree with; however, the results of this are interesting.

Mice were exposed to the scent of cherry blossom and at the same time, given an electric shock. As you can imagine, the electric shock caused the mice discomfort. That set of mice had offspring and when those mice were adults, the scientists exposed them to the same scent of cherry blossom, only this time they didn't give them the electric shock. They found that the physical reaction of the mice when smelling the cherry blossom was exactly the same as their parents who had received the electric shock: they ran about in their cage in a frenzy.

Then a third generation of mice were born, the grandchildren of the original group of mice. This third generation of mice were exposed to the scent of cherry blossom, and they ran around the cage in a frenzy too, without ever having received an electric shock.

What this study shows us is that learned behaviours to a situation are passed down in the genes through at least two generations of mice. During my research into human epigenetics in humans, some of the theories suggest that genetic coding can be passed down four generations, and others more than fourteen generations. From my personal experience with healing my family lines, I can see it lasting at least seven generations.

The seventh generation

In my ancestral healing work, I go back seven generations for two reasons. Firstly, because of the Seventh Generation Principle, which takes its name from the Great Law of the Iroquois, the five Native American tribes of northeast North America.[8] This philosophy isn't unique to just this nation, however, as many Native American nations, tribes and other indigenous people around the world still live by this code.

Under the Seventh Generation Principle, when a decision is made, consideration is given to what the impact will be to future generations, specifically seven generations down the line. I came across this principle when I worked in corporate sustainability. Sustainability professionals work to achieve 'sustainable development', which was defined by the United Nations in 1987 as 'meeting the needs of the present without compromising the ability of future generations to meet their own needs'.[9] However, thinking ahead this far is not a luxury the model of capitalism can endure. Capitalism is about growth today rather than holding back through a concern of future generations. During my time spent working as a sustainability manager for large corporations, I found that the senior management teams are not usually thinking more than five years ahead. This concept of sustainable development in the context of a capitalist society was perhaps only ever an ideal. However, it was one that stayed with me when I left that career.

When I came to explore the field of ancestral healing, my exposure to the Seventh Generation Principle shaped my focus. I was interested in what was happening seven generations ago. I began to think about what decisions my ancestors would have made that are impacting me now. This led me to wonder what decisions the privileged people were making around the same time: the laws that were passed that impacted on my ancestors, and in turn on me. What I found was that two hundred years ago there was an unprecedented change in my ancestors' lives. There was a mass migration of people leaving rural areas across the British Isles and moving into cities, the powerhouses of the Industrial Revolution. As their right to the land they had farmed for generations was taken away by the government, with no means to feed themselves, millions of people moved from country dwellings into the slums of Victorian Britain.

Many people who lived seven generations ago were the last who had land or access to land. With land came the autonomy of growing your own food. Once that was taken away, these landless people were forced to work for someone else, leaving them open to being controlled by the privileged. Many of my fifth and sixth generation ancestors moved to the Victorian slums where they and their descendants remained for the next century. It is these stories that grab my attention. I believe this powerlessness was encoded into their DNA and passed down the ancestral line. Six generations on, I'm finding it hard to step into a feeling of being free. I believe that until I can uncover my ancestral stories and expose the unresolved trauma experienced by my ancestors, I will always be caught in this pattern of repression.

GENEALOGY & STORIES

How do we go about exploring the lives of our ancestors in order to uncover these stories? For some people, it is possible to get back to the stories and information of our great grandparents by speaking with our parents or grandparents. A lot of healing work can be carried out at this level. However, in order to get to the root cause of an inherited trauma, it's often necessary to go back further in the ancestral line. This involves researching official records through the process of genealogy.

What excites me about blending the science of epigenetics with genealogy is that through the records, we can go back further and put names to our ancestors that lived hundreds of years ago. We can see where they lived, what they did for work, information about their family, how they died. In just a few days, this information can be found through online ancestral databases. I began this process over a decade ago. I researched back along a number of lines to build up my family tree and before long I had over two hundred names, all with occupations and the places where they lived.

However, it is necessary to look beyond the demographic census data to get a more in-depth understanding of a family member. Behind every one of these names is a hero or heroine in a story of their world. It is meaningful to look beyond the statistical information to explore the story people have to tell.

I combined genealogy with research into social and political history, have read books, visited museums, watched films and documentaries to inform me of the period in history when my ancestors lived. I have been able to see what it was like at the time these ancestors were alive and how this might have impacted them. Also, I have created a biography for many of my ancestors and considered what kind of traumas they might have experienced. I have given these people a voice. This is an important part of the work, as I believe my ancestors lost their voices when they lost their land.

When I began researching my family tree, Catherine's story was the one that most interested my family because my maiden name was Riley. The story my great-grandfather told my grandfather was that we came from Ireland, but no one knew when, how or why we came to live in England. The information I was most interested in was the hardest to find. It took me eight years to solve. I wonder now whether it was because it was waiting for me to be ready to find it. I was in a different space when I began this work and wouldn't have approached Catherine's story in this level of detail. Stones would have been left unturned.

THE TRANSFORMATION

This work has a funny way of unfolding. I was in a very different place in my life when I first embarked on this research. I felt trapped in a stressful job. I had constant demands on my time and felt I was being pulled in many directions, none of which felt like they gave me any choices.

Now I am in a very different place and I am in control of my time. I work for myself rather than for a corporation. I spend my days working from home or outside on Anglezarke Moor, which is a mile or so from where I live in Lancashire. I travel and work in the national parks in the northwest of England in my little red van. No day is the same and I have few places to be and few things to do for a specific time. Many things have played out for me to get to this place, including my ancestral healing work and the wilderness vigil.

Healing work

The writing of this book has been a part of my healing process. Through telling Catherine's story and reframing it from one of shame to heroism, I have rewritten my own core language. Mark Wolynn introduced me to the concept of inherited core language in his book *It Didn't Start with You*.[10] Wolynn shares examples of how he worked with clients to trace back the origin of their inherited core language. In his approach he goes back to their great grandparents, four generations ago. I have gone much further, to seven generations and have found great benefit in researching this far back. Catherine is my great-great-great-grandmother and my sixth-generation ancestor, and her parents are the seventh generation. Through Catherine's story, I have identified what my core language was, and through the writing of this book, I have rewritten this. In this process I have found my voice.

One of the concepts throughout this book is taking back control of my time. This is an ongoing process. It is also one of the things we teach at The Way of the Buzzard. This is a community of seekers who have a love and fascination for nature, and a thirst to learn about the old ways. Through The Way of the Buzzard, Jason and I help people unlock the secrets of ancient wisdom and nature's insights and lead a more connected, creative and empowered life. This book forms part of the work and is an extension of all of the techniques I describe here that we teach through our online membership site, The Mystery School.[11]

This work is a form of activism. I believe it is an act of revolution to live a life that was not accessible to our ancestors. Events in recent history, such as the clearances of people from their land, has led us to lose our connection to the Earth. My passion is to explore the lives of the people where this connection was lost. Through this process I can get a sense of the traumas that are unresolved, going back to the point it all started and reweaving the web. To do this ancestral healing work we need to understand the lives these ancestors lived, and then decide how best we can rewrite these stories through our lives.

It is said that there is one person who is born into every family whose role it is to do the healing on behalf of all the family. The fact you are reading this book suggests that is you. This is such important work. Without unpicking and listening to our ancestors' stories, how is the healing going to happen? Who else is going to care enough?

So, we are going to travel back in time now to Victorian Britain. We are going to follow Catherine's journey, which began in amongst the hedge-lined meadows of Ireland and finished in the smoke-filled Victorian power engine of London. Each chapter follows the same format. I will begin by giving an insight into Catherine's life, and then offer a narrative of how I have worked with this aspect of her story and the things it has brought up in me. I will conclude each chapter by sharing practices I have followed so you, too, can begin to heal the wounds that have been passed down your line.

Are you ready to begin the journey? Let's head off to nine-teenth-century Ireland together. May the adventure begin.

CHAPTER 2

Leaving the Ancestral Lands

Catherine hauled her tired body up the steps to the ferry ticket office. She had reached a new depth of exhaustion, and the uncertainty about the journey ahead weighed heavily on her mind. By her side stood her husband William, greatly weakened from the toll of the past few years living in famine-stricken Ireland.

They had set off two days ago and walked across County Down after selling all of their belongings to raise money for the journey to London. Hunger was a permanent acquaintance and their threadbare clothes hung off their slight frames, but their greatest concern was for the child Catherine carried in her belly. This was the point of no return and all they could hope for now were better times across the other side of the Irish Sea.

They had held out for as long as they could, but it was now time to make the long trip to England to seek out Catherine's brother who was living in London. He had emigrated years before to find work and had written to them several times. In his last letter, over a year ago, he described the terrible afflictions of the Irish in London and begged his sister not to join him. But how could anywhere be worse than Ireland right now? Catherine and William would surely both be dead by winter if they stayed. The only thing to do now was to look across the Irish Sea for a new life.

It had been heart-wrenching for Catherine to say goodbye to her mother and father, who were too old to muster the energy or desire to leave their homeland. 'We've lived our lives and we will die here in Ireland, but you Catherine, you have so much more life ahead of you,' they said to her.

Catherine took a glance over her shoulder at the crowds of people gathered in the harbour. So many people were all seeking passage to a strange new world, all with their own sorrowful story leading them to this godforsaken place. Pushing the ticket office door open, Catherine and William stepped inside and secured their passage to Liverpool on a ship leaving in three days time. They couldn't afford the fare to America and with family in London it was the best place for them to go.

With their ferry tickets safely tucked away, the next task was to find lodgings. They had two priorities in mind: cheapness and convenience to get to the docks. There was little choice as the city was so overcrowded, but they found a basement room in a street close to the harbour. They climbed down the stairs and entered a windowless room, where, entwined with the smell of damp, there were at least ten other people: men, women and children all lying side-by-side. A bucket was in the corner of the room for the necessaries, and as far as Catherine could see there was no room for more bodies, as slight as they were.

William guided her through the dim light to a space by the wall where they could both squeeze in. This would be their temporary home until the ship was ready to sail. They needed to be careful not to spend the money they had set aside for their journey across to England and onto London. They had heard stories of how some never managed to leave Ireland because their ship had been delayed. These people had ended up spending what little money they had and were forced to become servants without pay.

Catherine and William had managed to raise enough for the journey, with a little extra to tide them over until William could get work. They held onto their money tightly. The noise and the smells made sleep a challenge, but Catherine was so tired from her journey she managed to get some rest. At least this was a warm place to shelter from the cold night air.

The day came for their sailing and they made their way to the dock. As they approached the ship, Catherine looked up at its tall masts. She had never seen anything as big as this ship before. Her weary eyes moved across to the men loading sacks onto the ship. Barley, wheat and oats were being loaded on and stored underneath in the hold. She noticed the same happening to other ships further up the docks. All around her, there was food; food grown by the toil of Irish people, and it was setting sail for England. This food should have been in Irish bellies, but it was destined for wealthier lands. She spoke the same words to William she had said over recent years: 'Why do they let us Irish starve when there is so much food?'

They walked up the ramp to the deck and took their place standing alongside hundreds of other Irish emigrants, all ema- ciated and forlorn. They were human cargo, who were not given the luxury of shelter like the sacks of grain were. She was grateful that it wasn't a wet day. She had heard talk in the port over the past few days of the journey between Belfast and Liverpool being the worst an emigrant ever has to endure. When conditions were rough, cattle rather than people were given cover. People died on the deck in cold weather from exposure to the snow and hail. She was relieved they were leaving before winter.

The ship set sail and moved slowly out of the harbour. She grabbed William's hand as they looked back at the Irish coast. They would never see their homeland again. She felt a new emptiness running right through her core as she watched the green fields slowly diminishing until they were swallowed by the mist. All she had of her beloved country now were her memories. She allowed her mind to drift back to happier times for a while.

Before the famine

In 1834, on the summer of her fourteenth birthday, Catherine had gone to a hiring fair just as her brothers and sisters before her had done to find work. She was hired by a farmer and his wife and had enjoyed her time working for them. Over the years she worked her way up in service to attain positions with greater responsibility. It was hard work and she was on the go all day to well beyond teatime, but she had learnt a lot about how to keep a larger house. It was very different to growing up in her mother and father's cottage with only two rooms. The farmhouse had several floors with four rooms upstairs and four rooms downstairs. She had learnt to knit, sew, clean, tidy, wash and cook, but she enjoyed her work by the hearth most. There was a lot of cooking and mouths to feed, with three other servant girls and three labouring boys. Her day would begin early in the morning before the family woke. The first job was to build the large fire needed to begin cooking the day's food and to prepare the porridge, which had been soaked and cooked slowly overnight. Every day bread was baked. The main meal was prepared for the evening, which was either a stew or soup cooked in one pot over the fire. Overnight, bread would go as hard as a brick, so they would fry it in fat to make Ulster Fry. They also made potato bread from butter, flour and potato moulded into cakes, then rolled out and baked on the griddle. Catherine reminisced that during those years at the big farmhouse she never went a day without a meal.

She had fond memories of her time growing up as a young girl too. Catherine's mother and father were tenant farmers for a wealthy family who had come over from Scotland a few hundred years before and owned a thousand acres of land. Her mother and father rented sixteen acres from them, with around a quarter of this being rough grazing for sheep. The good land was used to grow oats, barley, wheat and flax for linen, which was sold to pay the rent. There were around eight or nine potato beds, where they grew their potatoes to have food to eat throughout the year. There were also cabbages and turnips, and they had a pig and some chickens.

Catherine's father was a weaver. The whole family lived and slept in one room, whilst the other room housed the weaving loom. Catherine, her mother and her sisters would prepare the flax they had grown and spin this into thread, ready for the weaving. Other tenants who didn't have their own weaving loom would sell their thread to her father and he would also weave this into linen.

They welcomed the steady income. The linen trade in the north was one of the few exports that Ireland had, as the government of the day imposed restrictions on trading anything else. These restrictions kept the rest of Ireland very poor, but here in County Down, there was a little more money to go around the tenant farmers.

Catherine had met William at the big farmhouse when she was sixteen years old. He was hired through the hiring fair too, a few years after she had first been employed. William was a farm labourer who had travelled from County Cavan looking for work in the wealthier Ulster provinces. For the first few years he had left each winter and returned the following spring. Each year she hoped he would return, and return he did.

She spoke of him to her family, but there was resistance as he was Catholic and her family were Protestant. There was tension in the years running up to Catherine's twenty-first birthday. William hoped to ask her father for his daughter's hand in marriage.

When William did ask, her father had said no, but Catherine prevailed. She had a strong spirit and talked her father round. She explained that William had many virtues that were well sought after in a husband. These were the kind a father would want from a man his daughter was to marry, if he hadn't been of the other religion. William was skilled with the soil and had a gift of turning poor land into good. He could turn his hand to any manner of building work. Her father eventually agreed on the condition that their children were brought up as Protestants.

Catherine and William married in 1841 and made their home on four acres of rough grazing land. They worked hard to improve the soil. They kept one-quarter of an acre of land for growing potatoes, which they would eat. They grew them in lazy beds that William created by piling up the soil and separating them with narrow trenches. He layered piles of manure on top to enrich the soil that he brought over from the big farmhouse. He would plant the seed potatoes in March and April and the young foliage was visible in May, but the first crop wasn't ready to harvest until late July at the earliest. A good harvest would see them comfortably through to the winter. They just needed to store the potatoes in an underground pit, sealed from the elements to keep them from rotting.

The rest of the land was planted with wheat, oats and flax to pay the landlord his rent. To bring in some extra money to help see them through the winter months, William would do seasonal labouring work for the big farmhouse. Catherine would spin flax for her father to weave into linen too.

Catherine and William had built their cottage themselves from local stone and given it a straw-thatched roof. They refrained from installing a window as this would increase the rent and instead, they had a half door to let the light in. Inside, their cottage was simple, but cosy. They had a mud floor and a fireplace on the far side of the room, over which hung a large iron cooking pot. There was a single chair on one side of the fire and, on the other side, a basket of potatoes. Catherine liked to always have something cooking on the fire. Their room was always filled with the smell of freshly baked bread, vegetable stew and oatcakes. She made these out of oat flour, salt and water; they were rolled first thing and leaned up close to the fire on a harnan iron. This is a round metal stand placed close to the fire. In the corner of the room, opposite the door, they had a settle bed with a straw mattress. This was a seat in the day and a box to sleep on at night. As their family grew, they would all sleep here together.

For the first years of their marriage, they got by comfortably and were blessed with two daughters. However, Catherine lost her first child soon after the birth. This was a heart-wrenching episode, but not unusual among families as children would often die before their time. Her second daughter was strong and determined to live, just like her mother. Catherine and William named her Mary. She was the joy of their life.

Catherine loved sitting by the fireside rocking Mary in her arms while they listened to William tell stories that his grandfather had told him. Her favourites were the ones about the great Fin McCall and the mighty Fianna, and she loved to hear the tale of Diarmuid and Gráinne. Catherine and William dreamt that one day they would go in search of those faery hills together: the Gráinne mounds that were never farmed. William would tell these old stories of what the faeries would do if those mounds were disturbed, and his words would sometimes send chills down Catherine's spine as she listened.

Catherine had fond memories of the times they made the short walk across the fields back to her parents' home. The whole family would gather around the fireside during the long winter nights. All her brothers and sisters and their children were there, and they would listen to her father's stories just as she had when she was little. These were stories her father had learned from his mother, and they would hang on his every word as he spoke the old tales. Then, there would be the music. Her uncle played the fiddle and her brother the bodhran. There would be dancing and laughing as sons spun mothers and aunts spun nephews.

When she was younger, Catherine would play on the mossy knoll, rising up from behind their home, with her brothers and sisters. Tearing down the hill, cushioned by moss, they would see who could roll down to the bottom the fastest. There had been some difficult years when the harvest hadn't been so good. She had known hunger, but her mother and father worked tirelessly to shield their children from the hardships imposed on the family. The income they had generated through her father's weaving had carried them through.

July was always the leanest month when everything edible was scarce, including potatoes and vegetables. That was when they would mostly just eat bread and porridge. During the more abundant months, she would dash into the cottage at supper time and be greeted with the usual smell of burning peat. As she entered the smoke-filled room, a bowl of steaming potato stew would be placed in her hands which she would wash down with buttermilk. Sometimes as a rare treat they would get sweet milk and apples too.

During these days, her mother was practically tethered to the fire, which was never allowed to go out, even at night, as this was thought to bring bad luck. A permanently lit fire was a strong symbol of family continuity. The hearth was at ground level, which meant they could build a great big fire on frosty nights in the winter.

They would burn turf, and the person who slept closest to the fire had the job of adding on a new piece of turf every few hours. This was harvested by hand from a nearby bog. It was the children's job to go and gather faggots, which were small sticks, from the hedges that criss-crossed the farm. They bundled these together and put them in the big basket by the fire, and it was these faggots that brought the fire to life in the mornings.

Throughout the autumn and winter, there would be a steady stream of women coming to the door to give her father spun flax to weave. The whole family were involved in preparing the flax. The children prepared it for spinning. Mother did the spinning and passed on the thread to Father to be made into cloth. Sometimes they would dye the cloth with onion skins or leftover tea. In the summer and autumn, they did this with flowers.

The whole family slept in the clothes they stood up in. They struggled to keep clean, but they did their best as Mother was a proud woman. They knew no different and were comfortable in their numbers. Catherine knew of other families who had to sell everything to raise money for a ticket to England or America, but she held no such dream herself. Her heart lay in the tree-lined meadows of County Down amongst the only people she had ever known. She felt it would forever be so.

Catherine's favourite time of year was autumn when there was an abundance of food outside for them to forage. She gathered berries from the hedgerows and nuts from the woodland. There would be blackberries, raspberries and wild mushrooms to feast on. She loved the excitement of Samhain, the old Celtic festival at the end of October, which marked summer's end. This was when they would gather around the hearth and play games such as catching an apple in their teeth – the apple was usually hung from a piece of string attached to the roof. They sometimes also played tricks on each other, which had been the custom for people on 31 October.

Her heart was entwined with nature and the natural flow of things. As a little girl, she would name the robins that came so close to her she could feed them out of her hand. She would always listen for the song of the returning garden warbler who nested in the trees above their cottage. Early May was always a delight when the first hawthorn blossomed. On the first day in May, she would go outside and wash her face in the morning dew as it was said that this kept your skin fresh and young-looking. Her life was a simple but happy one.

Changing times

Over the years, things started to change as Catherine grew from a girl into a woman, and there was more uncertainty for the family. The rent her father paid kept increasing, and it was getting harder and harder to grow enough flax to keep up with the payments. Many of the tenants said that it was legalised robbery. Hanging over them was the worry that they might be evicted at a moment's notice. 'Surely not us after the generations of our family who have been here sub-letting?' her father would say. They didn't have anything written on paper, and they couldn't read anyway. Any letter that did arrive would need reading by the priest.

The verbal agreement for the house had stood for three generations, agreed by her great-grandfather, and her father depended on it to prevent their home from being taken away from them. They had heard stories from other tenants who had been in the same situation only to be sent on their way. The threat of eviction seemed to be moving closer to them each year. It was deeply unsettling.

Some tenants had sold the interest in their land for a lump sum to raise money for their ticket to America. They were tempted by the lure of the New World, believing there was a better future across the Atlantic. Others only managed to raise enough for the ferry to England, which was much cheaper, just sixpence. Anyone poorer than this had to stay behind in Ireland. Catherine's family hadn't come so close as to have to consider leaving. At least they had an income from the linen, which so far they had been able to use to ride the storm.

The famine years

Late in the summer of 1845 when the potato crop failed, life changed drastically for Catherine and William. That moment was chiselled into her mind, when the strangest of fogs had rolled off the sea one September night. In the morning when Catherine opened the half door to their cottage to let in the morning sunlight, she noticed the potato plants had wilted. After calling William, they had run straight outside to investigate. Digging into the soil of one of the plants, they were overwhelmed with a stench of putrefaction, and each potato had turned into a black sticky mess. They both cried out in distress, moving from one bed to the next, frantically digging in the hope that there would be some of their crop that hadn't been affected. They were relieved to find the more sheltered beds behind the house were alright. They salvaged just over half of their harvest, which was transferred to the storage pit.

They dug through the morning and into the afternoon and could hear similar cries of angst from their neighbours' land in all four directions. These people had also discovered that potato blight had decimated their crops. Some people hardly salvaged any of their crops at all.

'We'll manage. We still have half our potato crop and our flax hasn't been affected, so you can spin it into yarn. This will bring us some money'. William spoke optimistically to try and lift her spirits. 'I also have my farm labouring and you can turn your hand to your seamstress work.' William had heard stories of famine that had travelled up from the counties on the west coast of Ireland: County Clare, Kerry and Mayo. These areas of Ireland had poorer soil. It was harder to grow crops and they had been subjected to several famines over recent years. William was fearful for what might be in store for his family in the coming months, but he put his hope in the good fertile land of County Down. He hoped this would be the only year that they would have to face such hardship.

Catherine reflected and took comfort in William's words. She had been a very good seamstress when she worked as a servant at the big farmhouse. There was a dressmaker shop in the market town, so she walked there the following day and made enquiries. As it happened, there was work available. There was a clutch of wealthy people living around the north coast of County Down, so there was work available for her that served their needs. Her father reassured her too. 'There has been famine before in this part of Ireland. Our family survived it then, and we will now. The income from the linen I weave will also help us buy food to make up for the lost potatoes,' he said.

Alongside Catherine's seamstress work, William took a small wage from building roads through a programme of public works. Wages were small and irregular, and in order to earn food, he had to endure long days of back-breaking work. Some poor souls were so weak they collapsed and died amongst the crushed stone. Nevertheless, it was much-needed income, and William persevered with the work. Along with the money Catherine raised through spinning flax and her seamstress work for the rich families, they raised enough to buy the additional food they needed and to pay their rent.

The government had provided some outdoor relief during the hardest months. The Indian meal, imported from America, played havoc with their stomachs and needed so much work to be made palatable, but they coped. They had no choice as the government saw it fit to export the good wheat grown on Irish soil with Irish hands and import this unpleasant corn. It was a tough winter, but they made it through to the other side.

In the spring of 1846, they spent the money they had carefully squirrelled away on seed potatoes, which they planted for that year's harvest. The crop failed last year, but surely it will not fail a second? They drank tea made from the tips of new nettles and gathered hawthorn leaves and wild garlic to eat in a broth. Despite growing thinner each month, they looked ahead to the time when they would harvest their early potato crop and did what they could to keep their spirits high.

Sadly, the evil hand did indeed strike a second blow. In July that year, the same peculiar fog enveloped the land and decimated the potato crop. Then to make matters even worse the price of linen dropped substantially, and the money Catherine earned for her spun flax plummeted with it. Her father was getting much less for the linen he wove and was struggling too. He had to work longer hours, up to sixteen hours a day, and for less money. It was taking its toll on him.

Famished and weak, Catherine and William looked ahead to the following spring. They wondered how they would raise

enough money to buy the seed potatoes they needed for plant-
ing in March. The small income Catherine and William earned
barely bought them enough food to survive the winter. In the
autumn the hedgerows were bursting with nourishing food at
least, as there were fewer people to share it with now. So many
people had left Ireland or died of hunger or fever. That was a
blessing, of sorts, but would they have enough food?

In winter that year the government set up a soup kitchen
that provided some relief. The soup was watery and tasteless,
but it provided a little much-needed nourishment. This was
only available to those who could walk to fetch their soup
daily. So, each morning Catherine, William and their daughter
Mary would set off on the two-mile walk to the town where the
soup was served. They took their cups with them and would
have to queue, sometimes for several hours, alongside other
famished souls.

By the following summer though, the soup kitchens were
closed. It was said the government was concerned that the Irish
were getting too dependent. They said the Irish brought the
famine upon themselves and that they needed to solve their
own problems without the government's help.

During this time a quietness had descended on the land.
The villages were different: silent and empty. More and more
people were leaving through choice, eviction or, worse still, had
died from hunger. Over those years, Catherine had become
familiar with the feeling of a total lack of control and fear as
she tried to make sense of their changing circumstances. She
felt this the most in the small hours of the morning when the
Devil himself came and sat heavily on her chest. She would
reach over to William and curl up in his arms as she cradled
their little girl. What a world they had brought her into.

They had sold many of their possessions and their tiny
cottage looked empty, not like before when it was simple but
cosy. They no longer had the chair by the fire or the small table
by the door that she used to prepare the food on. They did

still have the cooking pot and a bowl, and most of all they had each other. William and their daughter Mary were the most precious things in the world to Catherine.

They witnessed heart-breaking stories of others who lived in their townland: stories of starvation and eviction. But the spring of 1847 had brought their family hope as they received a letter from her brother in London. This included a small bill of money, which was enough to buy their seed potatoes for that year. Summer brought them a good crop of potatoes with no blight. At last, they felt a sense of calm they had not experienced for a long time. They were relieved that they had made it through to the other side. Again, it was a harsh winter, but the success of that year's harvest filled their bellies. They lost the gaunt look in their faces and they had the warmth of their peat fire, which despite everything never went out.

Wear your shadow like a cloak

All was well through the first half of that winter until a new level of despair arrived at the door to their little cottage. The fever. It was spreading among the poor and it was only a matter of time before it reached their family. The unthinkable had happened and it claimed the life of their daughter Mary. Her tiny, frail body finally gave up. As Mary took her final breaths in this world, Catherine held her in her arms. She sang softly to her, a sweet song her grandmother had sung to her in happier times. With Mary's final exhale, Catherine broke down and released a wail of a depth only possible from the lips of a grieving mother. She rocked and rocked, clutching on tightly to her daughter, feeling the last of the warmth drain out of her body. Surely this was the end of her sorrow? What else could be ahead of them that could tear her apart more than this? Surely no fragment of her could feel more pain than she did at this moment?

But then the potato blight struck again later that year in the summer of 1848. There was no food for the coming winter, nor any prospect of work. The opportunity for harvest work had stopped, and the affluent were leaving for England, so Catherine's seamstress work ended. What were they going to do? The threat of the workhouse was now looming over them if they stayed in Ireland. This was a last resort as they would be separated and a strict regime imposed on them, but at least they would be fed.

The workhouse was an institution built in every parish to house the poor, but conditions there were atrocious. There were damp beds, poor sanitation and back-breaking work imposed on people living there, who were known as 'inmates'. Despite this unpopularity, the workhouses had become inundated with people seeking aid during the famine and failed potato harvest. After people entered the dreaded doors, many died. The workhouses had incredibly high mortality rates.

The success of the previous year's harvest had given Catherine and William hope, and they decided to add to their family. After all, Catherine was approaching her late twenties and there were only so many childbearing years left ahead of her. Now she had come to regret that decision. What kind of hell was she bringing her baby into? Surely no child would be able to survive what lay in front of them. Aside from the workhouse, there was one difficult choice left. It was time to leave Ireland for the sake of their unborn child.

The reality of this moment struck Catherine like a bullet in her stomach. It would mean leaving their home, their land, her mother and father and all Catherine had ever known. There was an unbearable void running right through her core at the mere thought of doing this. She felt a new dread, a new depth to her not knowing. Nothing would ever be the same again.

They accepted their fate and her father helped by selling his loom to raise money for their passage to England. With the price that linen was fetching over recent years, it was impossible for him to earn any kind of living from weaving. Many farmers had closed up, sold everything and emigrated to America. Her father would not do that. He was too old to be travelling that distance. He was born on Irish soil and he would die on Irish soil, and had no need for his loom now his weaving days were over.

On the night before they left, Catherine and William walked across the fields for the final time to say goodbye to her parents. Her father could see the fear in her eyes and spoke words of comfort. 'Don't fear, my strong-spirited girl; you have a great determination still left in you. Go and find your brother. He will look out for you. You'll be able to get seamstress work down in London and William can turn his hand to just about anything. Do not grieve us. We have lived our lives, but you have yours still to live. Go, be strong, for your unborn child's sake. Wear your shadow like a cloak but hold your head high, for you are a survivor. The misfortune you have borne here has made you strong. You can ride the wave of sorrow and still find the strength to smile. You carry within you the next generation, so take yourself away now to a better place where you have a hope of living.'

The next morning, as William closed the door to their cottage for the last time, Catherine dared not look back for fear she would not leave. She walked down the path away from the hard-toiled soil, and a startled blackbird flew away crying a searing alarm call. A knot in her stomach twisted yet another time. Never again would she hear the spring birdsong here, or sit on the step to her home and watch the moon rise through the treetops. Never again would she gather berries from the hedgerows in the autumn, or feel the cool earth beneath her toes in the spring.

On the way to the road, she noticed how the pathways had become overgrown through the lack of feet to walk on them. Over time all the neighbours had left. After two hours of walking, she came to the place in her townland that marked the furthest she had ever been from home. It was a poignant moment. From this point onwards, she was in unfamiliar territory. How much sorrow could she bear? And yet she must struggle on for the sake of her unborn child. She took comfort that William was an adventurer and had travelled across two counties in his younger years to find work. She admired his strength and resilience, for every cell in her body wanted to turn around and march back home.

The walk to Belfast was slow as they were so weak from hunger and the toll of the last few years. The lack of food made them lightheaded and they would get out of breath just taking a few steps. Whilst resting at the side of the road, they watched poor emaciated souls pass them as they made the same journey. These were men, women and children, all scantily dressed in rags that hung off their bony frames. They brought with them only what they could carry – if they carried anything at all. All faintly held onto the prospect of a better life ahead on the horizon.

Along the way, Catherine and William walked through village after village. Some were completely deserted with no one living there. Catherine saw the evidence of the evictions. Tenants who failed to keep up with the rent payments had been evicted by landlords who wanted the Irish off the land. Maybe this was the fate awaiting her parents.

The famine had given the landlords the excuse they had been waiting for to turn the land over to the more profitable enterprise of grazing sheep and cattle. The evictions had been carried out with great force as the Irish clung onto the one thing they still had after selling everything else, their home. The bailiffs and the sheriff, accompanied by a military escort, evicted the tenants and burned the homes to prevent their reoccupation. As she passed through each village, Catherine saw home after home was ruined and roofless, with doors battered down and insides charred black from being set on fire. Some poor souls had tried to move back in. They'd made makeshift roofs from small pieces of timber that they could salvage, or by using fallen branches. Others must have left, to goodness knows where: the workhouse maybe, Belfast port, or perhaps an early grave.

The cries of the seagulls brought Catherine back to the present moment where she was standing on the deck. Waves were picking up and the ship was rocking from side to side. It was going to be a long crossing, taking the best part of the day. It would be dark when they arrived in Liverpool. It was a long time for them to stand being so weak. She pulled her shawl tightly around her and drew William into her arms. He was shivering in the cold sea breeze as he had sold his big coat to raise money for food. Her concern for him was growing as he seemed to be getting weaker. She took one last look in the direction of Ireland and buried her face into his shoulder. They had a long journey ahead of them to get to London with much uncertainty, but at least they had each other.

***

CLEARING THE INDIGENOUS PEOPLE

We will pick up Catherine's story again at the beginning of Chapter 3 as she arrives in England. For the remainder of this chapter, I will reflect on some of the themes that have arisen for me as I have traced back to my Irish roots. I will begin by describing these and then conclude with some practical suggestions on claiming back what is lost when we lose our connection to our ancestral lands.

Homeland

A huge part of my work over the past decade has been about returning to the land, to the wild places in the countryside, to immerse myself in the healing power of nature. Being in nature has always been such an important part of my life. During adulthood, I realised my time was not best spent in the sterile corporate walls of the city where I spent the first fifteen years of my working life. It took me a while to extract myself. Undoubtedly such choices were influenced by my experiences as a child.

When I was seven years old, my parents bought a small run-down orchard in Kent, which they gradually turned into a business, selling apples, homemade apple juice and cider from our shed.

The rural life was a blessing as we worked the land together. Children, aunts, uncles, cousins and grandparents were pulled in for various tasks through the year from shed dismantling to collecting the hay to picking the apple crop. We kept chickens and ducks and grew many of our vegetables. I was given my own patch of soil to garden and cultivate whatever I liked. I kept woodlice as pets and my best friend was a chicken called Elsa. I had eleven acres of playground and spent much of my free time imagining I was a squirrel living in the apple trees. I was extremely lucky when I was growing up.

When I was a little older and allowed to wander further afield, I expanded my turf and took to the back fields that stretched out to the horizon. I would walk the footpaths and climb barbed wired fences exploring the hedgerows, ditches and woodlands on an untold series of adventures.

My favourite go-to place was a wood that was full of bluebells in May. In the far corner there was an oak tree that I would sit under and look out across to the next village. This is what I would refer to now as my 'sit spot': a place in nature that I return to again and again and do nothing there but sit. As a child, I never used such terms. I just did what was instinctive to me. I think children know instinctively what is natural for them.

When I learned about my ancestors being forced off their land, it tugged at something deep inside. Growing up on the land made me who I am. It is in my blood and my bones. I am at my happiest when I am out in the meadows, woodlands or up on the moors. So, when researching my family tree, to see that my ancestors had to leave their homeland struck me as rather odd. It compelled me to look into why they did this.

This led me to discover the politics at the time that ultimately forced my ancestors off their land in order to make the land more 'profitable'. This is a scenario still seen today, where the privileged few make decisions that impact severely on the underprivileged many.

In this chapter, I speak of what happens when a person is forced to leave their ancestral land. This is a very sad and damaging consequence of civilisation. I begin by exploring the historical context behind what happened to Catherine and my other ancestors who were cleared from their lands during the nineteenth century. I share what I believe to be the trauma they experienced because of this and how it has played out in me. I finish with some examples of practical steps I have taken to heal the ancestral trauma that I believe has been passed down my family line.

The knowledge that my ancestors moved en-masse from the countryside into the cities first came to my attention when I began to map out my family tree. I have mentioned that I was interested in looking beyond the dates my family members were born and died and other general information. I wanted to understand the stories of my ancestors' lives. When I started the process of writing each biography, I noticed a trend. The adults in the mid-nineteenth century moved, and they moved a lot. There was a great wave of ancestors relocating from the countryside into the cities, which were the powerhouses of the Industrial Revolution. It made me wonder why.

This was when I began my research into social history. I was curious as to the reasons for the mass exodus. It seemed counter-intuitive to me. Why would my ancestors move from what might be seen now as idyllic countryside into the Victorian slums? At this stage I had no idea of my Irish origins, other than knowing my Irish ancestors moved to London for work because of a story passed down by my grandad from his father. I didn't know when this happened, or if it was because of the Great Irish Famine, or what the underlying reasons were for the famine.

Similar clearances were brought to my attention when I was trekking in Scotland in my twenties. I'm a wild camper and I love to sleep out amongst the hills, away from campsites. I thrive on that sense of freedom when I wake up and all I can see is nature surrounding me and breathtaking views. The natural place to be drawn to in the British Isles when it comes to wild camping is Scotland as it is permitted there. So, I often would go off with a rucksack on my back, catching the train to Scotland, then just walk and camp, walk and camp. One of the common things I noticed in these wild places, whether it be on the East or West coast, the Inner or the Outer Hebrides, was the number of abandoned homes. I learned this was because of the Scottish Clearances.

At times I would camp near some of these ruined crofts. I always felt I was impinging on someone else's land, as if a part of them was still there. I would be careful to camp as far away from the ruins as I could. I felt like a trespasser; like I needed to ask permission when I was near one of these old buildings. These were the most beautiful of places, but there was a haunting stillness. If I were to stay for a while I would begin to feel unwelcome after around three days, like I had stayed long enough. It felt as if I was picking up on the unsettled energy of what had happened in the past.

These experiences led me to read about the Scottish Clearances. During the eighteenth century, English landlords cleared entire communities by issuing each household with a compulsory eviction notice. At best, the people who were evicted would be given the boat fare to America. Many of the older people would refuse to go, not wanting to risk the dangerous journey ahead or simply because they couldn't bear to leave their homeland. They would stay behind and starve. At worst, the whole community was uprooted and left to find another patch of land to live on. They would walk miles to inhospitable areas that were near impossible to grow food on, and often they would also starve.

These stories stirred something deep within me, but I didn't know why. At this point, I knew my family had come from Ireland, not Scotland. Nevertheless, the Scottish Clearances' story triggered something in me as I reflected on the trauma these people must have felt as they were forcibly removed from their homeland. When I saw a similar pattern as I researched my family tree of my English ancestors leaving their homes, it led me to wonder why they had left.

I was aware that the circumstances around my English ancestors moving were very different to the Scottish Clearances. Still, the outcome was the same in that people lost their land and moved away from their homes and communities to embark on a very different life.

I wondered what happened to make so many of my English ancestors leave the countryside and move into the slums of industrial cities?

The Enclosures

I found the answer to my question by researching English social and political history. In England, for around four hundred years, a series of laws were passed called the Enclosures. This was a legal process in England where small landholdings were consolidated into larger farms from the sixteenth century onward. The Enclosures meant that people lost access to land they had farmed for generations and were the cause of riots across England through the centuries.

In order to enclose the common land, hawthorn hedges were planted, stone walls erected, and wooden fences built. The settled communities across England lost the common land where they grazed their horses and livestock. This cut off a lot of their food supplies and destroyed the agrarian way of life that had sustained families and villages for centuries. It must have caused unimaginable anguish to parents who could no longer grow food to feed their children. What had once been traditional access to public lands used for firewood, fruit, nuts and pig fodder was taken away. Instead, they had to seek work, which was far less secure and sent many further into poverty.

Up until the nineteenth century, a separate Act of Enclosure was required for each village, but that all changed in 1801 when the General Enclosure Act was passed. The General Enclosure Act (1801) outlined how common land farmed by the working class would be converted into private property for rich land-owners in any village where three-quarters of the landowners agreed to enclose the land.

It saw a marked rise in the rate of common land enclosure, and in the thirty years following the General Enclosure Act being introduced, I noticed my ancestors' patterns changing according to my family tree. They found themselves needing to move to the nearby towns and cities as the engine that drove the Industrial Revolution.

I first found this out when I looked into the origins of my mother's maiden name, which took me to a place called Tadcaster. This picturesque village is located in fertile lands known as the Vale of York, which is between Leeds and York in the north of England. It is perhaps best known as the place where John Smith's bitter is brewed.

On visiting this idyllic English place, it got me thinking about why my ancestors moved. They had lived there since the time of the English civil war in 1644. In just one generation, they had gone from farming their land to clinging onto exist-ence in Holbeck. Holbeck was among the worst of the slums in England, notorious for outbreaks of typhoid and cholera. Two hundred years ago, this generation saw a level of change never seen before or possibly since. Although the story that has claimed me is Catherine's story, I could go back to any family line and find a tale rife with poverty and the afflictions of the poor.

The Great Irish Famine

When I discovered my Irish ancestor had left Ireland during the Great Famine, my interest diverted away from England. I wanted to understand the underlying reasons that led to Catherine choosing to leave Ireland at this time. I drew on various sources when researching my Irish family's history and the sequence of events that led to the Great Famine.

One of the books I read on Irish history landed in my hands while I was in a second-hand bookshop in Scotland. It was *A History of Ireland in the Eighteenth Century* by William Edward Hartpole Lecky.[12] Lecky was a member of the Anglo-Irish Ascendency and wrote this book when Ireland was very much a part, albeit a controversial part at that, of English party politics. Lecky discussed the period of history leading up to the Great Famine. The book has a thorough account of Ireland's history, dating back to the time of the Normans. During this long period of English rule, the story of Ireland helped me understand the division between those with power and those without.

In Chapter 3, I will discuss the Norman invasion that began with the Battle of Hastings in England in 1066. I want to focus now on what happened after the Normans continued their invasion into Ireland. When William the Conqueror won the Battle of Hastings and became King, his control over England happened relatively quickly over a ten-year period. In comparison, across the Irish Sea, it took the Normans over four hundred years to 'conquer' Ireland, and Lecky goes into detail as to why this was. He writes that when the Norman colonists arrived in Ireland, they were rather taken by the Irish way of life. It was so attractive to them that instead of conquering the land and forming a central controlling government, they integrated themselves with the Irish clans. Without a central controlling government, the English failed to control the land.

Lecky goes on to explain how Queen Elizabeth the First all but destroyed Gaelic Ireland and shares the horrific details as to how this was achieved during the Nine Years War that ended in 1603. It makes for hard reading as entire regions of men, women and children were massacred.[13] Worse atrocities were to follow when Cromwell, along with his parliamentary troops, arrived in Ireland in 1649. His opening salvo in September of that year was to oversee one of the worst conflicts on Irish soil – the Massacre of Drogheda.[14]

Lecky goes on to explain what happened following the end of the Nine Years War, once Ireland was under English control. The Irish became tenants of the English aristocracy and steps were taken to eradicate the Catholic religion, forcing the people of Ireland to become Protestants. If they did not convert, they were not allowed any kind of professional employment, nor could they own any land. This meant they were left with just one option: to be tenants of farms run by English landlords.

Being a tenant to an English landlord was fraught with problems for the Irish. Many of the English landowners never set foot in Ireland, and their only interest in their land was for it to be a source of secure and long-term income. They disliked the difficulties of collecting rent from numerous tenants, and so they let their land out on long-term contracts to tenants who ran the larger farms. These tenants of the larger farms would divide the land up and let it out to smaller tenants. As demand for land increased and profits rose, the larger tenants would often themselves become absentees and sublet their tenancy. This went on until there were up to five people between the landlord and the cultivator of the soil. The tenants right at the bottom of the chain were the poorest. These people were called cottiers. Lecky describes a cottier as: 'A man destitute of all knowledge and of all capital, who found the land was the only thing that remained between him and starvation.'[15]

A cottier relied on growing enough food each year to feed their family and also pay their rent. When the cottiers couldn't pay their rent, landlords brought police and troops to evict them off their land. The conditions in Ireland were dire and showed how precariously close to famine so many people in Ireland were. Localised famines, predominately on the west coast of Ireland, were common during the fifty years preceding the Great Irish Famine.

There were other factors at play that made the Irish susceptible to famine. At the beginning of the nineteenth century, during the decade when Catherine was born, there had been a huge increase in population size. This meant that families were living on increasingly smaller plots of land as the land was divided up to accommodate the rise in the number of people. The quality of the land was reduced because land that had never been farmed was put into use. Both of these factors made people more vulnerable to potato crop failures, which I wrote about in Catherine's story.

There are several theories as to why so many people died in Ireland or had to leave the country during the Great Famine of 1845–1849. I will share a summary of some of the theories here. For a thorough review, I refer the reader to the Thomas Davis Lecture Series in *The Great Irish Famine*.[16] This book is a compilation of essays written by academics from Ireland and the United Kingdom, which were published in 1995 to mark the 150th anniversary of the beginning of the Great Famine.

Relief measures

One of the reasons mortalities were so high during the Great Famine was because there was limited aid from the British government who governed Ireland from Westminster. Just like it is today, parliament was made up of Members of Parliament representing regions across Britain. As Ireland was a part of Britain, this meant that some of these MPs were representing Ireland. Many Members of Parliament held the opinion that Ireland should support herself and so were reluctant to deploy relief measures. There was a strong feeling that the responsibility lay with the Irish landowners who had tolerated and exploited the rise of a potato-dependant population that was surplus to their labouring needs. The government was also committed to free trade and would not interfere with private markets. The public was divided in their opinions as to the plight of Ireland. For example, on the one hand, there were large sums of money raised through charitable donations from the middle classes. Then, on the other hand, the editor of The Times newspaper published that there was no natural disaster, and instead, the famine was the result of idleness and dependence on public money. There were also those who held the belief that the potato blight was inflicted on the Irish as a punishment from God against a sinful nation, whose sins included their abuse of the plentiful harvests in previous years.

For these reasons, the government relief measures in the first two years were pitiful, both in the form of soup kitchens and public works schemes. Yet, they did provide the means for many of the cottiers to survive the successive potato crop failures. The greatest devastation happened following a small but disease-free potato harvest in the summer of 1847. In this year, the British government declared the famine over and ended all relief measures. The soup kitchens were closed, and the public relief works ended. With the famine officially declared over, any further outbreaks of famine were regarded as 'normal' and were to be relieved by 'normal' mechanisms put in place by the Poor Law. Public sympathy in Britain had also waned, and charities stopped gathering donations following the 'official' end of the famine, according to the British government.

In addition, there was an amendment made to the Poor Law in 1847 called the Gregory Clause. This stated that anyone who occupied more than a quarter of an acre of land could not receive any relief under the Poor Law, unless that person surrendered their land to the landlord. Nothing facilitated the clearances of the tenants from their land more than this added clause, as it meant if a cottier was starving, they had to relinquish their rights to farm their land in return for aid. The Gregory Clause was the means by which English landlords could clear their land of tenants and make their estate more profitable.

When the potato blight struck again in 1848 and 1849, the cottiers who had survived the earlier famine years now faced almost certain eviction. In his book *The Irish in Britain 1815–1914,* historian Graham Davis wrote that:

> The landlord reaction varied, ranging from the selfless and humane to the cynically opportunistic. While some landlords impoverished their estates in relieving the distress of poor tenants, others exploited the situation, clearing their estates of poor cottiers and increasing the size of their holdings.[17]

Some landlords were tyrants by nature, with whole families being evicted and left to die on the roads or to take refuge in the overfilled workhouses. Those that had the means left for England, Scotland and the New World never to return.

I do not know precisely what happened to make Catherine and William decide to leave Ireland. It may have been because they risked starvation when their potato crop failed once again, or it may have been because they were physically evicted from her home for failing to pay the rent. I know Catherine had arrived in London by the winter, and so I felt the dates tied up well with the potato crop failing late in the summer of 1848. However, they could just have easily been the victim of the wide-scale evictions resulting from the Gregory Clause, which was voted in by 116 of the 125 members of the House of Commons.

The theories as to the reasons behind the scale of devastation during the Great Irish Famine range from government incompetence to calculated genocide. My research found a consensus that there was no intent from the British government for the mass deaths that resulted during the Great Famine. Instead, it was thought to be a result of neglect and ignorance rather than deliberate malice. What is clear from all the theories is that there were issues within the political system that led to the devastation during the famine years. The Irish did not have access to enough food provision or the means to feed themselves, courtesy of the impact of brutal government policies that favoured the English aristocracy.

What I have found alarming is looking at the volumes of food that were exported from Ireland as the Irish starved during the famine years. The numbers are startling. Researcher Christine Kinealy suggests that in 1847, at the height of the Irish famine, there were almost four thousand ships carrying food from Ireland to English ports, while at the same time, four hundred thousand Irish men, women and children died of starvation and related diseases. Throughout the five-year famine period, there was an average monthly export of food from Ireland worth £100,000. Ireland remained a net exporter of food for almost the entire duration.[18] This took place at the same time as millions of Irish people starved or resorted to leaving their country to find the means to survive.

In 1782–83, Ireland experienced an earlier famine. However, during this time, ports were closed to keep home-grown food for the Irish. Food prices were immediately reduced. This move was unpopular with the local merchants who lobbied against the measures, but their protests were overridden by the government. No such measures were brought in that protected the local Irish people's interests during the Great Famine. Kinealy's research shows that there was sufficient food in Ireland to prevent mass starvation, but the food was exported to England. Along the way, warehouses and ports were guarded by the British Army in order to ensure the cargos' safe passage and guarantee the landlords their profits.

Estimates vary, but it is thought that over one million Irish people died, and two million fled the country in the ten years following the first blight.[19] Every one of these people, like Catherine, had their own story of destitution and despair.

The Great Famine affected the whole of Ireland, including the wealthier counties of Ulster. Some areas were worse affected and the southwest of Ireland has been widely written about. This is especially the case for the period 1845–47; however, there were regions that were hit later, and it wasn't only the Catholics who suffered.

Many Irish Protestants were also affected by the famine. The ruling classes and landlords of the day had little consideration for the religion of the ordinary masses: if they couldn't pay their rent, they were evicted.[20]

This knocked the heart out of Ireland, as Irish novelist Edith Somerville (1858–1949) wrote: 'The Famine yielded like the ice of the northern seas; it ran like melted snow into the veins of Ireland for many years afterwards.'[21]

According to Somerville, the British Empire was the richest in the world. The British government had sufficient warning and enough resources at their disposal to help prevent the Great Famine. To read of the politics at that time and the decisions made is quite heart-wrenching, especially knowing the impact this had on so many people, including my great-great-great-grandmother Catherine.

THE YEAR OF 1842

To further explain the situation leading up to the Great Famine, I would like to describe a series of events in 1842. I have chosen 1842 because of two dreams I have had. I have already mentioned how my dreams reveal important information to me, and I have dreamt of the date of 1842 twice now. In the second dream, I saw three journals, and each of them was blank. I would like to write in each of these now, explaining three events that happened that year, which illustrate how powerless my ancestors were in the hands of the controlling elite. By describing these events, I hope to set the scene in the years that immediately preceded the Great Famine. This was at the time when Catherine and William were embarking on their life together as a married couple and laying the foundations to bring their own family into the world.

Hungry and powerless

The first event happened in Ireland, on the west coast in County Clare. This was the opposite corner of Ireland to where I believe Catherine lived. The west coast was more prone to famine. This story shows the government's stance with regard to the Irish.

County Clare was the centre of a famine in 1842 and food riots took place that year. June 6 was the date of the Wanton Massacre, in which three Irish people were killed and sixteen more injured. Forty police officers were deployed to protect a shipment of grain bound for export. Around one hundred Irish people had come to steal the grain they were guarding. It ended in bloodshed. Witness accounts of how the events unfolded differ, but one version said that the police were given instructions to shoot at the crowd if they did not back down, even though they posed no physical threat. No one was convicted for the killings.

This illustrates the hunger and desperation in Ireland, years before the famine struck the whole country. It illustrates that there was grain, but it was not made available to those who were starving. It is telling that firearms were used, allegedly 'by mistake' on people who posed no threat to others. This shows the power held by the privileged. The local Irish people were powerless to influence the government, so they resorted to stealing food to feed themselves. In response, the government used firearms against them. This leads me on to the second event that year I want to share.

Petition for reform

At the same time, across the Irish Sea in England, it was also a period of great unrest. The year 1842 saw continued efforts to bring about parliamentary reform through The People's Charter. The People's Charter was written in 1838 by a group of working-class men who called for a series of rights to be extended to all men over the age of 21, including the right to vote. A petition containing over one million signatures was submitted to parliament one year later, yet parliament voted not to consider it. In May 1842, the petition was resubmitted, this time with three million signatures. Again it was subsequently rejected by parliament. The Northern Star newspaper published this article in response:

> Three and a half million of the slave-class have holden out the olive branch of peace to the enfranchised and privileged classes and sought for a firm and compact union, on the principle of 'equality before the law'; and the enfranchised and privileged have refused to enter into a treaty! The same class is to be a slave class still. The mark and brand of inferiority are not to be removed. The assumption of inferiority is still to be maintained. The people are not to be free.[22]

I feel a great sadness reading this quote, hearing of the struggles of the working class in their fight for equality. To think that so many people's voices were gathered through signatures only to be silenced in parliament by the elite. The terms 'slave class', 'inferiority' and 'the people are not to be free' are all poignant, particularly when I relate this to my own ancestors' stories. Some may well have signed the petition. I can only imagine their disappointment when their request for equality was rejected.

1842 was also a significant year in terms of economic history. Britain had been in a period of economic depression that began in 1837. The downturn in economic activity led to wages being cut, which led to civil unrest and widespread strikes across Britain. The strikes spread to nearly half a million workers, and 1842 'was the year in which more energy was hurled against the authorities than in any other of the nineteenth century'.[23] Alongside the submission of the petition for The People's Charter in 1842, the working-class people made demands for their wages to be returned to previous levels as they were before the depression. When their requests were refused, there were violent outbreaks, including damage to property, and police convoys were ambushed. Later that year, the government arrested several leaders from the Charter movement along with hundreds of other people who had joined the riots. Many were sent to prison, and some were transported to serve long sentences of hard labour, never to return to Britain again.

Twenty-five years later, reform took place, and working-class men were given the vote in cities. Twenty years later, working-class men in the countryside were also permitted to vote. In 1918, this was extended to all men and one-third of women. It took another ten years before all women were finally afforded the right to vote after years of campaigning for truly universal suffrage.

Corn Law repeal

The final event relates to the issues resulting from the depression in the 1840s and the price of food because of something called the Corn Laws.

The Corn Laws were a series of trade restrictions designed to keep cheap American wheat, oats and barley out of the United Kingdom. The laws kept grain prices high for English landowners by artificially inflating food prices. This essentially blocked the import of cheap grain, making it too expensive to import from abroad, even when supplies were short. It meant English people worked long hours as the cost of living was so high. It also meant that grain was too expensive for cottiers to buy in Ireland, so they had no choice but to rely on potatoes as their only source of food.

Members of Parliament, who were also the aristocrat land-owners, fiercely protected the Corn Laws. In 1842, there was a campaign to repeal the Corn Laws, remove the tariffs imposed on foreign imports and open up a free trade market. Advocates of repeal promised not only a 'Big Loaf', which was the doubling in size of a loaf of bread, but also the passing of the 'Ten Hours Bill' to reduce working hours to ten-hour days[24] That year saw the first reduction in tariffs on imported wheat and was the beginning of a movement towards free trade and a reduction in living costs.

These three events that happened in 1842 illustrate the power of the elite and how they went to great lengths to keep working people poor. This demonstrates how the privileged use their power to control the people, and it is a theme I will speak about more in the next chapter. Now I would like to go back in time and explore how this situation came about. Has it always been this way for humanity, or did something happen to create this dynamic where the privileged few control the underprivileged many?

THE BIRTH OF CIVILISATION

Throughout this chapter, I have spoken of how, historically, people were removed from their land in England, Ireland and Scotland. By looking closely at the events of a single year in 1842, I have also illustrated how powerless the working class were as their lives were influenced by the decisions made by the controlling elite.

I am a theorist and I am interested in understanding why things are the way they are. I was keen to understand how long this pattern of the rich removing people from their land had been playing out. My enquiries led me to go a long way back in history, right back in fact to the dawn of civilisation. The author Daniel Quinn covers this well in his book: *Ishmael: A Novel.*[25]

Quinn highlights what happened to humanity over the last 10,000 years since civilisation was born. Civilisation came about when the way people fed themselves changed. There was a move away from the hunter-gatherer lifestyle to a life where the soil was cultivated and crops were grown for food. Quinn argues that there is a fundamental problem with the foundations upon which civilisation was built. He suggests that if anything is to last on Earth, it needs to be built on particular laws. Gravity is one law: it cannot be defied; it has to be worked with. For example, no matter how many times you push an object off a cliff, it will fall to the ground because of gravity. Another law is to: 'take what you need, and leave the rest alone.'[26] Quinn states that civilisation has ignored this law. If this law is ignored, then there will be consequences. One of those consequences is that some people will rise above others and displace them, taking more than they need at the expense of others. Another consequence is that, as there is a finite amount of land and natural resources on Earth, these will run out at some point down the line.

Ignoring the Law of Life, 'take only what you need', began with the discovery of wheat and the onset of agriculture, where land was cleared and crops planted for food. Agriculture began in what was known as the Fertile Crescent in what is now called the Middle East. The shift in the way of life was so significant that it was documented in the Bible through the story of Cain and Abel. Many modern scholars view Cain and Abel's Bible story to be about the development of civilisation during the age of agriculture rather than about the beginnings of 'humanity'. From this perspective, the Cain and Abel story is a fable about when people first began to apply the ideas from agriculture.

In a hunter-gatherer society, the survival of the tribe is dependent on what food is provided in nature. There is only a limited amount of food available to eat in any one ecosystem. So, the population cannot grow above a certain limit, otherwise all of the food will be eaten, and then the tribe will starve. In an agricultural society, this is no longer the case. The land can be tilled and crops grown that will support a much larger population. In the story of Cain and Abel, Cain was a crop farmer, and Abel was a shepherd. The story says that when each son sacrificed their food to God, God favoured Abel's sacrifice over Cain's. This angered Cain, and so he took his brother into a field and murdered him. The underlying message that can be interpreted from this story is that the hunter-gatherer life is the more sustainable way to live on Earth.

However, the person who farms the land has more wealth and therefore more power and can use this to remove the hunter-gatherers from their land. They then grow crops on their newly acquired land that, in turn, generate even more wealth for them. Greater wealth leads people to have larger families, and in this way, it is food that drives population size. Where there is more food, there are more people, and so it is this culture that prevails over others.

As the population size increased, there was a need to organise people, which was achieved through a hierarchical structure. People were told where they fit into this hierarchal organisation and how they would gain access to food. Quinn argues that this is how civilisation was born, and he calls this group of people 'The Takers'.

Takers and Leavers

This new way of life that depended upon agriculture within a hierarchically organised society, continued to be adopted beyond the Fertile Crescent. This had implications for indigenous peoples in other places as they were left without land and access to food at the hands of the 'Takers'. Over five hundred generations, the Takers have spread across the world. It was and still is considered by many that it is acceptable to colonise others in the name of 'advancing civilisation'.

According to Quinn's Laws of Life, the 'Leavers' were the indigenous people that refused to keep 'taking' from the land. They took only what they needed. Quinn made the case that these people throughout history have not joined civilisation by choice.

There have been many wars that have taken place in the name of progressing 'civilisation' over the past two thousand years. It's possible to see many indigenous communities or Leavers have been prepared to die for their way of life, rather than be taken over and controlled by Takers.

I suggest this relationship between Takers and Leavers has played out in England, Ireland and Scotland. Landowners in these countries have sought to increase their wealth by clearing the indigenous farming people from their land so it can be used for profit. In Ireland, people have been cleared so the land can be converted to graze farm animals. Scotland has been a playground for the rich as large tracts of land have been converted for use by hunters shooting game. In England, activities have also taken place to reap more wealth from the land, rather than sharing it with farmers.

It surprised me when I researched the Great Famine in Ireland how long the Irish clung to their lands. They didn't want to leave. This is seen time after time with indigenous people.

I sympathise greatly with the plight of indigenous people alive today who continue to fight to keep their land, such as the Native Americans and the tribal people of the Amazon rainforest. There is a part of their story that speaks to me at a deep level. It speaks to a deep wounding, a hidden ancestral wounding, a wound that is created when a person is removed from their land and becomes a refugee.

WE WALKED ACROSS EUROPE TOO

In Catherine's story, I get a whisper of the trauma she felt when she became a refugee. I thought more deeply than ever before about the trauma refugees experience after a night vigil during my late thirties. I used to be terrified of the dark. Despite my confidence in wandering the hills in daylight, my greatest fear was being in the woods at night. I have done a lot of work around this in recent years and am not quite so scared now.

Doing a night vigil was suggested to me by my supervisor Jayne Johnson, who is also my shamanic teacher and therapist. We have been working together for a decade now, and several years ago she suggested that I try a night vigil to work on my fear of the dark forest. This involved sleeping alone in the woods with a basic set-up of a tarp strung between two trees and a sleeping bag. She watched from a distance. This was a mini version, if you like, of the four-day, four-night wilderness vigil, although at the time it didn't feel the slightest bit like a mini version.

During this long night, I honestly believed that dawn was never going to come at one point. I convinced myself that I had slipped into another reality where the sun was never going to rise again. It was in this moment that I heard the words being whispered from the dark woods behind me: 'We walked across Europe too'. With the words came an image of two bedraggled people, walking slowly forward, exhausted and dirty. I couldn't place the meaning of the words or the people. I had a feeling that their condition was the result of being controlled and enslaved. The other messages I got that night made sense to me straight away, but this one was a mystery. Those words and their accompanying images have never left me.

I find when it comes to receiving messages from my spirit guides, often the most impactful messages are new, and I can't figure them out straight away. This makes sense, as this fresh information was unearthed from my unconscious.

My conscious mind isn't supposed to be able to fathom it out immediately. I find that given time, the meanings reveal themselves, and this process can take several weeks, sometimes months. This guidance has been the longest for me to understand as it took nine months for the meaning to come through.

In the autumn of that year, I had a conversation with someone who was telling me about their Jewish father leaving a concentration camp at the end of the Second World War. While we were talking, he spoke the words his father had spoken to him: 'We walked across Europe too'. I froze. It was that sentence again. It had been spoken back to me and in the context of refugees who were landless and homeless, victims of persecution. I knew it was significant, but I didn't know why. I couldn't at the time see the link between myself and refugees. This conversation happened around the time when Syrian refugees began trying to enter Europe by crossing the Mediterranean Sea. There was a lot of coverage in the British press, so I assumed that the message was related to that in some way.

Over the course of the next few years, I began to join two and two together and link the message with my ancestral work. The meaning became loud and clear: my ancestors walked across Europe in order to stay alive. My ancestors were refugees. They came to a new country to settle in order to stay alive. They had to leave everything, and they never went back to their homes. There are other examples from my family line of ancestors who have been displaced from their land due to persecution. They too will have walked across the land and may have died of starvation.

A wounding has been passed down my family tree. This has brought with it the trauma of moving into the unknown, a place of uncertainty without a home or community. Elders, wise men and women, are lost when indigenous communities are broken up. Traditions fall away and the people lose a piece of their story when they leave family customs and the only way of life they had ever known.

Land and identity

When a group of people live and farm the land, they create a sense of identity rooted in that area. This association between identity and place is intuitive.

In Western culture, geographer and poet Tim Cresswell terms it a 'metaphysic', a fundamental nature of reality. When individuals are forced to leave a place, their identity changes, and there is a chasm left within them from this loss. They endure this for the rest of their lives. Oliver Goldsmith's well-known poem, The Deserted Village, written in 1770, is driven by this sense of loss:

> A time there was, ere England's griefs began,
> When every rood of ground maintained its man;
> For him light labour spread her wholesome store,
> Just gave what life required, but gave no more:
> His best companions, innocence and health;
> And his best riches, ignorance of wealth.[27]

The words in this poem speak to me about what was lost when our ancestors were removed from their land. When they could feed themselves from their own land, they had their health and happiness, but that was lost to them as they left their village and moved to the city. The poem speaks of the grief that came over someone when they left their land and their home.

This grief is held in the body and is passed down through the ancestor line within the DNA of their children, their children's children, and so on. This is the science of epigenetics that I spoke about in Chapter 1, when information is coded into a person's DNA and then passed on to future generations. In his book The Wild Edge of Sorrow: Rituals of Renewal and the Sacred Work of Grief, Francis Weller speaks of this grief carried in our bodies from the sorrows experienced by our ancestors. He says:

Much of this grief lingers in a layer of silence, unacknowledged. What great sorrow there must be when
forced to leave your homeland after a long slow deci-
mation. What a feeling of powerlessness this must cause
when all that you love has been taken from you.[28]

The wounding experienced by a refugee who has had to
flee their homeland must be severe. They have had to leave
the soil that has sustained their family for generations and
their community: the only people and place they have ever
known. A part of them may feel broken, as if a chunk has been
taken, leaving a void. When there is a void, there is a space that
needs to be filled with something. In Western culture, this is
usually filled with addiction to alcohol, food, exercise, drugs,
tobacco or consumerism, to name but a few. In my opinion we
believe, or have been led to believe, that we can fill the sense
of this deep ancestral void within us with 'stuff'. The driver of
human consumption and destruction is a desperate attempt
people make to meet tragically unmet needs. Western society
cannot replace that which is lost when a community no longer
lives off the land together.

In my twenties and early thirties when I worked in corporate sustainability, I had friends who were also in professional
careers. Each was on their own particular career path and had
the objective of climbing higher on the ladder, becoming richer
and more successful. To an outsider we looked happy and
successful, and in many ways, we were. But, in the small hours
of the morning, when we had drunk our fair share of alcohol, the time for deep heart-to-heart chats emerged. I always
enjoyed these moments, when my friends would open up and
reveal their deepest inner workings. I remember that I would
revisit one conversation with a friend of mine who had very
quickly risen to a senior level within the organisation where
he worked. He would tell me that his all-time dream wasn't
the fast cars. He had a very expensive fast car already. It wasn't
the big house and, again, he had a nice semi-detached house.

What he really wanted, more than anything, was a patch of land we could all farm together. We would joke about what kinds of things we would do on this farm. We would definitely have goats and chickens and would live in small houses set around the land. We would come together to gather around the fire at the centre.

I believe my friend was intuitively tapping into the ancestral wounding I have spoken of, the void that needs filling. This was someone who had achieved so much so young. Linking to my previous discussion of Quinn's Laws of Life earlier in this chapter, my friend was a 'good citizen', being both successful and wealthy. But, deep inside, when he was reflective and baring his soul, something was missing. What he really wanted was a piece of land that he could farm within a community. I remember these conversations well. It is all I ever wanted, too.

Economists and psychologists have seen this trend reflected in research in recent years. Materially some people are getting more, but happiness is not increasing at the same rate. We are richer but less content. GDP is increasing, but life expectancy and quality of life are declining. As author Charles Eisenstein eloquently asks:

> How much wealthier would we feel if we had access once again to a black star-filled sky at night and to a silence in which the loudest noises were birds and insects and children? What deep need would that meet? We have to recognise what we have lost in order to find what we are looking for. Otherwise, we feel this void and we don't know why. We think maybe we are crazy as this is normal and the way things are. Only when we understand the magnitude of the loss do we realise that we are not crazy. And our inborn expectation that the world was meant to be more authentically beautiful, joyful and connected than what we have been offered, is real. Only then do we have the inner confidence to seek out what has been lost, we need to see that there has been damage done and something lost, so we know how beautiful it

can be and what to aspire to. We have to hold the pain in order to hold the possibility.[29]

The story of how to be human is breaking down for many people, leaving us in the space between stories. In recognising this loss, I believe that the most important work we can do here on Earth is to go about claiming it back. How is this possible? By returning to the land. I will spend the rest of this chapter talking about this idea.

***

HEALING THROUGH NATURE

I have mentioned that my work over the past two decades has been about returning to the Earth. When I first started to acknowledge this inner burning desire to return to the land, my initial vision was the one I'd shared with my friend at two o'clock in the morning.

I wanted to own a piece of land that I could farm alone or with others. I explored this idea more and considered seeking out a commune of people interested in living off the land. There are many of these groups across the world. In the United Kingdom they are particularly found in Wales. The Welsh government looks favourably on this kind of sustainable set-up and have made concessions to planning regulations to make it easier to achieve.

I have a lot of admiration for these people, but it is not my path. My place seems to be sitting on the edge, occupying a space much closer to the world and everyday way of living. I have mused over this a lot and concluded that the reason I am occupying this place is that it is the best way of seeing how the world might be in the future. It isn't realistic for everyone to move into the countryside and buy a piece of land. So, what is possible? What is available that will enable us to go back to the Earth, reconnect with nature and find a more natural way of living?

My place is living within the everyday world and changing things from here. What I have come to realise is that we can make changes to claim back what we lost when our ancestors were displaced from their land, without moving to a remote part of the country and achieving self-sufficiency. I can summarise what I do to reclaim my connection with the land in four ways: 1. Nature-time, 2. Relationship with place, 3. Flowing with the seasons, and 4. Growing food.

I will explain how I work with each of these and why I see them as important.

Nature-time

First, I have reclaimed my connection with the Earth through nature-time. This is time I spend outdoors enjoying all that nature has to offer. Although I can't know for certain, my sense is that my ancestors who lived in rural communities had a closeness to nature, and a love and respect for nature that I also hold within me. I wove this connection to nature into Catherine's story in Ireland.

Now it might sound straightforward to spend time out in nature in our modern-day lifestyle, but from my experience, as well as through working with people in our The Way of the Buzzard community, it is often harder than it looks. Within Western culture we have been spending gradually less time out in nature, and it is to our detriment. The health consequences of this lack of nature-time now has a name: Nature-Deficit Disorder. Author Richard Louv introduced the term with the publication of *Last Child in the Woods: Saving Our Children from Nature-Deficit Disorder.*[30] He coined the phrase to explain the human cost of alienation from nature, especially children.

According to Louv, the reasons why people are spending less time outside include: more time spent on electronic devices, a reduction in urban green spaces, more traffic, less emphasis on the importance of nature in schools, and fears around safety, which are amplified by the media. In recent years there is more evidence to show that Nature-Deficit Disorder dulls our senses. This contributes to attention difficulties, rising obesity, and higher rates of mental and physical illness. The benefits of outdoor time are widely recognised by the medical profession. Doctors in Scotland are even writing 'nature' prescriptions for their patients.[31]

Nature-time as a spiritual practice

Reclaiming nature-time has also been an important part of my spiritual practice. When I lived in cities, I sought out time in parks, but now that I have immediate access to the woodlands, meadows and moorland, I am at my happiest.

During my busy corporate working days, I would seek out any opportunity to spend time in nature. I spent my evenings and weekends in the national parks of the northwest of England, which was easier as I chose to live very close to one, and many others were just an hour or two away. I mentioned earlier in the book my love of wild camping in Scotland. This was a big part of my awakening. I ascribe this to being immersed in beautiful wild places for longer periods of time. I spent more and more time outside in nature, and my curiosity increased. I wanted to be able to identify the different species of trees and recognise every bird song.

We teach through The Way of the Buzzard that nature connection is a cornerstone of spiritual practice. There is so much we can learn from the trees, the plants and the animals. The definition of Shamanism is to travel to other realities to bring back the energy that is most needed by the community at that time. However, Shamanism is effectively the spiritual practice of many nature-based indigenous cultures. These people never broke their connection with nature. While we can learn how to journey to the other realms, we are missing an important aspect of connection if we don't immerse ourselves in the natural world and all the richness that is here in this reality. That is, in those places where nature thrives.

The benefits of spending time in and studying nature have been spoken of by some great thinkers. Einstein, for example, said: 'Look deep, deep into nature, and then you will understand everything better.'[32]

I love to catch the dawn on the moorlands behind my home and watch the changing colours, which are different every time. This means rising earlier in spring and summer, so my visits become more infrequent at that time of year. When I do go up there, I am rewarded with a great theatrical display. It leaves me tired for the rest of the day but with a renewed buzz and excitement about life and often a fresh perspective around something I am working with.

Throughout spring, my eyes are fixed on watching the leaves emerge from the bare trees. I look for horse chestnut first and then birch, sycamore, rowan, and oak. The last to show its leaves is the ash. I take the time to learn about each tree, understanding the environment it chooses to grow in, as well as its individual characteristics. For instance, the alder prefers the riverside where it stabilises boggy ground to give a firmer foundation. Knowing this teaches me to do the same in life, to spend time listening and working through my emotions, as represented by the element of water, in order to ensure I have a firm ground to stand on.

The oak spreads its roots far out across the soil like the base of a wine glass. This gives it the strength to withstand the toughest storms and live for over a thousand years. Having an awareness of such details reminds me of the importance of keeping a firm connection with the land in order to stabilise me during rocky periods in life. The birch tree, being a pioneer species, is the first to colonise new ground. It sheds its bark as well as tiny twigs that snap off in the wind. These fall to the ground and decompose into the soil. They build up and create suitable ground for other tree species to flourish. This reminds me of the importance of clearing when I embark on a new project or phase of life. To close off any outstanding projects and tie up any loose ends to prepare the ground for new growth.

The rowan, known as the flying tree, is able to move higher up a mountain than any other species. This helped me be determined to keep going when I have found myself wavering on a project. Branches from the hazel tree have been used in divination for water for thousands of years. This has taught me to tune into the inner wisdom that lies buried deep within me. When I am writing, I wear a small piece of hazel that I have had hand-crafted into a necklace. When I am struggling to find the words, I let my mind connect with hazel and ask for help to come through.

I have learnt these things by studying the natural history of each species of tree and then drawing out the lessons they have for me, as well as drawing on insights shared by author and teacher Glennie Kindred in her books *Walking with Trees and The Tree Ogham*.[33] I might go on a shamanic journey to the tree or go and find a tree of that particular species and lean against its trunk whilst pondering a question. Whatever approach I take, I always leave with a new perspective and a sense of clarity on the way forward.

Over the years, I have tuned in to the animals too, as they serve as insightful teachers. I have learned the song of the wren and how this differs from the nuthatch. I know that robins are one of the only birds to sing at night. I know how the great tit changes its song on the morning after the Winter Solstice to announce the return of the light. I have learned how all the animals are warned of potential danger through the alarm call of a concerned blackbird. I have learned what the call of the crow at dawn can tell me about darkness and emerging light. I know what the drumbeat of the greater spotted wood-pecker can teach me about taking care and cushioning myself from the impact of a challenging situation. I have discovered what the songbirds teach me about my own voice and the message I have to bring into the world. I have learned what a hare walking right past me in a bluebell wood can teach me about freedom. I know that a roe deer leaping over a wall can teach me about elegance and grace. I have even ended a career following an encounter with a blackbird messenger who crossed my path one morning. The animals have proven themselves to be faithful guides on my path, whether through sightings when I am out in nature, or through shamanic journeying.

There are also the medicinal qualities of the plants too. I have learned how hawthorn flowers and berries can help to lower blood pressure and how willow helps with pain. I have discovered how mint helps to ease digestive troubles and that nettles nourish me in spring. This coming back to plants and their medicinal qualities is something our ancestors would have known. It is another thread of nature knowledge to reclaim. In comparison with my work of tuning in to the messages and healing from trees and animals, I know less about plants. This is a growing interest of mine.

Relationship with place

The second way I have reclaimed back my connection with the Earth is to develop a relationship with my own patch of land. This isn't about travelling to far off destinations. This is about exploring my own country, and in particular, developing an intimate knowledge of the area where I live.

The sit spot

I have a special relationship with a place close to my home, which I call my sit spot. One of the things we strongly encourage our The Way of the Buzzard community to do is find a sit spot. This is a place in nature easy to get to from home that people can return to throughout the year. I have a sit spot by three sycamore trees in a small woodland that takes me around ten minutes to get to from home. I go there on a regular basis with no other purpose than to sit and notice nature around me. Sometimes I journal, and other times I just gaze, lie down, snooze, ponder, notice, and just simply be a part of this place as it moves through the seasons. I developed an intimate relationship with this patch of ground through regular practice. I mentioned earlier I had a sit spot when I was a child too, under an oak tree out in the back fields that took about twenty minutes to walk to. I would go and sit there throughout my teenage years. It is still an important place to me as it is my Axis Mundi: the place where I start my shamanic journeys to the Otherworld.

My intention is to connect with nature in some way almost every day throughout the year. Sometimes this is at my sit spot, other times it is whilst walking around Anglezarke on the edge of the West Pennine Moors, and sometimes I venture further afield to other beautiful parts of the northwest of England. Developing this relationship with a local place has had a profound impact on me. It is where I receive inspiration and understanding for the journey ahead. There are times when I don't manage to keep up as regular a connection with nature as I would like to, but awareness of this highlights that I haven't quite got my balance right, and I soon rectify it when I realise that the busyness of life is taking over once again. I always find my way back to nature eventually.

Solutions on our doorstep

I realised the importance of 'relationship with place' very early on in my spiritual path when I was a teenager. It was at the beginning of my enquiry into exploring the ancient, indigenous 'old ways'. I was drawn to learning about those things that my very distant ancestors knew because they lived so close to the land. I wanted to rediscover the knowledge that has been lost once we are disconnected from the Earth. One of the first spiritual books I bought was called *The Power of Place* by James Swan.[34] My spiritual line of enquiry led me to Waterstones bookshop to peruse the Mind, Body, Spirit section. The title drew me in during one visit. The book offers a perspective on the importance of place and its influence on a person's health and creativity. Even at an early age, this concept struck a chord with me.

Early in my adult life, I left the Evangelical Christian faith that I had been brought up in. I wanted to find a spiritual path, but I couldn't find one I felt I could get my teeth into. I bought books on Buddhism and tried to read them. I wanted to learn to meditate, and I sought out local groups, but it never gelled with me. In seeking my spirituality, I was aware people went on spiritual retreats travelling to faraway places such as India or Peru, but I was never drawn to such experiences. I travelled to Australia and South East Asia after I left university, but it wasn't to seek a spiritual experience, it was more about exploration and adventure.

I strongly believe that our solutions are on our doorstep and that we don't need to travel very far to find our spiritual path, or be happy, to have the experiences we crave. I have found deep fulfilment right outside my front door. It was waking up to the threat of climate change that stilled me and brought me to this realisation, and this led me down my spiritual path.

In my mid-twenties, my concern for the changing climate and warming of the Earth was heightened. I had been aware of this since studying a climate change module at university, but the knowledge hadn't changed my behaviour much. I didn't own a house at the time and so it wasn't possible to make many changes to reduce my energy consumption in the home. I enjoyed foreign holidays to Europe with my friends, but over time my concerns over climate change ramped up.

In the mid-2000s a new grassroots movement called Transition Towns began.[35] This empowered local residents to inspire others to monitor and reduce the community carbon footprint. Transition Town groups popped up in cities, towns and villages across the country, made up of enthusiastic local residents who embarked on all kinds of sustainable initiatives from growing food to installing community-owned renewable energy infrastructure.

With my background in corporate sustainability, I felt I had a lot to contribute and so I volunteered to lead a group of like-minded people in the cause. This was in my home town at the time, Bollington in Cheshire. We planted trees in the local area and explored the potential for renewable energy schemes. We set up local community gardens to grow food and helped families to understand and reduce their carbon footprint. We did very well and were shortlisted for national awards. In 2009, I was even invited for afternoon tea at Number 10 Downing Street with the then Prime Minister Gordon Brown and some of his cabinet members.

One of the programmes we ran in the community was a scheme called EcoTeams. The premise was that local residents would help each other understand how to monitor and reduce their carbon footprint at home. I became a case study to inspire people and began to meticulously monitor my carbon emissions. While I did this, I noticed the environmental impact of the flights I took, and it astounded me.

I spent four years making changes at home in order to reduce my carbon footprint, adding loft and cavity wall insulation, house timer-controls, reducing my shower time and getting A-rated electrical appliances. Despite these efforts, the reductions to my carbon footprint would be undone by just one return flight to Canada. I chose Canada to make this comparison as this was the country I most wanted to go to for my next holiday. I wanted adventure. I wanted to immerse myself in the wilderness and feel free in new ways. However, on discovering the huge carbon footprint of taking a long-haul return flight, I decided there and then to stop flying.

This was tough as I had a good job and could afford nice holidays, and it was the thing everyone did. I had to start saying no to foreign holidays with friends unless it was possible to travel by train. I spent some time considering what I would have done on that holiday to Canada. Why did I want to go? I looked for how I could have the same experiences somewhere I didn't have to fly to get to. This took me to Scotland and a course where I learnt how to trek. I was taught how to carry my camping equipment on my back and navigate my way across the hills to camp in wilderness spots. Scotland had it all for me, and I could get there by train instead of plane. My then-husband and I would travel on public transport and wild camp our way across the Cairngorms, up the west coast and across to the Outer Hebrides on a succession of holidays. We would set up camp at night in remote wilderness areas and catch the sunset and sunrise over the most beautiful views.

It was on one of these trekking holidays that I walked across the Cairngorm mountains and dropped down to the other side into one of the most magnificent valleys I have ever slept in: Glenmore Forest Park. It was here that I had my ancestral realisation I spoke about earlier in the chapter, whilst sleeping next to the abandoned cottages.

Choosing not to fly abroad for holidays has changed me. I grieve those places in the world that I would love to go and see. I find it hard sometimes to see photographs on Facebook of people abroad in the places I wanted to visit. However, my life is so much richer for stilling myself in this way. I do still fly on rare occasions for carefully considered reasons.

It has led me to realise that I am not going to find what I am looking for by travelling far. I realised over time that the Earth cannot sustain the environmental impact of people travelling in the way that they do.

I applied this 'no flying' principle when looking for teachers on my spiritual path. I wanted to learn how to help people reconnect and to fall back in love with nature. I trusted that I would find who I needed to learn from locally, and this happened. I set the intention that I wanted to find the right teacher locally, and just as I had hoped, they showed up. I received an email from a colleague about a year-long workshop called a Shamanic Medicine Wheel, run by my now shamanic teacher and supervisor, Jayne Johnson. It was ultimately through coming back to the land and flowing with the seasons that the deep transformations happened in my life. It brought me away from the corporate life and those unhealthy inhuman demands. It was messy. It looked like madness at the time, but it brought me to a much simpler way of living. I will share more about this throughout this book.

Flowing with the seasons

The third way I have reclaimed this connection is through aligning my life with the flow of the seasons. Agricultural communities organised their year by the changing seasons, and although many of us no longer farm the land, it doesn't mean we can't tune into the energies of the seasons. Following these energies brings me great benefits.

Ancient Celtic people would celebrate eight points in the year called the Sabbats. These fall on specific dates in our calendar in what is called the Wheel of the Year.

The Solstices and the Equinoxes lie opposite each other in the wheel and form a cross. The Winter Solstice as the shortest day of the year is at the top, and the Summer Solstice as the longest day of the year is at the bottom. On this axis, there is a horizontal line drawn across the midpoint. This line shows the Autumn Equinox on the left-hand side and the Spring Equinox on the right. These four points lie equidistant from each other and are three months apart. They form part of the wheel and are known as the quarter festivals.

What I find remarkable is that if an X is drawn over the wheel, this shows the cross-quarter festivals. The cross-quarter festivals mark the points in the transition of the season of spring, summer, autumn and winter. They are the festivals known as Imbolc, Beltane, Lammas and Samhain.

These eight festivals were so significant to our ancestors that they withstood the trials of religion coming in and wiping out the old ways, so much so that the Christian festivals overlay them. Let me explain.

Between the Autumn Equinox and the Winter Solstice, there is Samhain, which overlays Halloween on 31 October and lasts until 2 November. This is the transition from autumn to winter and is the time for moving into the darkness and slowing down, drawing in and hunkering down. The Celts believed that the darkness and the unconscious were where everything began, and so they made this Sabbat the beginning of their calendar year. This is an important time to go within oneself.

The Solstices occupy the extreme ends of the energy spectrum. At the Winter Solstice, which lands at a specific time between 20 and 23 December, we slow down along with the rest of nature. This is a time of stillness and peace. This is the time of the birth of the sun as it rests on the horizon, rising in the exact same place for three days before it begins to track its way back across the horizon once again. The Church chose this time of year to mark the birth of Jesus, the Son of God, aligning with the time of year when the sun is reborn.

When the wheel reaches the festival of Imbolc, there is a change outside again as we move towards spring, but it is very subtle. Imbolc is celebrated between 31 January and 2 February. I think of it as when the lights are turned back on. The evenings start to get slightly lighter, and the snowdrops show their faces as the first spring bulbs. Christians call this time Candlemas.

At the Equinoxes, there is a real sense of balance, as the day and night are of equal length. The date of the Spring Equinox falls between 20 and 23 March. The Spring Equinox is the rebirth of life after winter. It is a time to plant seeds and cultivate our hopes and dreams. It could be considered as the resurrection of life after the darkness of winter. This aligns with the meaning and timing of the Christian festival of Easter, which marks the resurrection of Christ, and its date is determined by the Spring Equinox and the full moon. Easter Day falls on the first Sunday following the full moon that occurs on or just after the Spring Equinox.

Beltane is celebrated from 31 April to 2 May. In our British culture, we know this as May Day. This is a time when the energies of fertility are celebrated. Folklore tradition is for people to dance around the Maypole, which is an ancient representation of the male and female energies entwining.

The Summer Solstice falls sometime between 20 and 23 June. This is a time of heightened energy as the days are at their longest and the sun is most powerful. In this moment, we can recognise our own inner power and strength and apply this to whatever aspect of our life that needs it.

Next, there is Lammas or Lughnasadh. This is the time of the first harvest between 31 July and 2 August. Our ancestors would depend on a good harvest to see them through the winter, and so the cutting of the first ears of wheat was an important moment in the calendar. It is a time to begin to reap what you have sown. In the Christian calendar, this festival is celebrated as Lammas, Loaf Mass Day, which falls on 1 August.

The Autumn Equinox happens at a specific time between 20 and 23 September. It is about celebrating the gathering of the harvest and making preparations for winter drawing in. It is a time for gratitude for all we have. Culturally in the United Kingdom, this is celebrated as the Harvest Festival, which falls on the first Sunday after the full moon that is closest to the Autumn Equinox.

So, we can see that modern-day Western festivals have underlying energies aligned with nature. What is the relevance of this in our lives? Well, these energies can be worked with through the year as they present themselves. We can flow with the Wheel of the Year to achieve goals in life and tune in with nature and her healing messages.

As I follow the changes through the seasons, each year I notice more detail around the time of the cross-quarter festivals. I notice at Imbolc the arrival of snowdrops pushing their noses through the frozen soil. They show their faces, as the wheel turns and the evenings get lighter. I notice, approaching Beltane, the moorland grass turns from yellow to green as the new grass grows. For me, there are few things more beautiful than an English woodland in early May. There is the heavy perfume of the bluebell carpet and the delicate, luminous green leaves of the beech tree at Beltane.

By Lammas, I notice a change in the evening temperature. I can literally taste autumn in the breeze. I mentioned at the beginning of the chapter how Catherine loved the excitement of Samhain, and I feel the same way. I have the feeling of breathing a sigh of relief as the nights lengthen. I look forward to the long winter nights to catch up on rest and things at home. I look forward to the slowness and winding down, and anticipation of what is going to emerge on the other side of winter.

Working with the Wheel

I observe these changes and seek ways to align my way of thinking and the things I choose to do, such as how I manage all my large projects, by the wheel. I take an idea into winter, marking my intention with a ceremony at Samhain. I allow ideas to emerge through the dark nights and begin to stir these into action from the Winter Solstice onwards, not putting myself under any pressure to start putting too much time and energy into a new venture until Imbolc has passed. By the Spring Equinox, I look at what I need to address in my life to bring more balance and so I can move my plans forward. When Beltane arrives, I have set myself up to go full pelt achieving my goals through the Summer Solstice and on to Lammas. When I get to the Autumn Equinox, I take stock of what I have managed to achieve and move towards the winter to begin the cycle once more.

On or around each Sabbat, I go on a shamanic journey to meet my spirit guides and seek their advice. I carry out a ceremony to set my intentions for the coming period of time. Sometimes I run large public ceremonies with Jason, and other times it is a small, intimate affair with family or friends – or just the two of us.

I took this approach of working with the Wheel of the Year as I wrote this book. Several summers ago, I went on a moorland walk on the day of the Summer Solstice and sat in an old farmstead ruin. It was around the time that Catherine's story had been revealed to me through my ancestral research, and I wrote down a series of paragraphs that I wanted to write about. I set the intention there and then that I wanted to write a book.

I didn't realise this at the time, but over the following twelve months, I carried out research into what Catherine's life might be like. Then, as I approached Samhain, I decided I would set the intention to begin the writing process. I spoke out my intention during a ceremony at Samhain. By the Winter Solstice a writing mentor had presented herself to help me and I had my first session in early January. I wrote each chapter with the growing sun, moving through Imbolc and the Spring

Equinox and ramping right up by Beltane. In the weeks after the Solstice, when the sun was still at its highest position in the sky, I completed my first draft and began the editing process.

This took until first harvest at Lammas in early August for the first round of edits. Then from the Autumn Equinox on to the following Spring Equinox, I worked on the proof-read edits. I completed my final proofread on the day of the Summer Solstice, exactly three years after I penned my first reflections of Catherine's story as I sat up on the moorland.

It was a process following the flow of the seasons. Had I not been successful in completing the book, I would have simply taken stock at the Summer Solstice, and readdressed what needed to happen so that I could achieve my goal later that autumn.

Jason and I run our shamanic business like this. We begin our planning in the autumn as we approach Samhain and then ease ourselves into the dark months to allow ideas to gestate through to spring. We ramp up our work through the warmer months, ready to draw back in again once the trees begin to shed their leaves for winter once more.

Flowing with the Wheel of the Year has taught me that I do not need to go full pelt throughout the year, which I was told was necessary when I worked in the corporate world. It allows me to bring about changes in my life following nature's way, with a flow of activity that involves periods of rest followed by periods of activity. If I don't achieve my goals in the first year, I get another go the following year after a period of re-evaluation and rest.

Alchemy doesn't happen overnight in nature, and transformation doesn't happen overnight in my life either, well at least not usually. Significant changes and growth take time. The Wheel of the Year gives me the permission and structure I need to go with the natural flow.

Growing food

The final way to claim back that lost connection to the Earth is to grow my own food. It doesn't take as much land as you might think to do this.

The book *Beyond Civilization* by Daniel Quinn highlights that when our food is under lock and key, we have to work to earn money to buy it.[36] However, if we can grow our own food, then we take back some control in our lives. I started growing my own food during my Transition Town days. I lived in a town with lots of terraced houses with small backyards, so people didn't have their own gardens. There were council-run allotments, but the rumour was that you could only get one if someone died and they were passed down to a family member. I waited on the list for an allotment for several years and then decided to take alternative action.

A group of us got together and set up a garden-sharing scheme. We acquired several large plots of land and set up community garden projects there. We accessed grant schemes to help get them started. Growing food together creates community cohesion. After all, working the land together has been done for thousands of years. But you can choose to go it alone if preferred, even if you only have a small garden or backyard. I have read in the past that hand-tended soil can be up to ten times more productive than agriculturally farmed soil. I've known people who used a third of an acre to feed their families. You can achieve a lot with just a small patch of carefully tended ground.

Growing your own food feels very empowering too. As my ancestral stories have shown me time and time again, the government took our land away from us. Anything we can do to reclaim the land can be part of the process of healing.

Earlier in this chapter, I referred back to a period in our history where the land was taken from the common person through the Enclosures. Following the General Enclosure Act

(1801) the first land that was given back to the people followed the Allotments Act (1922) after the First World War. The efforts to return the land to the people has been ongoing since the 1900s and has really taken hold in Scotland. For example, activist Alistair McIntosh describes his work in the book *Soil and Soul: People versus Corporate Power.*[37] McIntosh shows how it is still possible for ordinary people to take on powerful people and mighty corporations and emerge victorious. The Scottish people have claimed back a relatively small but still impressive percentage of their land to date. This includes the whole of the Isle of Eigg.

The importance of working the soil again came to me in a dream when I slept out at one of my ancestral sites. This time it was North Yorkshire. I dreamt that I dug up some soil with a spade, and there were so many worms it wasn't possible to tell soil from worm. The morning following the dream, I was sitting in my van enjoying breakfast when I saw a blackbird on a mound of earth holding a worm. I have already mentioned how a blackbird sighting profoundly impacted my life and led me to end my career. I felt a connection with this blackbird holding the worm and felt there was a message for me.

As I drove to my first ancestral location visit later that morning, I saw a person working their allotment. If I receive a piece of information in several different ways, it adds layers of importance. In this instance, initially I had a dream, then a nature sighting and finally an observation. The following weekend Jason and I began to clear a part of the garden, where there had previously been an old shed, to make a vegetable patch. This project is still ongoing, and we plan to turn our third of an acre into a permaculture garden, growing enough food to feed us for much of the year once it is established.

There are many health benefits to growing your food, such as being assured that the food is pesticide, herbicide and fertiliser free. It has been scientifically proven that getting your hands into the soil is good for you. Researchers have found clear evidence that childhood exposure to outdoor microbes is linked to a more robust immune system.[38] It is also possible to create a food-growing garden that is good for nature. We aim to have soil of high enough quality that it is full of earthworms and to create a habitat that encourages toads and hedgehogs into the garden to manage the slug population naturally. We already have many toads so we are off to a good start.

I feel this is the ultimate rebellion against the controlling system I have been born into, making myself independent from food shops and reclaiming the soil that was taken from my ancestors.

The simple life

All of the ways I have described to reconnect with nature can be achieved with little or no money and you don't need to have a garden or yard. You can develop a close relationship with nature in your local park or the countryside close to your home. You can begin to celebrate the eight ancient festivals of our land and align your life with the Wheel of the Year. If you have a backyard or garden, you can begin to try your hand at growing some of your own food or seeking out an allotment or garden-share. We all need to find our way back to nature. We need to simplify our lives. It is our choice. It isn't always a quick thing, to make the necessary changes to create more space in our lives for this essential practice, although it can be. Awareness is the first step. It isn't necessary to do all of these things at the same time. In my experience, I simply follow my line of curiosity and that which draws my interest the most. Treat this as a lifelong process of learning to come back home to nature.

I've talked about four ways of reclaiming our connection to nature but underpinning all of this is the need to do one more thing. That is, we need to claim back what has been taken from us: our free time.

Before the onset of the Industrial Revolution, our ancestors didn't work as much as we do in modern times. They had lots of rest time. This is going to be the focus of the following chapters. Firstly though, it is time to go back to the nineteenth century and follow Catherine into the next phase of her life as she arrives in Victorian England and makes her home in London.

CHAPTER 3

CITY LIFE

Catherine walked behind the cart as it rocked its way along the cobbled streets of Soho, towards the cemetery. It carried the bodies of five paupers who had died in the workhouse over the past few days. Among them was her daughter Charlotte, lying cold against strangers, no longer of this world. Her daughter's coffin was of the cheapest possible construction: rough pine wood stapled together with her name chalked on top. Inside Charlotte lay naked on a layer of sawdust under a covering of paper.

Bone-tired with grief, Catherine had no one to hold her up, or share the depths of the pain she felt as she was about to bury the last of her family in a pauper's grave. She was truly alone.

In those last few weeks, any hope left in Catherine had fallen away as she watched the life drain from her daughter's frail body day by day. It was the small hours of the morning when Charlotte passed, after eight months gripped with whooping cough. Catherine gazed desperately into her eyes for the final time and squeezed her tightly. Another life slipping away in her arms, just as her other daughters, Catherine and Mary, had passed from this world another lifetime ago in Ireland. For four long days, Catherine had stayed in that workhouse after Charlotte had died. She wanted to be as close as she could to her daughter's body, as she didn't want to leave her alone. Now, having discharged herself, and once again wearing her own threadbare clothes after changing out of her workhouse uniform, she hauled her way up the streets to Charlotte's final resting place. This was a pauper's grave in Euston where her daughter's body would be buried with other poor and desperate souls.

The Devil's tears frozen over

It was a cold April morning and there was a heavy layer of frost on the ground of the cemetery. The Devil's tears frozen over, no doubt, on this saddest of all days. Charlotte was all Catherine had left of her love William, who had died just weeks after arriving on English soil. That was two autumns ago.

The journey across the Irish Sea had been as treacherous as the stories she had heard before they embarked on their journey to England. Huddled together without shelter and packed shoulder to shoulder with her fellow Irish people, there was no room to even sit down on the wooden decking. She and William had stood there for hours feeling the storm gradually encircle the ship, rocking it from side to side. There was no protection from the rain, and they were drenched through and bone cold. It got so rough people were falling into each other. Some poor souls were knocked down as they were too weak to stand up again, and so collapsed in a crumpled heap. Others held onto each other and to anything else they could to keep them from being washed overboard.

The crossing took a gruelling twenty hours. As they approached Liverpool, they saw hundreds of ships sailing along the river. The air was heavy with pungent smells, and there was so much noise compared with the only life they had ever known in the quietness of County Down.

When they docked, the crew drove the passengers down the boarding planks with sticks. Drenched by sea and rain and suffering from the cold and seasickness, many of the passengers were so weak they were scarcely able to walk and practically crawled ashore.

Liverpool offered little comfort to the Irish immigrants, rife with thieves and con men of every kind. Keeping their wits about them and careful not to make eye contact with anyone, Catherine and William avoided the fraudsters, moving out of Liverpool within a matter of days. They began their journey to London on the packet boat that travelled through the canals. They had been on English soil for only a few weeks when William's health took a drastic turn for the worse. Worn out with the hard labouring on the public building works and famished with hunger, he caught the fever. He picked it up in one of the lodging houses they had stayed in. He battled with the sickness for almost two weeks before his body finally gave in.

Catherine cradled William's head in her lap as he took his last breaths in this world. She lost herself in his eyes, wanting to hold on to this moment for an eternity. She wished time would stand still for them both. The moment came when his last breath passed his lips and his eyes fixed upwards to the sky. He was no more of this Earth. She was numb with the fear of being alone in this unfamiliar land. She was frozen and frightened. Yet she must continue, for the sake of the child she carried inside her. This was the only thing she had left of William, aside from her memories.

Catherine had to press on to London in the hope that she would find her brother who would take care of her. Being Irish, she was an unwelcome traveller wherever she went. She had constantly been afraid as she made the last leg of her journey alone, but now she was almost in London. She felt a small glimmer of hope that she would soon be in the safe embrace of her brother. That was if she could find him.

The packet boat carried her into the city. The buildings grew higher and darker as the canal paths became noisier. Black smoke filled the sky. The trees had stopped growing and there was no grass left to blow in the wind. The ground was nothing but dirt and cobbles. Stepping off the final boat, she walked further into the darkness of the city, picking her way through the narrow streets and trying to avoid the most dangerous-looking places. She moved between the ghetto buildings. Never before had she seen such squalor as she did here in London. There was so much despair in the wealthiest city in the world. There were foul ditches, open sewers, and defective drains with offensive smells. She passed two slaughterhouses in a few minutes. The noise of the animals had cut through to her core, as she stepped over the blood oozing into the street.

She found her way to the address on the letter she had received from her brother a year before: Falconberg Court in the district of Soho. This was once a favoured location of the aristocracy. It was different now. They had mostly all moved out to more desirable suburbs of London like Kensington. Now the streets were filled with prostitutes, music halls and small theatres. The population of Soho had swelled, making the area one of the most densely populated in London. Houses became divided into tenements with chronic overcrowding and riddled with disease. The people who stood around on the streets had sunken eyes and shrivelled skin.

She had never laid eyes on such sights as the crowded tenements, and she found it hard to believe that this was the richest city in the British Empire. She passed a cluster of women all crouching in a line on the kerbstone. They had baskets of dried herrings before them and their legs were drawn up so close to their chests that a thick plaid shawl covered their bodies. She asked them for directions, and they pointed their bony fingers towards an alley, motioning that it was just up there.

Falconberg Court was a little yard surrounded by ramshackle buildings that were sitting as infilling behind a once-elaborate street frontage. Catherine walked up an alley between two blackened buildings where all colour had leached away, except for the dull greys of smoke and soot. The buildings were so close together that people were talking to each other from their windows. Ropes for drying blankets and shirts stretched and zigzagged from wall to wall. The gutter was filled with dirty, grey water that had been emptied from the washtubs. Barefoot boys played at boats with pieces of rubbish.

Catherine climbed several steps to knock on one of the doors. The basement beneath her was filled with rotting rubbish that looked as though it had been festering there for years. The man who answered was the landlord. He was an unshaven man with a gaunt look who explained that her brother no longer lived there. He took her up to the first floor and offered her a space to rent in a room occupied by two other Irish families. One of the families consisted of a haggard man, his hollow-cheeked wife and their four children. The whole family were engrossed in making matchboxes; even the three-year-old girl was given a job spreading glue on the paper. The other family were a couple who were employed to tailor shirts while they looked after their baby boy. The room was nearly empty of furniture.

Irish famine migrants would often come together in ghettos such as Falconberg Court. These were the poorest of districts that were called 'nests of Irish'. Catherine had found herself in one of these. It seemed scarcely possible that human beings could live in such places. There were holes in the floors and parts of the stairs were broken. Plaster was peeling off walls that were once whitewashed but now housed a layer of black grime. In the windows, lumps of brown paper alternated with shivered panes of broken glass.

Catherine questioned some of the other tenants who were loitering around the entrance to the court. They explained that her brother had stayed here for a good while before finding employment in the north of London. They didn't know where he had gone or whether he would be coming back. All Catherine could do was wait and hope that he might return.

It was here in this tenement that she gave birth to her daughter in the depths of a cold January night. Catherine named her Emily Charlotte Riley, after William's mother. As soon as she was strong enough, Catherine took her to be baptised at the local parish church. Should her daughter die in this godforsaken place, at least her soul would be saved. Catherine was running out of money fast, and it would be only a matter of weeks before she had nothing left of what she and William had brought with them from Ireland. She was unable to work because she was nursing her baby, so Catherine began to prepare for the inevitable. She would soon be evicted. She was left with two choices. She could try to survive on the streets, or she could go to the place of last resort that they had left Ireland to avoid: the workhouse.

The walk of shame

Catherine was evicted early in April on Easter Saturday. It was a cold, wet morning and the sky was thick with dark clouds. The wind pierced through her threadbare clothes as she stepped out onto the street, closing the door behind her. She pulled Charlotte close to her skin. Exhausted from hunger and afraid of what would become of them both, Catherine picked her way through the detritus of Soho and made her way to St James Workhouse in the neighbouring parish of Piccadilly.

She followed an Irish family who were walking in the same direction. The man led the group first, his body hunched forward with exhaustion and his hands pushed deep in his pockets. Behind him, his wife held one child in her arms. She sheltered this child and one other who was slung over her back from the rain beneath a flimsy shawl. She was nearly bent double from the weight. Four other children clung to her skirt. They reached the workhouse doors before Catherine, looked up and then walked on. They were most likely seeking a final day together before they walked through those doors and were separated forever.

St James Workhouse was a tall and foreboding building with a huge heavy wooden door and a large knocker that

Catherine lifted and let fall onto the wood with a heavy thud. She held her breath and leaned against the wall, listening to the faint sound of footsteps drawing closer. The keys jangled as they unlocked the door.

It was a tall man with kind eyes but a stern face who opened the door to let her in. She was so slight that he didn't notice she had a babe in arms swaddled beneath her shawl. He led her through to the admissions room, where she was met by the matron, who also had a stern look, although this time with harsh eyes and tightly pursed lips to match.

After a lengthy stream of questions asking Catherine where she lived, where she had come from, who the father of her child was, and who was left to support her, she was told to strip naked. Her hair was cut short, and she was instructed to wash in a cold-water bath and bathe Charlotte too. Her daughters' cries pierced through the air as she screeched at the icy water touching her skin. Catherine's clothes were taken away and she was given a grey workhouse uniform to wear, the same as the other inmates. Charlotte was wrapped in a swaddling cloth and they were led to the nursery.

What a place to bring a child into. The nursery was a damp and miserable room with nothing but two rows of beds with cage-like cots next to them. There were ten other single mothers, in various degrees of disgrace, each with a sad-looking child. There were no toys or comforts. Catherine was given a bed with no mattress: just metal springs and two blankets. This was to be Charlotte's world until the day came when she would be taken from her mother's arms and sent to an industrial school. Victorian society harshly judged single mothers as having no right to children. Catherine was the only one amongst the women in the nursery who had been married and was now a widow. This did not matter though; all the women were treated the same. Catherine was a nursing mother, so she was allowed to keep her baby until she was two years old. After this, Charlotte would be taken from her.

However, Charlotte didn't live that long. The workhouse was rife with disease, and Charlotte began to cough just months after they came through that workhouse door. This led to something more severe: whooping cough. Charlotte would have fits of coughing that were so drastic it would lead her to vomit or have periods when she would stop breathing altogether.

Catherine nursed her daughter for eight long months as the cough got progressively worse. She willed her daughter to hold on to life, but she didn't know to what end. What prospects did her daughter have here in London so far away from her home soil? Positioned firmly at the lowest level of Victorian society, pauper children had few opportunities ahead of them growing up on the streets other than a life of extreme poverty and all the turmoil that came with this.

The night came when her daughter left this world. Catherine traced her tiny fingers in hers and gazed into her eyes, just as she had with William when he took his final breath, less than two years ago. Her daughter was exhausted with the perpetual gasping for air. Several days before, Charlotte had turned a blue colour and her limbs were limp. Catherine willed God to breathe life into her child, but her prayers were left unanswered. In the early hours of the morning, Charlotte died.

In the minutes following her passing Catherine wailed the words 'don't go, don't go', over and over, rocking back and forth, holding her daughter's limp body in her arms as she felt the warmth drain away. She had nothing left from Ireland now. She was alone with just her thoughts and memories. How would she carry on? How would she keep on living? How would she make herself a life here in this abyss?

Into service

In Victorian Britain, the prospects for a single Irish woman were limited. They occupied the bottom rung of the employment ladder. Many of the Irish who found their way to London were not skilled for work in the city. Having only worked on farms, they could only resort to street selling. Thousands of women would spend their days on the streets of London selling fresh fruits, vegetables and flowers from baskets or handmade carts. Others would walk from alehouse to alehouse selling pigs trotters, or eels. They would also seek employment as needlewomen, working from dawn to dusk sewing shirts.

These were all options available to Catherine. Now that she no longer had her daughter to care for, she could work. Employers would come to the workhouses when they were seeking more skilled workers. Catherine's prospects were a little better than many Irish women as she had experience from cleaning to sewing and everything in between. She could draw on what she learned in Ireland during her time in service.

She found employment as a house servant in a fine town-house in a middle-class area called Brompton, a hamlet in Kensington. Irish women would often seek out employment like this to improve their low status in society. This felt like a different world for Catherine. She recognised that she had a new life, and that there were opportunities unavailable to her as a single mother. When she had Charlotte, she had been marginalised and seen as a disgrace to society. Now Charlotte was no longer of this Earth, there was a chance that she could perhaps find a place within respectable society. Mixed with the grief she felt, what could she do other than put her best foot forward and build a new life for herself? She thought back to the moment her father had spoken as she left, about how she was strong and heard his words: 'Don't fear my strong-spirited girl, you have a great determination still left in you'. She drew on this determination as she walked up the upper-class street in Kensington to her new employer and new home at the address 2 York Cottages.

Life in service in London was very different to what she had experienced in Ireland amongst her kin. She was the only house servant, so she had to do everything. The wealthy couple were rarely there as they chose to spend their time at their other home in the country. They had left their three children here in London with their cousin and governess Clara. There was Walter, aged ten, Emma, aged eight and Alfred, aged two. It hadn't escaped Catherine's notice that the children were of a similar age to hers, or at least they would've been if they had survived, and this was difficult to bear day in and day out. She wondered why she had been dealt such a cruel hand. Why had fate been so hard on her?

A servant's life in Victorian Britain was similar to that of a bird shut up in a cage: well-housed and well-fed but depleted of liberty. Catherine's day would begin at 7 am by bringing hot water up to the bedrooms. She would work right through to 10 pm with every minute accounted for. The work was boring, repetitive and demanding, and it was a lonely time for Catherine, despite there being a house full of children. Her tasks included emptying the bedpans, washing clothes, washing the dishes and keeping the house clean. She was living in a grand house surrounded by beautiful furnishings, the like she had never laid eyes on before. Yet, she was very much kept at a distance from the family and was reminded that she was not one of them and not of their class. She slept in the attic room, and at first, she struggled with the empty feeling of the grand house. There were so few people living in such a large space. She had to acclimatise to being on her own at night too. Up until this point she had always slept in a room with other people.

She was given time off on a Sunday to go to church. The message in the sermons incorporated the strong Protestant work ethic. It was always about accepting one's station in life, and the best thing that she could do to serve God was to do good and honourable work.

During the years working in service in London, Catherine didn't go hungry and was warm and well dressed. She was somebody. When it was just her and Charlotte, Victorian society had looked down on her with scorn. Although she was a widow with a child, people did not care for her story and saw her as a fallen woman, a disgrace to the Victorian people. Now she didn't have her daughter to care for, she was a little higher up the rungs of poverty. There were no opportunities to become richer in this line of work, only for Catherine to stay in her place. Catherine had to accept her station in life and stand still in a world that was shifting around her.

Then a change breezed into her life, and with it a glimmer of hope. A visitor from Ireland came to stay, a young barrister of law called John Hickson. Over the months that followed, he showed affection towards her. Catherine felt love blossoming, and he told her so. This wasn't the first time a man had shown interest in Catherine. They were entranced by her soft gentle manner. A man's affection went some way to filling the aching emptiness that throbbed in her body day and night since losing William. During her time in the workhouse, she had fallen for a fellow pauper, Henry Chard. Although men and women were kept separate in the workhouse, there were opportunities for the opposite sexes to meet whilst labouring. Catherine took some solace from this.

Catherine was drawn in by the barrister's eloquent charm, and she became close to him. He eased the grief in her bones and ignited hope for the future. She felt safe in his arms and trusted in his promises. It was common for the gentry to take advantage of the women in service, and Catherine learnt of this in the cruellest of ways. When she fell pregnant by him, he denied all relations. All the words they had shared fell away as he walked out and shut the door firmly behind him. John went back to his home where he could forget about Catherine and their unborn child, pretending they didn't exist.

Catherine held onto her service job for as long as she could. With her employers away, Clara took pity on her and allowed her to stay for a while. But a mistress's personal reputation is dependent on the moral conduct and behaviour of her servants. If society saw her servant had given birth to a baby, it was deemed the mistress's fault that she had failed to teach her the way of middle-class righteousness.

Catherine was sacked from her job when she could no longer hide her pregnancy. Once again, after this brief interlude of being a part of civilised society, she found herself back on the London streets once more. She turned her back on high-class Kensington and began the walk back to Westminster and the poverty that awaited her there. Her path took her alongside the gates of Buckingham Palace, where she was stopped from crossing the road because of a passing military parade. A long procession of horses and guards imposed their way past her. The might of the British Empire and the wealth of the royal palace lay in front of her eyes. Just a mile up the road was the government that made the decisions that had led her to this foreign place.

She had been ripped from her family, her community and her life in Ireland. She was a world away from the small croft she had shared with William only a few years before. She was only partly here in London. Her soul was still in Ireland. She was alone, numb with fear and apprehension, with just a few coins to pay for a few weeks' lodgings and food. She took her attention away from the procession to the life she carried inside her. What would be the fate of this child, she wondered, as she put one foot in front of the other and made her way back to the slums of Victorian London.

***

OPPRESSION & CONTROL

I am going to address oppression and control in this chapter as two of the overarching themes that speak to me through Catherine's story. Firstly, I will share my interpretation of how the dynamic of oppression and control has played out through recent history and my own life. Towards the end of the chapter, I will offer examples of how I have worked through oppression and control within my own life to find a place of greater freedom.

Catherine's loss of freedom, extreme poverty, and lack of choice are very apparent from the point she moved from her cottage in Ireland to the heart of the industrial world. This is the symbolism of the military parade, that mighty force keeping everyone in check. This illustrates for me how broken civilisation is. Catherine's story shows how inequality played out in Victorian times and illustrates the vast divide between the controlling elite and the poor. This division of wealth is still prevalent today, and it is a story that goes back a very long time, right back to the dawn of civilisation. In this chapter, I am going to share how the dynamic of oppression and control came about. Before this, I want to talk about how I came to gain the insights I have shared in this part of Catherine's story about her early years living in London.

Walking in ancestral footsteps

Many of the ideas and the story images came to me as I traced Catherine's footsteps through the streets of London, walking in the very places Catherine walked almost two centuries ago. In the final scene, when Catherine is crossing London from Kensington to Westminster, she reaches the gates of Buckingham Palace, and the military parade passes her. This happened to me.

A few months after the Summer Solstice in June 2018 when I first decided I wanted to write about Catherine's life, I got a strong urge to go down to London to explore where Catherine lived. This was a result of a supervision session with Jayne. Coincidentally, the only time I was able to go to London was Samhain, which is the Celtic festival when the ancestors are honoured. The synchronicity was not lost on me, and I made my plans to take a three-day trip.

The trouble was that I only had £100 to spend on my travel, accommodation and food. If I was to make this trip, it needed to be a London mini-break on a shoestring. I wouldn't usually try to do something like this. I would talk myself out of it because I couldn't afford it. This time I overcame my internal objections. I didn't want to stay with friends because that would take me out of my mindset. I wanted to be on my own. Once I had paid for my train fare, I only had enough money left to stay in a youth hostel. I paid for this in advance, which left me with a few pounds. It would be a very different kind of trip as I was leaving home with so little money to live on during my time in London. I was concerned about this, but I persisted with my plans. Then good fortune struck as I left our home for the train station – my mother- and father-in-law, who live next door, reached into their pockets, and each gave me a £20 note.

So, £40 is what I lived on in London for three days, and it meant that I took a totally different approach to the visit than I would normally. Interestingly, visiting London on a shoestring opened my eyes to more about Catherine's life than if I had more money to spend.

I haven't stayed in a youth hostel for over ten years, and I have never contemplated staying in one in London. I chose one as close to Kensington as possible, as I wanted to sleep where Catherine had lived. I was following through an idea that came to me to sleep in all the locations where my ancestors had lived. My intention was to observe the dreams that I had whilst sleeping in these ancestral places. I was given a bed in a basement room by the main door. There were thirteen strangers in that dormitory. It was noisy and smelly, and an argument broke out next to my bed in the small hours of the morning while I was trying to sleep. I feared for my belongings being stolen, and so I carried everything with me wherever I went. I got a flavour, just a hint, of what it might have been like for Catherine arriving in London alone and having to find accommodation with strangers, which I would not have experienced had my circumstances been different.

Having very little money also meant that I had to walk everywhere. Normally I would have bought a London Travelcard and found my way around London by bus and tube. This gave me a different perspective on Catherine's life as I walked the very streets she would have walked. Because of this, I discovered that the house she worked in as a servant was on the same road as the Harrods department store. And yes, I ended up walking past Buckingham Palace, and a military parade also stopped me. This was mid-morning at the time of the Changing of the Guard.

The stark difference between Catherine's life and the life of the aristocracy was made very apparent to me during those few days I walked the streets of London. I saw the wealth of London all around me, in the buildings in Piccadilly, Westminster, Kensington and Buckingham Palace. Catherine would also have seen these. I didn't have enough money to eat in restaurants and cafés, so these places were closed off for me. I had to carefully budget the food I bought from shops and then ate outside in public places. There was often no bench to sit on and so I would eat standing up. I felt set apart because of this and looked at London differently. I had inadvertently forced myself to leave my comfortable life, and in doing so, I had gained insight into the kinds of challenges Catherine faced and felt during her first years in London.

On arriving in London, Catherine was forced to live in the worst of the slums. The Victorian government blamed the Irish for the extreme poverty seen on the streets of the industrial towns and cities in England. They were convenient scapegoats for the problems that were already there before Irish people arrived during the famine years. Housing developers were allowed to build cheap housing of a very low standard. There was no requirement for them to develop infrastructural services such as sewerage and clean water. Landlords were not required to clean up the slums either. As more people arrived in London every day, seeking work, the demand for housing increased and vastly exceeded supply. This meant landlords had no incentive to invest some of their profits in cleaning up the slums. I have also explained the appalling land-grab process in the previous chapter, which forced millions of people off their land and into the cities in a very short space of time.

The situation in London didn't improve for the next two decades. Towards the end of the nineteenth century, there were improvements to sanitation and also slum clearances. As slums were cleared, the poor moved further east towards the docklands, so these slums became even more crowded. Landlords were eventually forced to improve their buildings for tenants, but this took them well into the twentieth century. It is a battle that is still going on today. The example of Grenfell Tower, which is also located in Kensington, helps to illustrate this. Due to the cost of fire defences such as sprinklers, the lack of provision was a key factor in the loss of seventy-two lives when Grenfell Tower burnt down in the summer of 2017. Landlords prioritised profits over the safety of tenants.[39] This battle of the nineteenth century still plays out today, with a disregard for people in preference to profitable gain.

'The Irish' were also blamed for employment shortages with job advertisements prefaced with words like: 'Irish need not apply'.[40] Newspaper headlines would lead with statements such as: 'Swarms' of Irish descending on cities and taking jobs. During Catherine's first few years living in the slums and her time in the workhouse, she did well to find such respectable employment after her daughter's death. The fact that she was Protestant would likely have been instrumental in this, along with the experience she gained in service during her early adult years in Ireland. To get a job as a house servant was the most respectable employment available to a single Irish woman.

Yet being a house servant was very difficult and lonely. It was a status symbol of the middle classes to have a servant, but they often couldn't really afford them, so they just had one whose job was to do everything. Servants never got a break and were often treated badly. This attitude is still prevalent in our culture today. Domestic service remains poorly paid, and it tends not to be appealing employment for many British people. Instead, in the twenty-first century, live-in servants or au pairs often fulfil this role and are required to work for around thirty hours per week without entitlement to the National Minimal Wage or paid holidays.[41]

It must have been incredibly hard for Catherine to live in a family home like this, surrounded by children the same age as her own children would have been had they survived. She had no breaks, and she was likely treated as lower class every minute of the day. What strikes me with Catherine's story is how few choices she had. In the nineteenth century, the upper and middle classes believed that the poor brought poverty on themselves, as some people still believe now. Through the cruel hand of fate, it seems that most choices were taken away from Catherine. She made the best of a terrible situation. If these things had happened to me, I have no idea how I would have coped. This speaks to me of the strength of Catherine's character and her determination to survive no matter what. I recognise this trait in myself, too.

From the moment Catherine became pregnant, her life changed drastically. This was her point of no return. From now on, Victorian society saw Catherine as a fallen woman and treated her very differently. Yet, as I will explain in the following chapters, she did have options available to her, and the choices she made showed her strength of character.

Catherine's time in Ireland before the famine was good in comparison to her life in London. This is despite eight hundred years of English rule that had brought the country to the brink of despair. The decisions that were made by parliament in

London had a devastating impact on Irish people during the Great Famine. Had it not been for the potato blight, the Irish would have managed. Conditions had to become really terrible for them to want to leave their homeland.

In the last chapter, I talked about how destructive it can be for a person to leave their land and disconnect from nature. When a person is separated from the soil and can no longer grow their own food, from that moment onwards, people are reliant on others to feed them. This enforced dependency means that they are open to being controlled. This whole story is an illustration of the drama that has played out in the world throughout history: the issue of oppression and control by the privileged few over the many who are underprivileged – and that continues today. For years I have wondered how this all arose. I found the answer in one of the most eye-opening books I have ever read.

THE FALL OF HUMANITY

The Fall: The Insanity of the Ego in Human History and the Dawning of A New Era, by psychologist Steve Taylor, is an excellent book to read if you are a person who questions what has become of humanity.[42] In his book, Taylor seeks to answer questions like: why do we think the way we do? What have we lost? What do we need to rediscover if we are to survive on Earth? Is there another option besides the atrocities that civilisation brings: war, greed, suffering, crime, homelessness, depression and inequality?

I was born into a world where there are dominant narratives that support war, genocide, mass murder, and atrocious inequalities between rich and poor as the only way, and this is seen as normal. Taylor presents his theory that this tendency towards certain behaviours that lead to these terrible outcomes is not a normal trait of humanity. These behaviours were born out of a single culture that existed in the Sahara region of the world around six thousand years ago. Something happened back then that caused those people to disassociate themselves from their bodies, each other and nature, dominate other cultures and eventually take over the whole world. He argues that this something was climate change. As the temperature rose, less rain fell, which resulted in food shortages. In two hundred years, a group of people emerged who were very different to anything the world had ever seen before.

This group of people have been extremely successful in spreading their way of living throughout the world to bring us to this current time, where we are at the brink of extreme crisis. Taylor argues that if things do not change, in less than one hundred years, this now very large group of people may very well wipe out the entire human species and much of the rest of life on Earth.

Taylor presents his work in three sections. Part One looks at the history of 'The Fall'. He begins by presenting evidence of what is known as The Golden Age. This was a period where cities didn't need walls, where men and women enjoyed equal status and experienced a sense of psychological well-being and connection to the cosmos. Taylor then shows that a transformation began from around 4000 BC due to dramatic changes in the climate of central Asia and the Middle East. He explains how this group of people spread civilisation, bringing an end to the indigenous way of life to many parts of the world.

Taylor then goes on to present the psychological problems that resulted from this change, which in turn led to an underlying unhappiness, including aloneness, perpetual sleep, and fear of death. In relation to the idea of perpetual sleep, he speaks of how indigenous peoples see the world in an animistic way: with animals, plants, rivers and rocks being sentient beings and very much 'alive'. He reflects on how in the modern world, many people pay hardly any attention to the natural world, and instead, focus on tasks, distractions and thoughts chattering in their heads.

Taylor talks of how people living in a Western culture seek to avoid unhappiness by embracing distractions through materialism and gaining status. He finishes the book by looking at what he terms 'The Trans-Fall Era'. He presents evidence for a gradual shift in consciousness in several waves over the last fifteen hundred years. For example, just three hundred years ago, back in the eighteenth century in England, the lack of compassion people showed for each other was quite shocking and makes for difficult reading. Public hangings were a spectator sport and considered a source of entertainment where people were put to death for minor crimes, such as theft, that would only attract a fine nowadays. Criminals were branded with a hot iron or would have body parts removed, such as ears and fingers. Other people who defied the law were immobilised within the stocks, and people were encouraged to throw stones at them, which often resulted in head injuries that led to death. In Catherine's story, we can see how the poor were so badly treated, and how little regard was given to a human being at the bottom of the social ladder.

Taylor argues that there was a particularly pronounced shift during the eighteenth century. He presents a positive view that there is also a renewed shift taking place right now. He offers that we can choose whether we want to be a part of this current shift in consciousness or not. He lists several contributing factors to this shift, one of which is connecting with nature and rewilding, quoting a poem by Shelley that was written two centuries ago. This poem speaks to me as Shelley summarises the importance of seeking out wild places and how they are a balm for the soul.

Away, away from men and towns.
To the wild wood and the downs—
To the silent wilderness
Where the soul need not repress
Its music lest it should not find
An echo in another's mind.[43]

Taylor's book has answered several questions for me. It has helped me make sense of the world in order to forge a path to a new way of life. I live in a culture in which terrible treatment of fellow human beings has been normalised because of the sequence of events that began over six thousand years ago. I agree with Taylor that a small number of people and a particular way of thinking has dominated the world. Extreme poverty is accepted and normalised as a necessity of civilisation. It makes me wonder what happens within someone that makes them feel they need to be master of other people's slavery. I believe it comes from a wound, a need to try to make oneself safe – and to feel safe, they need to have a lot of money.

As I've said before, what is clear to me is that civilisation doesn't work. It reminds me of something the Dalai Lama said when he was asked what he thought of civilisation. He said: 'I think it is a very good idea'. In his succinct response, the Dalai Lama is insinuating that civilisation is a good idea, but not good in practice.

Civilisation must prevail

If civilisation has such terrible consequences, why has it lasted? It has survived because there is a core belief that civilisation is the only way to live and it must prevail at all costs. It is incomprehensible to the majority of people living within a civilisation that there is any other way they can live on Earth.

Daniel Quinn presents this idea in his book *Beyond Civilization: Humanity's Next Great Adventure.*[44] Quinn explains that a culture is made up of a series of beliefs or myths. These are stories that the individual humans who make up that culture tell themselves this is the way that things have to be.

Those people who emerged from the Sahara region six thousand years ago held the belief that they should rule the world and that civilisation was the only way to live. This was a lethal belief, but it didn't have a lethal effect all those thousands of years ago, or even just hundreds of years ago. But, now, here in the twenty-first century, we have reached critical mass, and the devastation caused by people holding this belief is plain to see. Without a change in belief, it is now a matter of life and death for humanity and much of life on Earth.

Quinn offers hope by describing cultures who have adopted this belief and embraced civilisation, only to change their mind and abandon it later on. He cites several ancient civilisations as examples, including the Mayans who occupied a large area of what is now Brazil, several thousand years ago. The Mayan culture flourished for nearly three thousand years. Then at the beginning of the ninth century, the cities began to be abandoned. Quinn presents the theory that the Mayans walked away from their cities under their own steam, simply donning their tools and moving back into the jungle. It is a controversial view, and there have been many alternative theories as to why the Mayan civilisation collapsed, including overuse of the soil, climatic changes and disease. However, Quinn argues that this theory of simply abandoning the cities and disappearing back into the jungle seems so mysterious to historians because it is unfathomable that cultures would not pursue civilisation at any cost. When they no longer liked what they were building, the Mayans were able to walk away from it.

Walking away from civilisation is incomprehensible to most people in our modern-day world. People know civilisation doesn't work but see no alternative. Culture says that civilisation must prevail at any cost, even if that means humanity destroying itself.

In his book, Quinn presents some practical suggestions on what a new model for society might look like. He makes the case that:

> No single person is going to save the world. Rather (if
> it's saved at all), it will be saved by millions, and ulti-
> mately billions of us living a new way. A thousand living
> a new way won't cause the dominant world to topple.

But that thousand will inspire a hundred thousand, who
will inspire a million, who will inspire a billion, and
then that world order will begin to look shaky.[45]

When I look at the scale of change that is required, I can feel
quite overwhelmed. However, I take comfort in what Quinn
describes here. Change happens at an individual level. If a
thousand people choose to live a new way, this will influence
a thousand more. The first step begins with an individual
choosing to live a different way. I have the capacity within
me to make that choice to live a different way. From my own
experience, there have been several things I have had to work
on to enable me to be able to do this. One of these things is
to recognise the oppressive world that I have been born into
and how this impacts me and my choices.

As part of this work, I have found it helpful to look back
at the oppression in my country over the centuries. By understanding the history of oppression, it has helped me see the
story I have been born into. In turn, that has helped me decide
how I choose to live within this story.

The last of the free folk

Here in England, we have had our fair share of oppressive
regimes. For example, there was the Roman invasion two thousand years ago. This came to a head with the last rebellion of
the Celtic tribal people against the Romans, which was led by
Queen Boudica in AD 60. Fast forward one thousand years
and there was the invasion of the Normans, led by the Duke
of Normandy. The Duke crossed the channel from France
and crowned himself King after his victorious win against
the Anglo-Saxon king, King Harold II, at the Battle of Hastings
in 1066. He was named William the Conqueror and we still
live under the shadow of the Norman Conquest to this day.

I grew up in Kent and learned about the Battle of Hastings
in my history lessons at school. I was taught that it was a

pivotal moment, bringing much-needed order and prosperity to Britain. Kent has its fair share of Norman castles and at the time, I never thought to ask who the enemy was that the Normans wanted to protect themselves from. As I lived on the coast, I saw that the castles I visited pointed out towards the sea. I assumed the Normans built these to protect themselves from foreign invaders.

It never occurred to me that it was the Normans themselves that were the invaders. It was much later on in my life when, seeing that towns and cities located inland also had Norman castles, I realised that the Normans built them as protection from the people of England, and as a means to keep them under control.

At the moment when King Harold II of England was killed during the Battle of Hastings, land ownership immediately changed. The native people of England went from owning 90 per cent of the land before the battle to 10 per cent after. William the Conqueror declared that all land, animals and people belonged to him personally and then divided control of these between his lords and barons. From this, a form of modified slavery developed as well as devastation to the countryside, and famine.

This period in history is described brilliantly and creatively by Paul Kingsnorth in his fictional novel *The Wake*, which tells of an Anglo-Saxon freeman named 'Buccmaster of Holland' who came to terms with the effects of the Norman Conquest of 1066.[46] The months and years following the conquest marked one of the worst periods of massacre in the history of Britain. Those who survived retreated to the cover of the forest.

It is believed that this is where the legend of Robin Hood began. English legal records suggest that as early as the thirteenth century, 'Robehod', 'Rabunhod' and other variations of the name had become common labels for criminals. There was a band of survivors, many Robin Hoods across the country who were the last of the free folk. They launched attacks on the Normans over the centuries that followed, fighting to hold on to their autonomy and everything they knew.

The story of Robin Hood is one of our most well-known and well-loved legends. It is the great story of the oppressors and the oppressed: the fight against power and control and holding onto freedom, and the redistribution of wealth and giving back to the common folk what is rightfully theirs. The ongoing popularity of this legend tells me that this is a story that the British people can relate to in their psyche, despite it being almost one thousand years ago. I believe we love it because it speaks to a deep part of us, and one we may not be consciously aware of. When I internalise the story, I can see that the legend of Robin Hood wasn't just about stealing from the rich to give to the poor, it was about holding onto freedom, and fighting for what they saw as right and true.

The Norman invasion of England in 1066 predated the Scottish Clearances of the eighteenth century and the Great Irish Famine of the nineteenth century by seven hundred and eight hundred years respectively. The scale of the devastation to the settled people of England is no longer in collective awareness: the loss of land ownership and the genocide. For example, William the Conqueror took extreme steps to quash a rebellion in the north of England several years after he crowned himself King, known as the 'Harrying of the North' in 1069–70.

This resulted in the genocide of 75 per cent of the people who lived between Chester and Shrewsbury in the west to Cleveland in the east of England. Livestock, crops and farming equipment were all burned to ensure that rebels wouldn't be able to support themselves. The consequence of this was famine. It is a telling statistic that in the 1086–7 CE Domesday Book, which is a carefully compiled record of land assets and property in Norman England, entries that describe northern areas of England often said it was 'a waste land'. Northumberland was not deemed worth recording at all.[47]

The impact of the Norman Conquest on the common people is still prevalent today. Some families proudly claim they are direct descendants of the nobles who fought in the battle of 1066, forming the ruling elite and governing the country through their seats in the House of Lords. Queen Elizabeth II herself is a direct descendant of William the Conqueror as his twenty-fourth great-granddaughter.[48] Still in the shadow of the Norman Conquest, Britain has one of the worst land-to-people ownership ratios globally, second only to Brazil, as half of the land in Britain is owned by just 1 per cent of the population.[49] Knowing this helps me realise that the scenario that is so apparent in Catherine's life is still playing out today: that is, the landowners and the landless. This disparity is illustrated well in an extract from an article in the Guardian newspaper which tells the story of a working-class man who drew to the attention of the government the impossibility of him ever owning land:

> In May 1981, unemployed, thirty-two-year-old Dave Batty walked from Hull to the Houses of Parliament to deliver a note to the Prime Minister drawing attention to the plight of the unemployed. Mr Batty, an ex-farm worker and ex-lorry driver had called at every Jobcentre along the way, but none had been able to offer work. As he waited in the Commons Central Lobby, he said: 'My idea of heaven would be 10 acres of land. If I had that, I'd happily go away and not bother anyone about work ever again.' The chances of Mr Batty getting his hands on 10 acres of Britain are virtually nil. In 1981 that amount of land would have cost him about £17,000. No bank would have advanced him that sort of money ... even if he were in work; on a farm worker's wage (£5,000 per year for a 46-hour week in 1981) he would have had little hope of saving the sum he needed.

> In August 1984, Simon George Strangways Morrison was born. Baby Simon is the heir through his mother to a 3,000-acre estate in Nottinghamshire, 15,000 acres

of Dorset and a valuable parcel of London. Without any
exertion on his part, Simon can look forward to joining
a small elite whose grip upon the broad acres of rural
Britain is as absolute as that of the Norman Barons.
Simon's good fortune is bad news for Dave Batty. But
what does it mean for the people of Britain as a whole
that the land is in the grip of a privileged few?[50]

If you are interested in reading more about this disparity
between land ownership in Britain, I recommend *The Book
of Trespass: Crossing the Lines* that Divide Us by Nick Hayes.[51]
Hayes presents an excellent account of the legacy that followed
William the Conqueror's victory spanning the last thousand
years right up to the present day.

The internal voice

I have found it helpful to have an awareness of how broken
civilisation is and how this came about. I have also found it
useful to have a knowledge of the history of oppression in
my own country and how this is still playing out today. This
understanding has led me to explore the answers to several
questions. Firstly, what impact has living in an oppressive
world had on me? Secondly, how can I use this awareness
to navigate my way to take more control of my life and the
choices I make?

To answer these questions, I am going to focus on
how I broke away from a controlling workplace: the corporations. I will share my views about my own internal oppressor,
which is that inner voice telling me that I have to work above
all else. I will also share how I have broken away from the
traditional workplace to find my way to personal freedom by
working for myself.

I can relate to the story of Robin Hood in my own inner
workings. I call my internal oppressor my inner Sheriff of
Nottingham. It was easy to externalise the oppressor, as I did

when I was working in the corporations. I saw my employers as the oppressor, telling me what I had to do. It was a lightbulb moment for me because when I left the corporations and didn't have a manager instructing me on what I had to do, I found that I still had an internal boss. I was under a similar amount of pressure, but I was the one orchestrating it, not a senior management team. I was setting my own goals and putting myself under an immense amount of pressure to achieve them. In time I managed to reconcile this inner conflict so that working for myself was more freeing in the long term.

I continue to recognise this voice in me. Even after all these years of being self-employed, it is still there. It is the voice that says I must work rather than play. It is the voice that says I must do this thing that earns money over the thing that brings me joy. It's an ongoing process to quieten this voice and create more time to play. In Chapters 4 and 5, I will explore this idea of replacing work with play in more detail.

Breaking or leaving

The story of oppression begins in childhood for many people. Children are powerless in relation to their caregivers, and what happens to us up to the age of seven is stored in our bodies. I will speak more about this in Chapter 4 as I go into detail about the therapeutic process of Embodied Relational Therapy as a method that works to release trauma residing in our bodies.

It can be the case that as parents follow their own patterns, they become part of the oppression of children without necessarily wanting to or being conscious of this. I had a happy childhood and was brought up in a loving home, but it still left me with my inner Sheriff of Nottingham voice that had a controlling force over me.

When I left home, I unconsciously sought out a controlling environment to function in, which was the workplace. Having become aware of the devastating impacts humans were having on the planet, I wanted to 'save the world'. The best way I decided I could do that was by positioning myself inside the places where the problems arose, the corporations. I set myself on a career path to help change the way businesses were conducted. Looking back, it was only going to end in one of two ways: by me breaking or me leaving. I had had a breakdown once before, and after a decade of working inside the corporations, I was on the verge of this happening a second time. I chose to leave in the end.

Back then, mental health was still a taboo subject, or at least it was in my circles. I had my nervous breakdown early in adult life when I was twenty-one. I was coming to the end of my third year at university, and I couldn't cope psychologically with that academic structure and living in Liverpool. It was at the end of the recession in the 1990s, and there was a lot of poverty in the city. I lived in one of the poorest areas in the country, just on the edge of Toxteth, where the legacy of the Poll Tax riots was still heavy in the air. There was a lot of crime. Our terraced house was repeatedly broken into, and the police were regularly there.

A series of circumstances mounted up that got me down. A good friend died in a car accident. My boyfriend and I broke up. My housemate was physically threatened by a burglar one night as we slept in our beds. We had just rows of terraces with no green space around us, and many of the shops were boarded up. All of these challenges left me with a deep feeling of loneliness. This was confusing as the university years were supposed to be the best years of my life, and I felt like a failure. I feared that no one liked me and that I was all alone, and yet this couldn't have been further from the truth. I had some very good friends, and we are still close to this day.

What I have learned about mental health is that the mind isn't rational. Looking back now, I wonder if the environment I was living in triggered an ancestral memory in my DNA, for I felt desperately lonely. At my worst, I was afraid to go outside and didn't open the curtains for days on end. I rarely talk about this period in my life, yet it was pivotal for me. Once I had recovered, my decisions were all based on what I had learned from dropping into that place, determined that I would never let myself go back there again. This paid off because in the following decade or so, when I noticed the signs of depression returning, I managed to avoid breaking down a second time.

The overarching theme during my early adult years continued to be loneliness and not fitting in. I always had very close friends and we cared for each other deeply, but there were many years when I felt deep down there was something that wasn't quite right about my life. I didn't feel like I truly belonged. This was a recurring theme until I found my way to Shamanism, and back to the Earth. I came home.

The signs of the oncoming of a second breakdown came when I was at the height of my career as a senior sustainability manager for a large global construction firm. It was a good job for a sustainability professional, and I should have been happy: only I wasn't. I was desperate, and two things had brought this on. I felt desperate because of the impending climate crisis. I could see that climate change was imminent and that we were on course to reach the tipping point in the next decade or so. I was panicking, but, around me no one else was. In an attempt to stem climate change, I worked tirelessly to raise awareness of climate change and influence people to reduce their impact on the Earth.

However, the level of changes required to stop climate change was not happening. One of my inner battles was how we needed to raise the alarm within the organisation I worked for. It had to be done calmly and reasonably, otherwise people would tune out. It also had to be within the business case. By business case, I mean the senior management team would only look at reducing the company's environmental impacts if it either saved money or made money, but not purely for the good of the cause.

The other thing that brought on my feeling of depression was that I was a 'yes person'. I really struggled to say no, and this was not ideal in the organisation I worked for. People knew that if they wanted something done well, they would ask me. The sustainability team was a small department. There were just eight of us in an organisation of thousands. We were charged with advising the company on ways to become more sustainable, with a reduced impact on the environment. Yet people would see it as our responsibility to make change happen. With budgets slashed after the 2008 financial crash, we weren't able to grow our team or employ external consultants, and yet the performance demands increased. I was getting busier and busier, and working longer hours with sixty-hour weeks being the norm.

Reaching out

These pressures caused me to seek help, and help came in the most interesting of ways. I initially went to my doctor, but he wanted to prescribe me anti-depressants. Having been on these during my first experience of depression, I declined them. I didn't feel it was what I wanted. Looking back now, being depressed at the looming threat of climate change and overworking was a normal psychological response to what I was facing. Taking medication wouldn't have been a long-term solution. It would only have enabled me to tolerate being in a broken place a little longer. This was my situation though I appreciate that many people benefit from prescribed medication to manage their mental health and that it is an important route to recovery for them.

I was in the process of waking up, where I was questioning the world I lived in and the life choices I had made. This led me to want to try out new things. The path to my solution began with a weekend festival in the southwest of England called the Sunrise Festival. It was in its first year, and the festival webpage came up on a Google search as I was looking for weekend experiences to enjoy with my friends. I posed the idea to my camping friends, who gave a unanimous yes. What was different about this festival was that in addition to the music there were lots of talks. I attended the spirituality workshops and, through these, was introduced to the practice of Qigong. When I got home, I sought out a local class and found a local teacher.

After I'd started the classes, she sent me an email one day with the words: 'You are open-minded and interested in trying different things, Nicola, so this might be of interest to you.' It was a flyer for a labyrinth at Gorton Monastery in Manchester. I had never heard of the Monastery or a labyrinth, but I was drawn to giving it a go.

A labyrinth is a pattern on the ground that provides space for a meditative walk and it has been used across the world for thousands of years. I believe the energy of this labyrinth pulled me in, and this was a turning point in my life. For on that day, I met my psychotherapist, Liz Clarke, and we were together for ten years until she retired. I was tearful when I met her that Sunday as I was in a difficult place. I remember the day well as it felt odd driving into Manchester on the first properly sunny Saturday of spring, in early May. Normally I would be out walking the hills of the Peak District, but instead, I was driving in the opposite direction. Liz owned the cloth labyrinth, which was a replica of the one at Chartres Cathedral in France.

I wanted to have therapy with Liz after meeting her, but my diary was so full at this point that every minute was accounted for over the next two months. I explained this to Liz and she was happy to meet up with me at 7:30 am in the morning. That was what my life was back then: a never-ending to-do list and feeling I had no control of my time. I needed to be seen in the office as well as being expected to travel all around Britain.

I went to Liz to learn to say no, and it took me four years to crack. That was four years of therapy every week to unpick why I was struggling to say no and build up enough courage to say it and say it enough times with gravitas to be effective. I learnt that once I was able to say no, I could claim back my time for myself. The managers at the construction firm were nice people, with whom I got on well. However, they were also trained in managing people to achieve their end goals, which meant that they were skilled at getting people to say yes to requests. This, coupled with the fact that I found it hard to say no, meant I was very busy all of the time. I wanted to please. Internally I had an inner child fear of displeasing the parents, and this parent and child dynamic played out in the workplace.

I still have dreams about being controlled by the corporations even now, and I left that job ten years ago. I believe that there is also something ancestral at play here in addition to the inner child fear. If my ancestors were to displease their employers, they would lose their jobs, and they would be that bit closer to needing to go to the workhouse. Employees needed to toe the line, otherwise the worst of fates awaited them. This was the control the elite, the privileged, had over people. If you were controversial and stood up to them about something you disagreed with or asked for higher wages or improved working conditions, then you stood to lose everything. This is what kept the machine turning.

Much of my work in psychotherapy with Liz has been about finding my voice: recognising that I have a voice in the world. I particularly remember working with this when I became self-employed after leaving working inside the corporations.

Following the financial crash in 2008, the company I worked for underwent a series of restructures. It took a while to filter through to my position in the company, but I was made redundant from my job three years later. I took it hard: the kicking out from the tribe. My rational mind told me it was an opportunity, yet I was frightened and felt abandoned. However, rather than go and get another job in a similar firm, I decided that I was brave enough to try something different.

I used the redundancy money to carry me for the time I needed to set up my own consultancy business. This was an interim measure as I tried to figure out what my purpose was in the world. I became an independent consultant to take back control of my time. I had come to realise that employment with a big company was an imprisonment for me. I would sign a form to say that for so many hours every week I gave my time over to someone else. When I wanted to be released, I had to ask permission and have a form signed. I had to put in an application to be released from my desk. I realise this is normal to many people, but this began to seem nonsensical. I now feel this way with regards to signing one's life over to someone else to achieve their ends.

What I discovered when I had my own consultancy was that I hadn't broken free of the work ethic. I was still saying yes, and still working very long hours. But that voice that I had assumed was my boss in all the organisations where I had worked had been internalised. I had my own inner boss putting the pressure on me. It was an interesting realisation, as I could no longer blame someone else external to me. I had to look within. I will talk more about how I overcame this later in the chapter. What I want to explain here is how I found my voice and left that culture altogether.

Moving towards a simpler life

Finding my voice happened through a combination of shamanic journeying, nature connection and mythology. In Shamanism, we work with the messages of animals that we meet when we shift our consciousness through journeying and noticing animals we see out in nature. I will explain more about shamanic journeying in a moment. The process of finding my voice came to its head when I met with Dragon during a shamanic journey over the Spring Equinox. What I would soon discover about dragon energy is that if you have something to say, it will suddenly become difficult to keep it in. This was normally the other way around for me as I was a master of not voicing controversial opinions. It came as quite a shock. One of the contracts I delivered through my sustainability consultancy involved advising a group of organisations in the media sector. It was a long-term contract about creating a set of training materials they could use to teach employees about climate change and how to take action. At the start of the project, I was told in strict terms that I was to only focus on production, not editorial. This meant that we could teach about how to reduce carbon emissions generated from the production of media, but we weren't to try to influence the messages about climate change broadcasted through the various media channels.

This is the quandary about being a sustainability professional: you need to do things that stand against what you believe in order to get paid. The single thing some of these organisations could do that would have the biggest impact would be to change their messaging to communicate with the public about the climate emergency, detailing the impending situation and the action that needed to be taken. Instead, I had to help them create a less impactful course around reducing carbon emissions during the production of television. After two years, when I came to work with dragon energy, I could no longer do this. I could no longer advise businesses in this way and I wanted to find a way out.

I was about four years into working for myself as a sustainability consultant. At the same time, Jason and I had created The Way of the Buzzard, which we had set up soon after we met in 2012. We were running shamanic drumming circles and workshops and I thrived on the spiritual work. It seemed like I had an unlimited amount of energy for it, yet I couldn't see how I was going to close the door on the consultancy work, which paid well. I thought it was valuable work in the world too, greening the corporations. One Autumn Equinox I went on a workshop run by Glennie Kindred and Annie Keeling as part of my celebrancy training and pulled a card with the word 'simplicity'. I set the intention there and then that I wanted a simpler life.

The following spring, in 2015, all four major consultancy contracts that I was working on came to an end in the same month. I didn't have any more work, and I wondered if it was time to close the business. But I was scared. This work had been my lifeline, and I didn't want to have to rely on spiritual work for my only income. This would change the feel of the work that I did, or so I thought.

A friend gave me a lead for some new business with an architectural firm. I set off for the meeting, but my heart wasn't in it. Then, on the way, something really sad happened: a female blackbird flew out and hit my windscreen. There was nothing I could do, she died immediately on impact and I didn't have time to brake. I scooped her up and buried her in our garden.

I tried to put this to the back of my mind as 'one of those things', but it just didn't feel right. I was on my way to green another organisation, which was a good thing, right? Yet I had killed a bird on my journey there. Ignoring the signs and the uncomfortable feeling in my body I carried on as usual. I wrote the proposal for my potential new client and went on with life, experiencing the same knocks, the same highs and lows.

I picked up and read *Snowy Tower* by Dr Martin Shaw just a few weeks later.[52] It's the great Welsh myth of Parzival. Early in the story, Parzival's mother Herzeloyde hides her son in the forest to protect him from the same fate as his father fighting in battle. As Parzival grows into a young man, upon a chance meeting with three knights from King Arthur's Round Table, he starts to get the urge to become a knight himself, as his father was. He goes to his mother and speaks of his encounter with the knights and his desire to become one himself, as well as his love for birdsong. As she listens to his longing, she feels a faint echo of the bad old days. In anguish, she instructs her woodsmen to strangle the birds in the trees. Martin speaks of his own relationship with this point in the story, and how when he killed a bird while driving in America, it made him realise he needed to change his direction.

It was this story, this analogy, and the bird falling out of the sky onto the road I was driving on, which was the tipping point. Over the next week, other things happened. A blackbird visited the bird table at my house for the first time, and then came back again and again. Twice I pulled the blackbird card out of my animal spirit guide deck, which has the message of going from the outer to the inner. During one of the weekends on a five-weekend immersion course with the Westcountry School of Myth, I told my first story 'Finding Your Battle Cry'. This is about finding your voice and standing up for what you believe in. It had all become too much. I realised it was time to step out, turn my back on the corporations once and for all and walk out into the unknown.

I find so often that I need to firmly close one door, so I am not tempted to walk back through it, and once I do, the universe gives me so much in return. Rather than follow the motto, keep your doors open in case you need to walk back through them I am now quite the advocate of burning your bridges so that you aren't tempted to go back, and more to the point, so that going back isn't an option.

So, I did just that. Sure enough, as I closed that door firmly behind me and burned several bridges along the way, all manner of other doors opened up. I began to make and teach drum birthing. Not having to work all week meant I had the energy at the weekends to run retreats with Jason. I began to hold one-to-one shamanic healing sessions. I became a celebrant, helping people hold alternative ceremonies at particular junctures of their life.

All those years I had been attending courses, following what I loved, but never with the intention to work in this field. All of a sudden, I was ready to step into new and fulfilling work. At the time, it seemed very risky putting all my faith into a somewhat shaky field of work, and yet it felt so right in my body. Now, in the midst of a pandemic and with the UK having left the European Union, my old career is actually a very dubious one. Yet, the spiritual field is growing as more people wake up to realise that they want to live in a different world and help create it. What seemed crazy back then seems so sensible now.

When I set off on that uncertain road, I finally felt as if I was starting out on my life's adventure. I could no longer see what was ahead, but it didn't matter. The road to the unknown that once made me so afraid was instead becoming exhilarating.

I often get asked what steps I took to break free from corporate life, and I have mused over this for many an hour. The truth is I didn't just break away from the corporate world, I also made changes in my personal life too. I am sharing my story throughout this book and will summarise the five steps I took in Chapter 5. For the remainder of this chapter, I would like to share recommendations I give to anyone looking to break free from controlling forces in their life and their own inner Sheriff of Nottingham.

***

BREAKING FREE FROM CONTROL

What has become so clear to me from Catherine's story and other stories of extreme poverty in my family tree, is my ancestors' lack of choice. Catherine was faced with little choice when the time came and she decided to leave her homeland and step off Irish soil. Had she stayed, then the likelihood was she would have either died of starvation or disease in her home, or been separated from her husband and child in the work-houses and suffered a similar fate. Likewise, when she arrived in London, there were few choices available to her as a widow with a newborn child. Through her life in London, there were no opportunities available to her to climb the social ladder any further than she did.

When I first learned about my ancestors who lived in the workhouses and slums of the Industrial Revolution, I felt guilty about my life. I felt guilty that I lived in relative ease compared with them. This awareness of how little choice they had to improve their lives flagged up an important realisation. At the time, I was working for a large construction company and doing twenty hours of unpaid overtime each week. I didn't feel in control of my time or life choices. Yet knowing these stories of my ancestors' lives, and having an awareness of these, made me realise that I did have a choice. By staying to work in the corporations, I was choosing to stay and work in the corpora-tions. I am fortunate. I live in a time where there are perhaps greater choices available to someone born into a working-class family than maybe any other generation in history. This was a wake-up call, and I asked myself why I was feeling trapped in a job. Realisations came to the surface just by asking this question, as well as insights about my inner workings that were blocking me.

It wasn't a quick process to release myself from working within the corporations, and it wasn't easy. It was agonising at times. But just having the awareness that I was preventing myself from taking advantage of other options in front of me ultimately led me away from work that I didn't enjoy and a work environment that wasn't good for me.

When I reflect on this time, I can summarise what I did to release myself from the oppression in four ways: 1. Finding an elder, 2. Choosing my response, 3. Developing a relationship with my spirit guides, and 4. Following my gut. I will explain each of these in turn and why I see them as so important.

Finding an elder

The first step I took was to find an elder to help me. In an indigenous tribe, there is a person you go to for advice who isn't a parent or a friend. This is someone with deep wisdom who is detached from the scenario. I see therapy as like going to an elder. For me, a weekly session with a therapist has been key to moving from one view of myself and the world to another.

I engaged in long-term psychotherapy with someone who was not connected to my dramas. Someone who was trained in techniques to help me break out of my old patterns. Someone who could empathise with my story and help me find my own way to rewrite it. Someone who had created a caring space and was willing to listen. I am an advocate of psychotherapy because I was offered a space with all these things and feel this can benefit others.

I've noticed when I mention this to many people they withdraw. Fear of change is one reason. Money is another, and it was for me too. I cut back on other things so that I could afford it, such as meals out and holidays other than camping holidays. I recognised that this was an essential investment in myself and knew that this was fundamental to making the shifts I wanted and needed to make. I knew that it wouldn't be forever.

I had started this process during my mid-twenties with hypnotherapy. I had a feeling I wanted to try this, and one day happened across someone when I was out walking with friends in Castleton in the Derbyshire Dales in a place called Hope Valley. The word hope in the name was the decider for me. I was a negative person back then. I didn't want to be, it was just that I couldn't seem to shift my mind to think positively about situations. I walked past a house with some flyers displayed in a box hanging from the gate, which advertised hypnotherapy with a therapist called Christopher Gill. Later that day I gave him a call and embarked on a series of sessions to help me shift from a glass-half-empty to a glass-half-full person. This was pivotal for me, as since those sessions, I look for solutions to problems. I am now an optimistic person.

I went to my psychotherapist, Liz, initially because of problems I had already identified: struggling with certain work colleagues, not being able to say no and not having any time for me. These were red flags at the time, but once I got into therapy there were many layers and issues here to resolve.

Having a person to talk to every week ultimately helped me understand what it was that I wanted from life and this was the foundation of my great escape. I needed someone to help me break through my old patterns: feeling voiceless, feeling like I ought to do things, my anxiety, my fear, lacking confidence in my own ability, trusting that I was enough.

A few years after I had met Liz, I met my second mentor, Jayne Johnson. Jayne became my shamanic teacher and supervisor and I still have regular sessions with her. She is also a psychotherapist, body therapist and shamanic practitioner, and I've completed many of her training courses that have helped me on my path. I can't imagine a time when I stop seeking the advice of an elder such as Liz or Jayne.

Finding a psychotherapist doesn't seem to be a step everyone needs to take to change their work in the world. I have asked a few people I am close to, what helped them move away from unfulfilling work to work that enriched their lives. What they all did was learn from other people who had made changes, and presented a vision of what was possible. If finding a psychotherapist is something that chimes for you, then I would recommend someone who works with transpersonal psychotherapy or psycho-spiritual psychotherapy, and/ or with the body. The most important thing is that you work with someone you like and get on with. The UK Council for

Psychotherapy or the British Association for Counselling and Psychotherapy are two registering bodies that have databases you can use to help you find a therapist. The Embodied Relational Therapy database lists qualified practitioners.

Choosing my response

I was born into a controlling system. The effect of this is amplified in Catherine's story, and it is easy to see how decisions made by a small number of powerful people drastically affected her, leading her to a life of extreme poverty. Although my life is very different to Catherine's, living within the same controlling system does impact on me. What I have learned from finding my own way to live through this, is how important it is to choose my response.

For example, I could let myself be victimised by it. I could still be working for corporations and struggling with a culture that is driven to make me work for someone else's gain. Or I could rebel. I have been through rebellious phases and can still fall into this now, especially with regards to the actions of our current government; I feel it is OK to rebel and that it has its place in driving me to act. However, I find I need to be careful that I don't polarise against the repressor, otherwise I become like the oppressor and end up contributing to a divided society.

There is a third option, and that is the one I have chosen. I have decided to walk away and find a different way to live. I have opted to occupy a space where I can still create change but not be directly involved in the fight, like when I worked in environmental protection within the corporations. I have chosen to leave my career and give up a secure salary, company car and good pension. I now follow a different line of work that feeds my soul, taking each year as it comes.

The hut with seven doors

In my former life, I was happy: I loved my friends and my now ex-husband. We had a fantastic, fun time. But it wasn't enough. Something wasn't right deep down and it was agonising not knowing what the problem was. I had to stop and let that life fall away, and that wasn't easy. One day I walked away. I just left it and closed the door behind me, quite literally, much to the shock of my then-husband, friends and family. What happened in the immediate aftermath of my courageous great escape reminds me of a scene early within the Irish myth: The Pursuit of Diarmuid and Gráinne. This was one of the stories I heard Dr Martin Shaw tell during my first weekend of the five-weekend training programme I attended at the Westcountry School of Myth.

In this story it was said that Gráinne was the most beautiful woman in Ireland and the daughter of a king. She was promised to the great warrior, prince and chieftain, Fionn mac Cumhaill, who was grieving the death of his wife. At their betrothal feast, Gráinne is upset that Fionn is older than her father, and during the meal notices the handsome warrior Diarmuid. She catches sight of the love spot on his forehead that makes him irresistible.

Gráinne slips a sleeping potion into the guests' drinks, enabling her and Diarmuid to run away together into the forest. When they reach the forest, Diarmuid builds Gráinne a hut with seven doors. A very angry Fionn and his warriors, who are called the Fianna, arrive. Gráinne escapes on a wind that blows through the hut. However, Diarmuid stays behind. He tries to walk through each of the doors, but in each of the entrances, there is someone or something from his past beckoning him to return to all that he knows. They whisper and try to draw him out. In the seventh doorway stands Fionn and four hundred warriors. Diarmuid walks through this door, leaps into the air, and the wind picks him up and carries him to safety. He reunites with Gráinne, and the rest of the story is about their relationship of love and turbulence as they are pursued by Fionn mac Cumhaill and the Fianna.

When I heard this Irish myth, it was this particular scene that stood out. It spoke to what happened to me. When I walked out of my old life, I had many friends and family standing in each of the doors beckoning me back to my old life, to return to my husband and beautiful home, to restore things to what they were.

My soul had different ideas. For as much as it would have been easier to turn right back there and then to the security my previous life offered me, I knew it wasn't what I wanted deep down. My head said, 'go back', and my heart said, 'don't'. There was something not right about my old life. I wanted something different. The trouble is, I had no idea what that was at the time.

This realisation that I needed to drastically change my life happened during the first six weeks after I embarked on a year-long shamanic medicine wheel course with Jayne Johnson. I met Jason on this course and had the inkling of a dream of a different life being possible. Six weeks into the course it was Beltane, the time of fertility, and everything around me was full of life and beckoning me forward. At that moment I decided that I needed to leave my current life. As the wind picked me up and carried me to where I needed to be as the whole world fell apart around me. I had enough support to get me through, with Liz, Jayne, and some new spiritually minded friends. I hadn't known many of these people for very long, but they supported me and gave me a shoulder to cry on. I also had my oldest and closest friends. The shamanic medicine wheel helped me to work through various aspects of myself and to build a foundation beneath me on what was a very wobbly world at that time.

I stayed with my friend for a few months and found a cheap car and a caravan to live in on a lovely site in a wood. It was an old quarry, and my caravan was perched on the top of a rock face with views out over a valley. I stayed there for two years and slowly built my life back up piece by piece, whilst saying goodbye to many aspects of the old one, including my then-husband, whom I divorced.

Looking back now, I was in the wrong life. It was a fantastic life, but it wasn't *my life*: it was someone else's. When I entered adulthood, I set out my ambitions and reached them. Once I got there I noticed something was missing. My goals, my vision for how I wanted my life to be, were built on shaky ground. I need-ed to return to the Earth and start again.

When people come to Shamanism, they often feel fear. I felt it too. I have mused at length over the years as to what this fear is about, and I have a few theories. I was brought up as an Evangelical Christian. I was taught that in this faith there were people who worshipped the Devil, and this was the worst kind of thing you can do. This is, in part, why I think I was afraid of the Earth path. I was taught from a young age that this was to be avoided at all costs. I still felt that twenty years on.

I think that there is something else at play here that made me fearful, and that was change. I wanted to feel better, but I didn't want to lose what I had. I didn't want to shake things up. I just wanted to be happy with the life that I already had. One of the things that happens when a person turns to the Earth, is that there is an equilibrium that unfolds. There is a descent as the Earth shakes us up to allow parts of life that are not aligned with the soul to fall away. We see this in every fairy tale: a person has an encounter that then sets them off on a whole adventure and a different course in their life. This shakeup isn't easy. There are times where we find ourselves crawling in circles at the bottom of the well, dragging ourselves forward, pushing our fingernails into the dirt. This is a rite of passage that happened to me when I returned to the Earth, when I stepped out onto the shamanic path, and it turned out just fine, eventually.

I can see I was presented with three options on how to live within a system of oppression and control: allow myself to be victimised by it, rebel, or occupy a space where I can work to create change but not be directly involved in a fight. I have chosen my response. That is all we can do about anything really: make a choice. So, the questions I pose to you if any of this strikes a chord are these: Are you going to stay in a place where you are victimised? Are you going to rebel? Or are you going to choose which parts of the system you do not want to contribute to anymore and walk away?

Walking away can look like many different things, but in my case, it meant walking away from my home, my then-husband, and ultimately my career, which is probably the extreme end of the scale. Walking away brought me to a place where I am happy in my life, where I have control of my time, and choose what I do every day. I don't have a boss, except for my internalised boss. I don't have to get things approved. I can go and write on the hills with my laptop or sit in the woods. I can take a trip in my little red van when I like and sleep over in the national parks of the northwest of England at a moment's notice. The walking away process probably took around ten years to complete. It was a slow process of waking up and finding my new world, preparing myself to be strong enough to make the changes I needed to make in my life. Some of this was unconscious.

Waking up and building a new life has helped me, but I believe it is also helping the world to heal. I set off to help the Earth heal by working in a job that sought to encourage people to stop polluting and slow down climate change. I spent two decades working in this field in the heart of the corporations, and yet I was guided to work in a different area to the same end. With that said, however, I am still living in the physical world and there will always be boundaries and constraints that give shape to who I am and what I do, and what is realistically possible. The freedom in my life comes from the choices I make within the conditions that present themselves.

This brings me to the third factor in breaking away from the oppression, and that is through building a relationship with my spirit guides. I gained a great deal from learning how to seek spiritual guidance without needing to go to anyone in the physical reality. The main way that I do this is through shamanic journeying.

Meeting spirit guides

The traditional definition of a Shaman is someone who travels to the other realities to bring back the healing that is most needed at this time. What is remarkable is that each of us can shift our consciousness to travel to a different reality through what is called shamanic journeying. Our brains evolved with this ability many tens of thousands of years ago. It is only until relatively recently that we have ceased shifting our consciousness to seek guidance from the spirit realm. I believe that a big part of our awakening is about claiming back this ability and connecting with a far greater wisdom than our conscious minds can hold.

What is amazing about shamanic journeying is that it is possible to move very quickly into the spirit world and meet with a spirit guide, ask for their advice and insight on an issue, and then return to the physical world. There are many ways that a person can shift their consciousness and travel to the Otherworld to meet with their spirit guides, including listening to a repetitive sound, dancing excessively, and taking hallucinogenic plants. At The Way of the Buzzard, we journey on the drumbeat.

It takes time and practice to learn this skill, although not as long as you might think. Some people pick it up immediately, and for others it takes a few attempts. Also, spirit guides don't always give you the information you are asking for in a way that can be understood straight away. It can take a little time to unpick the guidance received from spirit guides, but I am consistently reminded of the effectiveness of the messages once I figure them out.

In Core Shamanism, which is the shamanic tradition I am trained in, we see the spirit world as divided into three levels: the Middleworld, this world; the Upperworld that is above us, and the Lowerworld that is below us. With Christianity as the main religion in the UK, it can be common to think of these worlds as the physical world, with Heaven above and Hell below. This isn't the case with the shamanic path. The Lowerworld and the Upperworld are places we can travel to and meet helpful spirit guides who can guide us along our path. The Lowerworld is the domain of the ancestors and our animal spirit guides and power animals, the gods and goddesses of the Lowerworld, and the nature spirits. The Upperworld is the domain of our spirit guides and spirit teachers, the angelic beings and the ascended masters. Some places are to be avoided unless you are experienced and travelling there for a specific reason, just like in this reality. However, people who go on shamanic journeys for their own personal and spiritual development, setting their intention for particular support and journeying with what we call a companion guide, will not be taken to those places.

We each have an entourage of spirit guides who can help us, giving advice relating to their specific expertise. One of the things I teach early on in the process of ancestral healing is to meet up and begin to build a relationship with an ancestor guide, who I call the ancestor ally. It is this particular kind of spirit guide that I would like to focus on now.

We all have an ancestor ally from our lineage who has a vested interest in our ancestors just like we do. They are waiting for us in the Lowerworld. We most likely won't recognise them, but they will know us. The first meeting might be brief, with not a great deal of sharing, but then that is to be expected. This is the beginning of a relationship, and you need to get to know each other, just like with any relationship in this reality.

Your relationship with them will build as you progress and continue to seek their advice over time. You are in this together, and your ancestor ally will be an incredibly useful guide for you. They are likely to be one of your ancestors from a long time ago, or what I call an 'unknown ancestor'. They lived at a time before the ancestral wounding you are looking to heal took place. They are positioned in the spiritual realm and stand 'up' the ancestral line.

Conversely, you are here in the physical reality living at a time after the ancestral trauma happened, and you stand 'down' the ancestral line. Ancestor allies are often, although not always, from a time before the Industrial Revolution, and may have lived right back to the Palaeolithic period, the Stone Age before the onset of agriculture when people were hunter-gatherers. They will guide you and give you advice, since they are just as interested in your family tree and family's healing as you are. They will guide you to what you need to do every step of the way.

Once you have an ancestor ally, they will help you with your ancestral healing work by introducing you to the ancestors you seek in the Otherworld. From my experience, it is good to work with your ancestor ally throughout any genealogy research you undertake in the physical reality.

My ancestor ally's name is Elder. I met her many years ago when I went on a journey to meet an ancestor at Samhain. When we first met, despite being strangers, there was a shared familiarity between us. Over the years we have become closer, just like a friendship would develop in this reality. She is an elderly lady, quite plump with a soft face and warming energy. I meet her in the same place every time I journey: a small cottage with a steep staircase. I walk through the kitchen and up the stairs and she is sitting in a rocking chair in the bedroom. I ask her my question and look around to see if anything in the room has changed. This often gives me the information that I am looking for as I find a message through the objects I see in the room or something is intuitively picked up through the act of looking and noticing. Other times Elder will speak to me, or hand me something that represents the information I need.

On one occasion I could smell cakes baking, which gave me the insight I needed at the time. Sometimes when I journey to Elder, I might see one of my ancestors standing with her. I might engage with them or simply be in their presence, but I always speak to Elder first. Elder calls me to her when she has something that she wants me to know. Over the years we have developed a 'calling card' system, much like the ringing of a telephone. If I see beads lying around the house, or a bead catches my attention in a particular way, I know Elder is telling me to journey to her.

Learning how to seek and interpret advice from my spirit guides in all the realms has been a really important part of my awakening process. It feels empowering that I can access wisdom in the Otherworld. There is another important skill I have learnt over the years to support me in breaking through my internal oppressor and finding my way to a life of greater freedom, and that is to trust my gut instinct.

Trusting my gut

When I think back to times in my life when I have ignored my gut feeling, I have to admit it didn't pan out well. When I have trusted my body over my mind, this has led to wonderful things, such as in the aftermath of killing that blackbird. My gut was telling me it was time to close the door on that career for good. Yet, going around in my rational mind was enough chatter to convince me to head off that morning and go and pitch for more work in the field that was causing me so much mental and emotional pain.

I believe an important part of the spiritual awakening process is learning to listen beyond what our minds are telling us. Minds have been conditioned to think in a certain way and see the world through a particular lens, and this process starts at a young age. Yet, if I move out of my mind and trust what 'feels' right in my body, I am rarely disappointed. It takes guts to listen to your gut, but it pays dividends in return.

When I think back to other times when I have trusted my gut over my mind, I recall the bodily feeling that I had when I moved into the caravan and left my old life. In my mind it seemed illogical that I would risk so much, and yet in my body it felt like I was in exactly the right place. When something feels wrong, I feel like I am almost outside of my body. I am off-centred. When something feels right, I feel solid and firm in my body and on the ground I am standing on, even if the whole world is falling down around me.

I also put a lot of weight into trusting the different ways that messages come through from the other reality, such as dreams and synchronicities. Throughout this book, I share many different dreams that I have had that have guided me along a different path than I might have taken otherwise. I also share all kinds of synchronicities that I have noticed, which have helped inform my decisions. For example, synchronicities such as killing a blackbird and then pulling the blackbird card from my animal spirit card deck, or planning a trip to walk in Catherine's footsteps in London and the only time I was available was over Samhain, the festival of the ancestors. Over the years I have become more self-determined. I have become more resilient and learned to trust myself more. I have learned how to look for the signposts to guide me on my next turn, and to follow the breadcrumb trail laid out in front of me by my spirit guides, perhaps even my soul.

This brings me to the end of this chapter sharing my views around the dynamic that is playing out in our world today – oppression and control – and how I have worked to overcome this in my life through finding an elder, choosing my response to living in a controlling system, building a relationship with my spirit guides and learning to trust my gut instinct over my chattering mind. Now it is time to go back to Catherine and her story, to journey back to the streets of Victorian London and pick up where we left off to see what becomes of her now. She has firmly closed the door on being a respectable member of society, so let's see where this leads her. Let's go together now back in time and see what happens in the next phase of her life.

CHAPTER 4

Inside the Workhouse

Catherine found herself once again at the workhouse door. As she stood and waited for it to be opened, she clung to her boys tightly. Little William was wrapped firmly around her legs and was shivering. His bare feet were cold on the cobbles and his ragged clothes offered little warmth against the biting April morning frost. George, still a babe in arms, was swaddled beneath her shawl and was barely noticeable. Catherine had held her family together for as long as she possibly could. These next few precious minutes would be their last. They were destitute with nowhere else to go. Another night on the streets would surely kill little George, and perhaps all of them because they were so frail.

It had been an incredibly tough four years since Catherine left Kensington. The brief time in that grand house where she worked as a servant was the last comfort she had known. She had been living back in the slums of Victorian London since then.

After leaving Kensington, she had sought temporary refuge in a lodging house for her first few nights back on the streets of Westminster, while she looked for work. There were nearly one hundred beds in the great rambling old house, which at one time would have been a mansion. Those days were long gone, and the house was something very different now. Each room was crammed with poor lost souls, just like her. It was cramped and stuffy, and there was a pungent smell lingering in the darkness. She took a bed in a room apportioned for women. Clean sheets were long overdue and there was black grease covering the headboard. Here she lay surrounded by strangers, barely sleeping through the night from worry about where she might find work, and fear that what little she had left would be stolen from beneath her.

The next morning, she began her hunt for employment, and found work in one of the sweatshops in Westminster. Here she lived and worked in an attic room at the top of the building with two other women. They were all employed as tailoresses sewing shirts for a pittance. This work was known as the slops trade. It was the lowest end of the seamstress work, and the pay was pitiful. It would take Catherine one full and long day to sew one shirt. She sewed by hand in poor light, and would be lucky to earn six shillings for a dozen completed shirts. There would be little money left over for food after paying her rent.

It was here in this attic room where she lived and toiled that she gave birth to her son. She named him William to keep alive a part of her husband who was slipping away and becoming a faded memory. She gave him a second name of John after his father so he would still have some link to his aristocrat lineage. William John was a bonny boy, but Catherine feared for the future he had ahead of him living in such poverty. Being a bastard child without a father and having an Irish mother would mean they were both firmly on the lowest rung of Victorian society.

She had several choices open to her, but she could only bear to consider one, which was to keep William with her. She could have sold him to a baby farm. Baby farms were awful places available to single mothers where the child would be taken off them for a fee. Fallen women would do this as their only way of redeeming themselves against the disgrace of having a child out of wedlock, but the chance of survival in these horrific places was slim. Nine out of ten babies died in baby farms. Another option for Catherine was the workhouse, only she didn't dare go back. She would rather take her chances raising William in the slums of Westminster.

Catherine shared the room with two other single mothers, and they would take it in turns to look after the children while the others sewed shirts. Women got paid half of what the men did and it was impossible to survive on such low wages. Women were made into slaves of the needle through the slop trade. It was a cruel and heartless exploitation of needlewomen in the backrooms and attics of London. Some women had been driven to kill themselves and their children, such was the hardship of this life.

Catherine's fingers grew weary and worn, and her eyelids heavy and red. She would sit by the light of her candle and sew through the night as William slept. She sewed through the seasons, from autumn into winter, and then spring when the light was brighter and kinder to her eyes. She would sit in her room in unwomanly rags, poor and hungry, working and working until her heart was sick and her mind was numb. She would wish that for just one hour she would feel how she used to feel. She remembered back to a time when she felt free and content, relaxed on the doorstep of her little cottage in Ireland. She could smell the potatoes cooking over the fire and hear the sound of her husband William digging the soil. How she wanted to breathe in the scent of hawthorn blossom that heralded the arrival of spring and hear the song of the wren pierce through the summer air. How she wanted to taste autumn through the blackberries picked from the track running between her and her parents' cottage. How she ached to belong, to be wanted, to matter.

Here in Westminster, Catherine's determination and resourcefulness in finding opportunities got her through the next few years of her life. When William was almost eighteen months old, she had been forced to leave her job as a needlewoman when she was evicted by the landlord for failing to pay her rent. She managed to find work as a charwoman, cleaning through the nights as William slept. Exhaustion and low pay made it impossible for her to make ends meet though, and this was why she found herself back at the workhouse gates once again. This time she spent a few nights in the workhouse casual ward where the tramps went to take refuge. It had been the most frightful of places: evil-smelling, badly ventilated and with no means of warmth. Catherine and William had slept on straw-filled pallets on the floor with rats running underneath them and fleas and bugs crawling across their skin. She couldn't bear to remain there any longer. She stayed just long enough to get some dry bread in their bellies before they left to take their chances on the streets once more.

She found another cleaning job. Each week as she struggled on, a little more inside her broke. It was the burning ache through to her core that drove her to drink. She was tempted into this by the other fallen women and joined many other poverty-stricken Irish in the back-street gin shops. For just a moment's respite, she could find happiness once again at the bottom of a bottle. At first, it felt like a harmless means of escape for Catherine, a way to find temporary peace. When she was drunk, she lost her senses. Sometimes she would not know who she was and preferred it that way. She could feel hopeful again and gain some happiness in this place. But over time, the love of liquor got a tight hold of her. It was the only comfort left to her in a desolate world, aside from her toddler son William. She could not escape its grip. When she ran out of money to buy drinks, still craving that feeling of belonging, she would take drinks offered by the landlord. Lost from her senses and in debt to him, she found herself in a position that no respectable woman wanted to be in and slept with him. It was through this unfortunate situation that she fell pregnant.

Catherine gave birth to her second son in the slums of Westminster and named him George Nobel. She had always dreamt of having a family. Now she had two children to cherish, but it was far from how she had pictured family life.

She was determined to do all she could to shelter them from the desolate world they found themselves in and keep them from harm's way. She managed this for the first few months of George's life when he was tiny and would sleep through the day and night. But she had to care for William too, and he was turning into quite the adventurer. She was spending less and less time working. Then the moment came when she could no longer pay her rent because she wasn't earning enough for her poorly paid work. Once again, she was evicted and back out on the streets. This time she was looking after two small children.

Final days together

Catherine closed the door of her lodgings behind her and stepped out onto the empty road. It was early morning and there was a nip in the air. She had nowhere to go, and two young boys to shelter from all that the streets of Victorian London could throw at them. She would hold off going to the workhouse for as long as she could, taking her chances sleeping rough and seeing if anyone might offer any charity towards them. But no charity came. Were people to look at Catherine and her children, they would do so with contempt. Some would even look at them as if they were carrion.

Catherine's last few days before she went to the workhouse were dreadful. She hid George under her shawl, and William walked slowly alongside them, a shadow never more than a few inches from her side. They spent two nights walking the streets and sleeping wherever they could. The first night they had joined one hundred or so other desolate souls sleeping in Trafalgar Square. They took a seat close to the sheltering wall and shivered their way through the night. Her sons were buried under her shawl close to her half-starved body. The government had ruled that it was illegal for someone to sleep lying down on the streets, and so policemen would approach the paupers with lanterns at frequent intervals to rouse those who were slumped over, including children. Catherine needed to make sure that she and her boys slept upright and weren't tempted to lie down or even recline, or else they would be moved on.

When the temperature became the coldest just before dawn, she felt most conflicted. She wanted the sun to rise so the deep chill would be over as the sun warmed them. Yet it would mean she was one day closer to making that most frightful of decisions: going to the workhouse.

The last time she and William had eaten was three days ago. They'd had a dry crust of bread. Her milk was drying up, and George's pitiful cries grew weaker underneath her shawl. They would not survive out here many more nights.

Catherine was unspeakably weak and worn as she began to make the journey through the streets back to the workhouse door. It was early in the morning when the rain started to fall. She gathered her children up and walked to a shop entrance for shelter. She stood there with strangers, and not a single word was exchanged. Catherine shared the streets with these poor souls, who were all utterly broken. The hardships they suffered knocked the spirit out of them. They retained hardly anything of their former selves, with no craving except for food and shelter and no ambition except to hang onto life a little longer.

This was no place for her boys. She had but four options in front of her. They could walk the streets until they dropped, or they could move between the workhouse casual wards every few days. Their third choice was to take refuge in the work-house. The fourth was unthinkable, although many had been driven to taking their own life and the life of their children to end the torment. It had taken Catherine all night to make up her mind that in the morning they would go to the workhouse. To go to that place was like burying oneself alive, but what other option did she have to give her boys the best chance of survival?

On the walk through the streets of Westminster, her legs would hardly carry her along. She paused frequently and took a seat wherever there was one. She was ready to drop with the cold, fatigue and hunger as she turned the corner and walked down the blackened cobbles of Poland Street. She reached the door of St James Workhouse, knowing that these were her final moments of freedom outside of those walls. This was the last time she would be with her children as a family. Once they were behind the workhouse door, nothing would ever be the same. She contemplated walking straight past but knew that starvation and death awaited them on this side of the door. On the other side, there was untold horror and grief, abandonment, and separation, yet they would still have their lives. This was the only thing she could do to keep her children from dying, as she had tried everything else. Life, however, was not assured on the other side either, as this place had stolen the life of her tiny daughter Charlotte. Her sons could meet the same fate, but the workhouse was their only hope now.

Separation in the workhouse

Gripped by fear, she lifted the door knocker and let it drop heavily on the wood, just as she had all those years before. She knew the horrors that awaited them as she stood there and listened to the footsteps drawing closer. She heard the jangle of the keys and the creak of the door opening. Once inside, the adult paupers are subjected to stringent rules and useless tasks. The children are chastised and disciplined in a manner that is the opposite of justice and charity. To the old, it is a house of slow death. To the young, it is a house of torture. Paupers are seen as failures of society who deserve to eke out the rest of their dismal existence within the walls of the workhouse.

The same porter met them as five years ago, but there was no familiarity or welcome. He led her through to the admissions room, with William hugging her skirt and George wrapped up beneath her shawl. She was subjected to a terri-fying interview just as she was before. It was degrading to be asked all the personal questions, and this task seemed to go on forever. There was no smile from the workhouse matron: just hard eyes, an icy-cold stare, and a rasping voice. She looked at Catherine and her children as if they were dirt, nothing but a burden on the ratepayer and everything Victorian society despised. From this moment, Catherine would be treated with scorn. She would not be permitted to have any rights, not even the right to have feelings of any sort. Victorian society placed Catherine at an exceedingly low level alongside the other tens of thousands of workhouse inmates across the country. They were repulsive rogues who had no just claim to life.

The doctor came and examined Catherine and her sons for skin diseases, and other ailments that could be passed on. After passing the examination, they were taken to the bathroom and told to strip naked to be washed. Their clothes were folded and taken away, and they were issued with the workhouse uniforms. There was no need to cut Catherine's hair this time as it was already short. She had sold it for money for food several weeks earlier.

Numb with grief, she knew that in a few moments, the time she had been dreading since William was born would come. He would be taken from her arms, as was the way in the workhouse. During her final goodbye, she clung onto him tightly and cried softly into his hair, not wanting him to notice her grief or alarm him. He picked up on her tension and began to cry even before the matron grabbed hold of him roughly and passed him to a workhouse officer to carry him out of the door. The door slammed shut behind them. Catherine stood there helplessly, listening to William's hysterical screams grow fainter as her boy was taken up the corridor to the children's ward. She wept deeply from her gut, now knowing the pain a mother feels when her child is taken from her, torn away from her.

Eventually, Catherine could hear him no more, and yet those wails were etched into the core of her being. She was helpless to comfort him. There was nothing she could do. She would have laid down her life for him if she could, but if they had stayed on the streets they would have all died. This way they were still alive.

The life they would have now would however have little hope or joy for any of them. At least she still had her younger son George, who was settled in her arms, unaware of the magnitude of what had just happened. The matron led them to the nursery ward that Catherine knew all too well. As she walked in, Catherine saw the same beds with the cage cots. Here she was again five years later, this time holding her son George in the same room she had cradled her daughter Charlotte to her death. Although now they had food and shelter, there were still perils to face here inside these walls.

Catherine and George shared the nursery with scores of fallen women and their disgraced offspring, constantly surrounded by some of the vilest and abandoned women that the lowest degradation of poverty could produce. The glum room was always overcrowded. Scores of preventable deaths of mothers and children took place in these horrible workhouse nurseries, as Catherine knew only too well.

Children over two years old were kept separate from the adults. They were deemed to be the property of the parish now, as the parish owned the workhouse. The parents had no say in their children's upbringing and were only allowed to see them for one hour on a Sunday, and only if the parents and children had been 'good'. Catherine was desperate to see her boy William more often, but if she tried to break into the children's ward she would be punished, with up to twenty-four hours of solitary confinement in a cell with no windows. It was a long wait through the week for that one-hour reunion with her son. All she could do between these meetings was hope he could feel her love through the cold stone walls. She counted down the days, hours and minutes to the time they were allowed to be together once again.

When she saw William, it was under the interrogating eyes of the matron. William's face lit up when he saw Catherine and George, and she held her boys so tight that neither of them could breathe. William fixed himself onto his mother's knee and nestled into her chest with arms wrapped around her neck, so they were cheek to cheek. Here they stayed locked in this embrace for the whole hour. The time came when William had to be parted from his mother, and the pain began all over again. Catherine would listen to his harrowing cries as William was carried out of the room, whilst she was led back to the nursery carrying George. She would once again have to wait for the next Sunday to see William … and the next.

The visits lasted for three months until it came to the last Sunday that she was allowed to see him. William was to go south of the River Thames to Battersea Industrial School, which was five miles away. He would stay here until his sixteenth birthday. This final meeting would normally have been the last time Catherine would see her son until he was an adult; however, there were problems with William adjusting to the industrial school away from his mother. He returned to St James Workhouse on two occasions over several months, only to be taken away again and sent back to the industrial school. When William was five years old, Catherine saw him for the final time as he never returned after that. She would not set eyes on him again until he was much older.

Gripped with grief from losing William, Catherine dreaded the day that George would also be taken away from her and sent to the industrial school.

George's baptism

Several months after Catherine had arrived at the workhouse gates, she was given the opportunity to have George baptised.

It was a warm day in late spring and her first time outside of the confining walls. She carried her son through the narrow streets that led to Piccadilly Circus. All around her was wealth: this was the middle and upper classes' play area. Catherine was invisible to those around her as she walked with the workhouse chaplain to St James's Church, just off Piccadilly Square. The people here saw just another poor person wandering the streets looking for salvation.

Walking up the steps, she went through the side entrance into the church and up to the font. The church was ornate, with carvings and gold-plated trinkets. The ceiling stretched up high, and there was pew upon pew. She had never been in a church so big or elaborate. The baptism font was carved out of a single piece of marble. Around the base was the main scene of the story of Adam and Eve. It was an illustration of the deviousness of women, where Eve had tempted Adam to take a bite out of an apple, the forbidden fruit.

Catherine thought she deserved her fate, the life she led. She wondered as she held George in her arms what his chances would be. He had been born into a world as the lowest of the low, where even the poorest people looked down on him. Undoubtedly people would think he had inherited her unsavoury character and lack of morals because he was born of sin.

On her walk back from the church to the workhouse, two boys ran out in front of her. Catherine would never see her children do this. She would never see them grow into boys of this age. The place was filled with people going about their business, but Catherine felt a world apart from them. She was down on her luck and had been victim to an ever-worsening set of circumstances. So much inside her had died, yet she still had one bright spark left – George. They were at least together for a while longer.

She thought back to her life in Ireland and how her boys would have grown into strong men, just like her husband William had been before he had to leave his homeland with

Catherine to survive. Her boys would have had a life surrounded by green meadows. They would have watched the seasons move and eaten the food they had grown. Catherine remembered how something would always be cooking over the fire when they were in Ireland and how they shared stories around the fireside in the evening. She remembered the day she met William, how they fell in love and how she had, at the time, dreamed they would be together as husband and wife. She thought of the first night in their own cottage and how she was filled with hope for the future.

How far her dreams were from the life she lived now in this hellish place. She didn't have a friend in the world. What was there to hope for now? She hadn't committed a crime, and yet she was treated as a criminal. There was nowhere to go but be locked up behind the workhouse walls. Catherine felt desperate.

She spent a precious eighteen months with George until the time came when he was taken from her arms, just as William had been. When William had left for the industrial school, he was returned to her several times. Catherine hoped that she would see George again as she had done with William, but it wasn't to be. George didn't come back to St James Workhouse. He was taken from her at just two years old, and it was the last time she was to see her younger son until he was a grown man. Catherine was alone once again.

Able-bodied

Catherine was moved to the women's ward and set to work doing mind-numbing monotonous tasks now she didn't have a child to nurse. Each inmate in the workhouse was classified into one of two categories: able-bodied and infirm. The infirm were those people who were too old or ill to be put to work. Everyone else was considered able-bodied and given work to do for six days of the week.

Catherine was surrounded by hundreds of people but experienced that familiar cursed feeling of utter desolation. Her thoughts ate away at her heart in the silence. She didn't care about the present. She lived only in the past and the future on the memory of lost happiness and the hope of meeting her boys again one day.

Her day would begin with the ringing of a bell that would continue ringing at intervals throughout the day to mark what the inmates needed to do and when. After rising in the morning, Catherine would wash and dress herself and tidy her bed. This was a metal-framed bed with a straw mattress, which she often had to share with other women when the workhouse was overcrowded. The matron performed a roll call before all able-bodied inmates were assembled in the dining hall. Communal prayers were read by the workhouse master before breakfast and after supper every day, with grace said before and after each meal. For the able-bodied like Catherine, breakfast was followed by five hours of work. By contrast, the elderly and infirm retired to their day rooms with some undertaking duties such as nursing or the supervision of children. Catherine was put in the sewing workshop. Here she sat out every day, with other lost souls, sewing for hours. Once again, she was a slave to the needle.

The inmates ate in silence in the dining hall at mealtimes, sitting on rows of wooden benches. The food was tasteless, with many of the meals just watered-down oats with dried bread, known as 'workhouse skilly'. The hour-long break for dinner at midday was followed by a further five hours of work, and then it was supper and bed. Catherine found the boredom excruciating; every day was the same. The work was designed to be monotonous and from 7 am to 8 pm, she was told exactly what to do and how to do it. She was no longer able to think for herself. All she did was follow instructions or else risk being punished.

Sunday was a day of rest. The inmates had an afternoon of leisure time following the church service. There was nothing to do other than sit on the wooden bench or take a turn around a yard covered with gravel from side to side. There was not a leaf of grass or green thing to be seen anywhere. Even the sparrows avoided the place and there was none of their chatter in the eaves.

There was nothing whatsoever to relieve the boredom. Luxuries such as newspapers, books and games were banned by the strict workhouse rules. Some inmates would occupy themselves with writing letters. Catherine couldn't read or write and would never ask anyone for help to send a letter home to her parents in Ireland. She was too ashamed, and anyway, her mother and father had most likely died from the famine.

The hardest hours were those at night, when her mind had nothing to distract it from sad reflections and shameful memories. The dormitory doors were locked each night and opened up again every morning. Between these times the paupers were left to themselves. Often the sound of snoring and coughing would be pierced with the workhouse howl. In the dead of night, some poor souls were unable to contain themselves any longer and let out a prolonged cry of grief and utter despair. This was of such a volume that it would echo through the walls and down the corridors into the adjoining rooms. It spoke of an agony beyond all words.

Catherine wasn't afraid of dying. Death would be a welcome rest from the drudgery that was life for her. Whilst in one sense she had nothing worth living for, she had her two children. Although not near her, they were still hers. Were she to die, her children would be told they were orphans. They would have to live in the cold, harsh world without the knowledge that she was alive. So, battle on, she must. At least they had this silver thread running between them all. Amidst all the heartbreak, there was the untampered force of a mother's love breathing life into an all-but-desperate story of surviving adversity.

Living in the shadows

In the months after George had left, with nothing to live for, Catherine reached a new level of depression. Her boys had been taken away to spend their childhood in the most desolate of places. This was their only chance of becoming someone and living a good life. At least they were fed and clothed and were being given an education. But they were alone. They would not feel the love of their mother. They would not have her embrace to comfort them through the nights. The abandonment they must be feeling broke her heart, and she came to the point where she felt the madness setting in and needed to escape. She needed respite from the constant pain.

One day it just got too much. She had to leave. She couldn't bear being inside those walls any longer. Catherine bypassed the official workhouse discharge process and ran out of the door, back onto the streets of Westminster. Still wearing her workhouse uniform, she hurried up the road, not knowing her plan or where she was going. She roamed the streets feeling the conflicted sense of having escaped a terrible situation, but knowing she was far from free. Where could she go, or what would she do when she got there? She didn't belong anywhere. She passed alehouse after alehouse and eventually was drawn into one to find peace in the drink once again.

For the next few days, Catherine lived on the streets and walked about the dirty bars, catching drinks where she could. She searched the faces of the crowds as she moved through the streets, hoping to catch a glimpse of someone she knew, someone who might be a friend. She wanted kin that she could speak to about her feelings of losing her babies. But there was no one. She was entirely alone in her dark night of the soul.

Eventually, she crumbled and returned to St James Workhouse and all that awaited her there. This sequence of events happened five times more over the following two years. She would tolerate the place for so many months, and then another part of her would break inside and she would escape the workhouse for several days, sometimes for up to a month. Without the ability to support herself though, she always returned. Catherine was unable to bear the pain of being inside the workhouse without her children, and yet not able to control her urge to numb the pain when she was outside the walls. She lived in the shadows, earning money through sewing slops, the grief in her unspoken, and the pain going on and on. Only the drink relieved her momentarily, and she could for a brief spell of time feel a glimmer of happiness and hope.

The landlords of alehouses would say they would rather have twenty poor English drunks in their taprooms than a couple of poor Irish men or women. Mostly they fought. They fought after they drank. Men fought men. Men knocked down women, often their wives or daughters. Women knifed and tore the hair out of other women. Catherine was caught up in one of these brawls; over what, she could not remember. She was wounded with a deep cut to her arm. Bleeding and distraught, she walked back to the only place where she now knew to go: the workhouse. Lying in the infirmary ward, injured and in pain, she succumbed to the pressure of her life and broke completely. The final spark in her died. She remained within those walls of St James Workhouse for eight years after that fight. She dared not to go back out onto the streets again: her spirit was broken.

Care for others

The infirmary wards in the workhouses were the early hospital wards. These rooms housed the elderly and the infirm who were too ill or frail to take care of themselves. At the time Catherine entered the infirmary they were very dismal places. It was the able-bodied inmates' role to look after the people who, on entering the workhouse, were assigned to these wards. The inmates were given no training and were largely left unsupervised to carry out the day-to-day care of the patients.

The quality of care received by patients very much depended on the personalities of the able-bodied inmates charged with their nursing. This changed during the following years that Catherine spent in the workhouse. This was due to the work of Florence Nightingale, who campaigned for improvements to hospital wards and established a training school for nurses. Florence Nightingale's efforts to reform healthcare greatly influenced the quality of care provided to patients during Catherine's latter years of life, right through to the following century.

It was Catherine's time in the hospital ward that led to her becoming a nurse. She was cared for by a fellow inmate as the cut on her arm healed, and this inspired her to request a nursing role once she was able to work again. As a nurse, she took care of the elderly and infirm in this early hospital ward. It felt good to care for others, and she felt valued, at least by the patients themselves.

Catherine thought of William and George over the years and imagined them growing up, wondering what they looked like, what they thought of her, whether they felt that silver thread of love running between them. When William was fourteen years old, Catherine discharged herself from the workhouse. She met with both of her sons as young adults, old before their time from the toll of a childhood without play. They were strangers, unfamiliar to each other. They had missed out on so much.

For the remaining years of her life, Catherine spent periods back in the workhouse, as well as out in Westminster working as a charwoman, domestic servant or needlewoman. During her time in London, she spent longer outside the walls of the workhouse than she did inside. The pain of losing her boys had numbed her, and she didn't feel as though she was in her body anymore. She was somewhere else; though where she did not know.

Catherine was fifty-five years old when she closed the door for the final time on St James Workhouse and she took the walk back to Kensington. There was so much more greenery here, and it reminded her of home. She could hear the birds sing and she could watch the squirrels playing under the trees in the park.

Her final months were spent here working as a laundress. Then she took ill with her lungs. They played up terribly as she grew older, damaged through the years of toil working in the sweatshops and living in the cold and the damp. She was admitted to the elderly and infirm ward at Kensington Workhouse, which was St Mary's Hospital.

As she moved between the worlds, moments before she died, Catherine could see her husband William coming to her. His bright warm eyes were a welcome sight, a familiarity she hadn't known for many, many years. The final sounds she could hear were the chattering of her brothers and sisters as they sat around the fire in her parents' cottage, listening to her father's stories and her uncle's fiddle. The last smells were of burning peat mixed with baking bread. Her final taste was of hot potatoes washed down with sweet milk. This was a world apart from her life alone in England. Her sons were Londoners now, and so it was the last her Irish bloodline would know of what life was like in Ireland.

Catherine died of pneumonic phthisis in the early hours of the morning of 12 June 1876. This was a form of pneumonia that was common in people who had led an exposed or dissipated life. She was fifty-six years old. She was buried in a shared grave along with other paupers in Kensington cemetery. Her coffin was made of rough-cut pine, and her name was chalked on the top. Her sons were not informed of her passing and there was no one to mourn her at the graveside.

Fate had dealt Catherine a cruel hand. Misfortune set her on a painful course through life. There was a grief that lingered down her family line, a pain that carried on. For Catherine had left behind in the world two sons, and what had become of them? This next part of the story is for the next chapter, as now I would like to continue with my explorations as to how Catherine's story has impacted me.

***

WHAT NEEDS TO DIE?

Before I left base camp to begin my four-day, four-night wilderness vigil, I had an evening to prepare around the camp-fire. There were six of us who were about to embark on our extended time in the forest. It was a poignant time, and I could feel the tension cut through the air as we each were about to set off on a prolonged period of solitude in the wilds of the forest without food. The Westcountry School of Myth ran the vigil. Dr Martin Shaw has been running these wilderness rites of passage for over two decades and joined us for the evening.

I spent some time reflecting and sharing why I had been drawn to carrying out this rite of passage in the depths of the Dartmoor Forest. I voiced the things that concerned me most and listened to the stories of my peers. I tried my best to prepare myself for what was to come. As Martin walked away at the end of the session, the last words he spoke to us were: 'What needs to die out there in the forest? What needs to die?'

After the vigil had started, as I lay in those woods alone, anxious through the days and terrified through the nights, time took on a new shape. Ninety-six hours is a long time in the general humdrum of life, but alone in the woods when the boredom sets in, that stretch of time is something else entirely. I grappled with the hunger and exhaustion that increased as each day unfolded during my vigil. During these four days and four nights, Catherine was very much in my mind.

The final morning of my vigil was Tuesday, 12 June 2018. I had been awake that whole night, staring right at the thing that terrified me the most: the dark forest. It had been a long night, and I was weak packing up my things and making the walk back to base camp. At the time, as I stepped out of my transformational wilderness on that final morning and made my way back to base camp, it was exactly one hundred and forty years from when Catherine had died. As I mentioned in my introduction to this book, I had no idea of this synchronicity at the time. I was to discover this remarkable alignment on the approach to Samhain six months later.

In a wilderness vigil, the participant doesn't necessarily get a moment of enlightenment there and then. This is a process that unfolds over time. When I emerged from the forest, I felt immensely proud of my achievement and also braver, as I had faced the thing that scared me the most. Other changes that had happened within me were much more subtle and were going to take a while to show themselves.

Two years on, I am writing Catherine's story at the same time of year as when I was preparing and then undertaking my wilderness vigil. Looking back, I feel that one of the things that needed to die in those woods was shame: the shame Catherine felt, the shame her son, my great-great-grandfather George felt, and the shame that has been passed down to each of the generations that followed.

I was born into the same oppressive system Catherine was born into. In this system, in the nineteenth century, it was not only acceptable to take the land from people, but laws were passed explicitly with the intention of forcing them to leave their country. When the Irish arrived destitute in the ports of Glasgow, Liverpool, Bristol and London, they did their best to find a way out of poverty, but it was an impossible task. This nation of people was looked down upon even by the poor. These immigrants lost their Irish culture. In Catherine's case, everything was taken from her, even her right to her children and her feelings.

In the twenty-first century, this system of oppression is dressed up differently, and it's a far cry from the atrocities that

Catherine had to endure. But as I have already mentioned, the paradigm is the same: the privileged elite makes decisions that control the underprivileged many. Shame is one of the methods of control used to limit the views and choices of the many. What needs to die in me is my response to living in this system, to ensure to the best of my ability that I am not affected by the same oppression Catherine was impacted by so severely. I want the decisions I make about how I want to live my life to be my decisions and not ones imposed on me. I want the opinions I hold to be my opinions and not opinions I have been manipulated into adopting by someone else.

I will address in this chapter how ancestral shame has played out in me and the steps I have taken to work through it.

Workhouse shame

On the eve of Samhain, just over six months after my wilderness vigil, I cooked a meal for Catherine and set a place for her around our kitchen table. Jason also invited his grandmother, who passed several decades ago. I researched Irish dishes and cooked turnip and potatoes. We left our two ancestors' food laid out on plates overnight and a candle burning. This is an age-old tradition that is still practised by some cultures today, such as the Mexican 'Ofrenda' tradition on the Day of the Dead.

The next day I caught the train down to London. I walked to Piccadilly to see the church where Catherine's youngest son George was baptised, and then onto Poland Street where St James Workhouse was located. It has been demolished now and a multi-storey car park occupies part of the site. I walked through the entrance and stood in the location where the nursery ward would have been according to the floor plan I had obtained. This was where Catherine had spent her days and nights with her babies, and where she had held Charlotte in her arms as she drew her last breath. I wrote some words in my journal to mark the moment as I stood on this ground.

As I visited these places on that cold November evening, I felt quite overwhelmed that I was walking in Catherine's footsteps. I was standing in the very places my great-great-great-grandmother had stood. I wondered how she felt. I reflected on the grief she would have felt when her daughter Charlotte died in her arms. I considered what her thoughts might have been as she watched as her son George's head was wetted by holy water at that ornate font. I didn't feel fully present in the twenty-first century. My body was here in modern-day London, but my mind was very much somewhere else, tapping into Catherine's world. I found it surprisingly easy to find some words to write down standing in that multi-storey car park in the heart of the bustling nightlife of the West End. Here is what I wrote:

> This is the spot that shaped me. This is the spot where the woman whose life is entwined with mine spent so many years. This is where her daughter died. This is the street she walked along with her two sons, knowing when they walked through those workhouse doors, they would be parted for good. This is where she lay alone at night crying, as she remembered the green meadows back in Ireland and the moment when she first met her husband. She recalled the twinkle in his eye. She remembered their wedding and then celebrating their first child on the way. This is the spot where she left the confines of the workhouse, again and again, only to return. This is the place where she tried to shelter from the world, a world she desperately needed to find refuge from. Where was her shelter now Ireland had gone?

After leaving the site of the former workhouse in Poland Street, I went to seek out the graveyard where Charlotte was buried. I walked up the streets to Euston as Catherine would have done, as she followed her daughter's body that was lying in a rudimentary coffin. I wasn't able to see the paupers' grave-yard. Coincidentally, at the time when I was uncovering Catherine's story, the grave of her daughter Charlotte was being dug up as part of the London Crossrail infrastructure works at Euston Station. I saw the exhumation of Charlotte's body as symbolic of the unearthing of her story that had been lying hidden in the pages of archived records for approaching two centuries.

I made my way to Kensington to find the place where Catherine had died. Catherine passed away in the newly built infirmary adjacent to Kensington Workhouse. This hospital was purpose-built and had several hundred beds, mainly for the chronically sick. The wards were designed according to Florence Nightingale's standards, with spaced-out beds and good natural light, and the patients were tended to by trained nurses. The site where the hospital and workhouse once stood is now a gated housing estate. It is not possible to enter past the barrier. Although the workhouse buildings have been demolished, much of the original infirmary building still survives, positioned behind tall black gates. I found it interesting that I wasn't able to get inside the very place that Catherine wasn't able to leave.

I haven't been able to determine why Catherine came to Kensington for her final years after spending so much of her life in Westminster. I know from the workhouse records that she worked as a laundress before being admitted to the hospital ward, so perhaps she found employment here in Kensington before falling ill. What is interesting to me is the symbology of the remaining workhouse architecture that still stands here in Kensington.

The gates to Kensington Workhouse still exist, as do the brick pillars and the original eight-foot-tall brick wall that surrounded the buildings. The black gates feel oppressive. I felt frustrated about not being able to enter through them, as I wanted to have the freedom to walk on the ground where Catherine died. In this experience, I tapped into the frustration that Catherine must have felt having to spend the second half of her life largely behind the workhouse walls, not being able to leave.

Not being able to pass through the gates meant that I spent some time outside them. I noticed that there was a small stone font set in the wall. Above this is a plaque on which these words are written:

Lord from thy blessed throne
The griefs of the earth look upon
God bless the poor
Teach them true liberty
Make them from strong drink free
Let their homes happy be
God bless the poor

Had Catherine been able to read, she might have read those words. They would have been right there in front of her just as they were in front of me. I wonder what she would have thought if she had. I expect she would have believed that her demise was all her own doing and would have felt great shame.

I am someone living in the twenty-first century and take something different from the message. It uncovers a rage that lies deep within and comes up through my veins. As I read those words my heart quickened and my blood curdled. I imagine Catherine had a happy home and was drink free earlier in her life. She didn't need prayer or pity. She deserved recompense for the terrible injustices she encountered during her life.

I laid out a mandala of ferns and heather I had brought with me by those gates in memory of Catherine and all that she endured. She would have had a most unceremonious burial in a pauper's grave, and she undoubtedly died alone. At that moment, around the time of Samhain when the old ones are honoured, I remembered her. I carry her story in me, and I grieve for her pain.

The week before, in preparation for my trip, I had undertaken a shamanic journey to my ancestor guide, Elder. I asked what I needed to do when visiting London. She told me to lay a mandala of heather and ferns collected from the woodland and moorland by my home in Anglezarke. I believe I was guided to use heather because I had seen the image of Catherine running through the heather moorlands as a child during an earlier shamanic journey. For me, heather holds the energy of fortune, peace and generosity. I believe I was told to use ferns because I love them so much: their vibrant green leaves give me a feeling of wildness whenever I see them. As I laid down the mandala, I expect anyone who was watching from the other side of the road in Kensington may have thought my actions strange. To me, it felt so right at that point in time.

As I researched the horrific conditions of workhouses during the seventeenth to twentieth centuries, I was shocked. As I set out to write this book, I wanted to portray how awful they were through the telling of Catherine's story. Workhouses had been around for over two hundred years before Catherine entered the doors of St James Workhouse. They were the early form of state-provided poor relief dating back to the final days of the reign of Queen Elizabeth I at the beginning of the seventeenth century. The idea behind them was that the institutions would provide a home and employment for the poor. They would be funded by a poor rate tax collected from local property owners. Until the nineteenth century, workhouses existed alongside grants of money, clothing, food and fuel given to those living in their own homes who needed state support. However, in 1834 there was an amendment to the Poor Law, called the Poor Law Amendment Act 1834, which ended all out-relief to able-bodied paupers. This meant that the poor could no longer get help outside of the workhouse walls. Steps were even taken to ensure that it was difficult to live out on the streets, as policemen would patrol the towns and cities at night and move anyone who was lying down, as I mentioned in Catherine's story.

These establishments supposedly existed to help the poor, but the government were terrified of encouraging those that they called idlers: people seen as too lazy to work. They ensured that the workhouses were so terrible that people would do anything to stay out of them. These places were designed to break a person's spirit, and the threat of going into one hung over generation upon generation. I recently asked my mother- and father-in-law about them, as workhouses still existed when they were children. They told me how these places were used as a threat: 'If you are naughty, we will drive you up to the gates of the workhouse and leave you there.' I believe the fear of the workhouse is still entrenched within our culture, and certainly it resides within the DNA of many people with British heritage like me. This is the fear of being so poor that we will need to go into the workhouse, and that we are so terrible that we deserve to be locked up behind their walls.

The stories that exist about how people in the workhouses were treated are heart-wrenching. The management of work-houses was open to abuse, and there are accounts of inmates dying of starvation and neglect. Everyone seemed to have a keen sense of disgrace on entering the workhouse, as there was a great shame and stigma attached to having to walk through those doors. Rules had to be obeyed to the letter on pain of harsh punishment, which included flogging and solitary confinement. Any complaints about living conditions invited punishment too. Poverty was treated like a crime, and prison was often seen as a better place to be than the workhouse.

The people who entered through the workhouse gates were seen as soulless. I've always felt pain when I think about these places, ever since I found out about them. I remember reading *Call the Midwife: A Memoir of Birth, Joy and Hard Times* and having to stop at the chapter where a woman called Mary-Anne Jenkins had been incarcerated in a workhouse.[53]

All five of her children were taken from her. One by one, each of her children died. She was notified each time, helpless to do anything. She was a shell of a woman when she was finally let out of the workhouse when they were closed down in the 1950s. What happened to her and her family was so excruciatingly sad I stopped reading that book after that chapter and never picked it up again.

Whilst researching my family tree I was surprised to find that members of my own family had been in workhouses. Some had grown up as children there, separated from their parents. Others had lived there as adults when they couldn't get work. A few had died there alone. Each time I found this out, the information would hit me as a force of energy overcoming me.

Along with the shame of being in the workhouse, Catherine would have felt this for other reasons. Back in Victorian times, it was shameful to be Irish. I have mentioned already that no one liked the Irish, they were the lowest class, and even the poorest English people had contempt for them. The Irish, who lived in rooms with two or three other families, had less rent to pay and would therefore settle for lower wages. For this reason, the working man blamed them for a reduction in their living wages too. It was perceived that the Irish were content to be living in overcrowded tenements. These were dirty, disease-ridden conditions where people slept on straw, often sharing their homes with pigs, and allowed their children to go barefoot in the streets. The Irish were known for their drinking, fights and debauchery too. In his book *The Irish in Britain 1815–1914*, historian Graham Davis writes:

> The belief in the existence of an abyss, a moral cesspit, below the level of respectable society with the threat of a savage mass rising up to destroy the institutions of civilised society – church, monarchy, parliament and property – was the dominant fear in early Victorian Britain.[54]

Catherine would also have carried the shame of being a mother out of wedlock. As mentioned previously, Victorian society perceived women who had children out of wedlock as 'fallen women'. As a rule, bastard offspring and their mothers were treated appallingly. It was perceived at the time that it was a woman's downfall to have an illegitimate child. Abuse of all kinds was tolerated, and the blame always pushed on women for birth out of wedlock, even if they were raped. The alleged father was absolved of any responsibility for his offspring, and the law singled out women to face the humiliation of illegitimacy. The woman's guilt was apparently evident, and she would serve as an example to others to inspire virtue, thereby putting an end to the birth of illegitimate children. This was considered a way of deterring unwed mothers, as they and their infants were considered immoral, an insult to society. They were scorned and ostracised through the government policies developed, the public relief provision subsequently offered and through the action and inaction of charitable organisations with the remit to support mothers out of wedlock. It was deemed that children conceived 'in sin' had no doubt inherited their parents' lack of moral character and would contaminate the minds and morals of legitimate children.

To be an Irish immigrant, a fallen woman, and living in the workhouse, was possibly as low as you could get in nineteenth-century Victorian society. The rich and poor alike would not have wanted to associate with people like Catherine and her boys.

A story of survival

It would be easy to judge Catherine when viewing her through a Victorian person's lens. In 1855, she was standing at the baptism font in St James's Church in Piccadilly, having had two boys, both illegitimate and born to different fathers. But there is a back story to this that paints a very different story.

It is important for me to reframe her story as I believe there is great healing in this retelling. There is healing for Catherine, as after centuries of silence, she is listened to and understood. This creates a shift in energy in the family line as the shame is released. There is also healing for me, as I can make sense of my internal workings and understand why I am the way I am. With this awareness, I can then choose to make different decisions in my life than I would otherwise. Hearing Catherine's story makes me question how she survived all that happened to her for so long. It makes me wonder how she could possibly have carried the grief that continued to blight her life, which was a long life by Victorian poor standards. She is a heroine to me, which is a far cry from the villain she was made out to be when she was alive.

Catherine was a survivor. She did the best she possibly could for her family, given the choices she had at the time. She tried to look after the children on her own and she did an amazing job for so long. When her first son William was born, she managed three years on the streets and in the slums of London. Working as a charwoman it would have been possible to bring her children to work, as the working hours went well into the night. As a needlewoman, she could work from home sewing through the night by candlelight. I cannot know very much about what Catherine did to survive, but I do know she was far from lazy as society perceived her. She worked at all types of jobs that were available to a woman of her class: needlewoman, laundress, charwoman and house servant and, while she was in the workhouse, a nurse. During the thirty years she lived in London, she spent more time out of the workhouse supporting herself than inside those walls.

As relief from the despair, Catherine turned to the drink, and this was perhaps her downfall. This was however somewhat understandable given the adversity she faced. I believe she fell pregnant by a publican, presumably one who took advantage of women who could not pay for their drinks. I have come to this conclusion as her son George Riley stated this was his father's profession on his marriage certificate, whilst also replacing his father's name with his brother's name. People like George would do this so that they did not have to declare that they were illegitimate. They would use their brother's or uncle's name in place of their biological father's name.

Having an awareness of what sorrow Catherine had endured, I can look at her circumstances with compassion and empathy. The drink was the ruin of so many of the poor. The temptation must have been high with a pub on every street corner of Soho where Catherine lived. If I had been subjected to this level of trauma in my life, how would I have coped? Would I have turned to the drink, like millions of other poor Irish immigrants? Would I have even survived the Great Famine of Ireland or had the bravery to leave my country? Would I have been able to make the transition needed to move from rural Ireland to the poorest areas in London, knowing I could never leave or work my way out of destitution? How would I have coped if my husband had died and left me heavily pregnant? How would I have coped living in a workhouse with a baby daughter, nursing her through eight months of sickness where she fought for every breath? How would I have coped when she died? Would I have been able to protect myself from all those people who were looking to take advantage of the vulnerable, those living in the shadows of Victorian London? Would I have been able to bear living after my two sons were taken from me, knowing they were being brought up without love? Would I have been able to handle such loneliness?

In Victorian times it was the luck of the draw what kind of life a woman had who was living in poverty in London. If your husband survived, then you had a chance of having a room in a tenement. If your husband died, it was touch and go whether you would end up in the workhouse. This was pretty much a certainty if your children were too young to send to work to earn money to help keep the household. I found it interesting to watch the developments during my research of another couple called Catherine and William Riley who were around the same age and living in the London slums at this time. This Catherine was also widowed, but much later in life. She had her children around her as she grew old, and her daughter was present when she drew her last breath as she died in her home.

My Catherine hardly knew her boys when they were children, and barely knew them as adults. I know that George remembered her. When George had his second daughter, he named her after Catherine. It was unlikely that he ever spoke about his mother's background, and certainly the story about her was never passed down our family line. George may well have never revealed to anyone that he was illegitimate. But I remember Catherine now, for if she had made different choices, then the lives of subsequent generations in my family would have been very different. We would have remained poor in London for many generations, most likely, and maybe the family line wouldn't have continued at all.

Part of this work in healing ancestral trauma is rewriting the story that has been hidden for generations because of shame. Catherine's life and choices were not shameful, far from it. But there is shame in this story, and that is the shame that should be owned by the elite. Feelings are energy. When a person owns their feelings, then this energy stays with the person. However, when a person disowns their feelings then it remains in the world for someone else to potentially pick up. The behaviour of the elite, those that passed laws and inflicted poverty on millions of people across many generations, was shameful. As those people in positions of power failed to own their shame, then this energy, this emotion was left for others to pick up. In this instance, the shame of the elite was picked up by the poor, who were powerless. Victorian society saw

Catherine's behaviour and choices as shameful, and yet the shame did not belong with her.

Take me home

Over the festival of Samhain, six months after undertaking my wilderness vigil, I went on a shamanic journey to meet with Catherine and ask what I could do for her. This was the first time I had spoken to her in a journey. She looked tired, and there was a glaze over her eyes. She stared right through me despondently and spoke the words: 'Take me home.'

I realised at this point that this meant a trip across the Irish Sea. I needed to decide on where in Ireland to go as I do not know where Catherine was from. I mentioned in the introduction to this book that earlier that year I had had a vivid dream of a location where Catherine was from in Northern Ireland to the east of Belfast in Ulster. This didn't make sense to me at the time, that she could come from both Belfast and Ulster. That is until I did some research and found that Ulster is the name of one of the four traditional Irish provinces. I find it fascinating to have received information as precise as this through my dreams. It confirmed to me that Belfast was the place I needed to go to.

As I approached Northern Ireland my eyes scanned the horizon, looking for land. The moment I first caught sight of it felt really significant. I remembered those words 'take me home' as I took my first step onto the ground. I thought about this being the first physical connection my family had had with this soil since Catherine left. I noticed the words 'freedom' and 'spirit' written in advertisements when I was waiting to collect my hire car. These synchronicities are important to me in my ancestral healing work.

After Catherine spoke the words 'take me home' to me, I found an Irish folk song through a Google search. The lyrics speak so true of how I sense Catherine felt throughout her life living in poverty in London:

I sit here thinking
As the sun is sinking
Over the mountain
And the dry, dusty ground

As the night is falling
I start recalling
The nights
In my own town

I see the faces
In familiar places
I hear the music
That they played way back then

My heart rejoices
As I hear the voices
Calling me
Home again

Home
Oh take me home
Oh to the people
I left behind
Oh to the love
I know I'll find
Oooh take me home

As the sky is burning
My mind is turning
To the cold winter evenings
By my own fire side

So far away now
But any day now
I'll sail
On the morning tide

Home
Oh take me home

Oh to the people
I left behind
Oh to the love
I know I'll find
Oooh take me home

Take me home
Far across the sea
Home is where I long to be.[55]

I stayed in a B&B in a small village to the east of Belfast,
which was close to the location I had dreamt about. On my
first morning I went on a shamanic journey to meet with Catherine. I wanted to ask her what she wanted from me in order
to take her home.

She was standing in front of me, wrapped in a shawl. Her
dark eyes held such knowing. She had seen so much, and she
had experienced great pain. She had had two boys and left a
legacy. She had survived. She told me she wanted me to lay
her to rest in consecrated ground with her fellow country-
folk. I replied that I didn't know where she came from. She said
it didn't matter, just lay her to rest with the others: a coming
back home to complete her and bring her soul back to her
land. I was reminded about the place in my dream to the east
of Belfast up on the north coast of County Down, so I decided
to drive up there.

I have to admit, I was rather disappointed at first about
Catherine's request at being laid to rest in consecrated
ground. I had visions of going to a windswept moorland edge
on a cliff overlooking the sea. It felt far more evocative for me
as this is what has always drawn me to Ireland: the wild feeling
the land has about it. I didn't expect to end up prowling around
the suburbs of eastern Belfast searching for a graveyard. But
this wasn't about me, it was about Catherine. She was a Protestant. This has been confirmed to me through records I have
of her. With her being a member of the Church of Ireland, her

request made sense. Revelations such as these that I receive through shamanic journeying have helped me trust information I glean from journeying. That this isn't something I have 'just made up'. Left to me and my own devices, I would have spent my time roaming the moorlands of County Down, not the conurbations.

To find the right church I needed to follow my nose and trust my gut. After driving past several churches, I found one that was accredited to St Philip and St John. Philip is a family name and John was the middle name of Catherine's first son, so it seemed like a good fit. However, there wasn't a graveyard. Also, it was a relatively modern church, having been built towards the end of the nineteenth century long after Catherine had died. I carried on driving around and found an old graveyard with a ruined church. I pulled over and didn't think it was suitable as this was a Presbyterian church. Then as I read the information board outside, I saw that during Catherine's life it was of Church of Ireland denomination. Not only that, but it was the church of St Philip and St George that was later moved to the new site where I had already been. These synchronicities spoke to me. This was the place I needed to lay her to rest.

I walked into the graveyard and found a small patch of ground without a headstone. I set out the mandala of heather and ferns I had brought with me. The ferns were rather wilted, to say the least, as they don't travel well. I said a few words. Then it was done.

Ceremonies like this can often feel functional when I carry them out. I like to think that I will be moved, that I will be swamped in feeling, but often I am not. I don't worry about this as it is the fact that I am doing it that is important. Sometimes I get caught in the moment and something stirs inside me. I always write a few words, and this sometimes brings something through, but often it is just a record of what is happening for my ancestral diary of healing work. I usually snatch a photograph. There is always a feeling of completion at the end though, like I can finally draw a line under something and move on. I think this in my mind consciously, and do not doubt that there is closure in my unconscious too.

The unknown ancestor

Catherine was the unknown ancestor. When I first began to research my family tree it was this story that I set out to uncover. Yet, after a relatively short time, I had the names of all my ancestors of that generation except hers. She was the secret. She was the one they never spoke about. In ancestral healing work, secrets are very noisy.

My great-great-grandfather carried the shame of his origins throughout his life and I will talk more about this in the next chapter. His mother's name was hidden from the world and her story brushed under the rug. Maybe this is why it claimed me when I did finally discover it. I find in ancestral healing work, time again, the secrets have the loudest voices. It is as though their silencing in the conscious world turns up the volume within the unconscious.

When I found out she had been in the workhouse, it hit me like a wave of energy through my body. I made the discovery after finding George's baptism record. For years, I tried to find information about him in the census records and find his birth certificate. I ordered so many bogus George Riley birth certificates that I hit double figures. In genealogy, this is commonly referred to as hitting a brick wall. This is where you follow a line of enquiry, locating paper records that reveal information about a particular ancestor or ancestral line. You have success up to a point, and then there is a break in the paper trail: you can't find a particular record that should be there. In this case, I could follow George's life as an adult, but I couldn't find any records for when he was a child, either in the censuses or his birth certificate. When this happens, I sometimes stop and forget about that line of inquiry; however, I didn't give up in this instance. I'd take a break for a year or two and then pick up my research again. This process lasted for seven years, as George Riley was someone I was interested in right at the outset of researching my family tree, with Riley being my maiden name. One day in the autumn of 2016, I told myself that this was the year. I would have a final push to see what I could find out and then put it down for good if I wasn't successful. I decided to go down to London, visit the archives. This decision followed a special experience I had during the five-weekend *Stalking the Rebel Soul* programme run by Dr Martin Shaw in the Westcountry School of Myth.[56] One of our assignments was to create a story of an ancestor. I chose a different family line, and went up my maternal grandfather's line, but I remember feeling frustrated that I didn't know the story of my paternal grandfather's line, the story of my Irish roots.

While I was preparing for my London research trip during the early spring of 2017, I found that the Westminster Parish records had recently been published online. By the time George was born, it was a legal requirement to register the birth of a child with the civil records, but many poor people didn't do this. This was especially true with poor Irish people. This was partly because it cost money, but it was also out of ignorance. Catherine may simply not have known this law or how to register a child's birth. For many Irish people it was also because of concern over being deported. Irish people would prefer their name to be on as few legal documents as possible so there was no paper trail to follow. When there were people frequently sent back to Ireland by the parish in which they were seeking refuge, the less paperwork they had saying they were Irish and where they were from, the better. Catherine didn't register George's birth, but she did, however, have him baptised.

It was discovering George's baptism record that led me to his mother's name and that they both lived in the workhouse. This in turn led me to locate the admission and discharge records for St James Workhouse. I am very lucky that these records still exist as they have been destroyed for many other workhouses. It is through these records that I have been able to build up a detailed picture of Catherine's life. Catherine has become known to me because of this. I now know more about her life than any of my other ancestors of that generation, or even the two generations to follow her.

During one of my visits to Northern Ireland, I stayed in a B&B run by a couple in their eighties. I noticed a book about Victorian Manchester on the coffee table and got chatting to them about this. The man who ran the B&B had lived in South Manchester for many years. This was the same place where I had lived. His mother had lived in Piccadilly in London during Victorian times. The synchronicities were stark. He told me his mother had lived to old age and died in her nineties. He could recollect her stories about what it was like to live in Victorian London. I didn't even know it was possible to have a link with an eyewitness account like this and I asked lots of questions. This was a way I could under-stand what it was like for Catherine to live in this place at that time. He said his mother had talked of the children running barefoot in the streets, polishing shoes for money and selling newspapers. I asked him about the workhouses, and what she had said about them. He asked why, and I said my ancestors spent time in them. His face dropped and he looked very sad and melancholy and said: 'No, she never spoke of them. The workhouses were so terrible that people never spoke about them. I am sorry your ancestors had to live in those places.' The atmosphere in the room shifted and a heaviness lingered in the air.

The workhouse was a place deeply feared. People would commit crimes to be sentenced to prison rather than go to the workhouse. I read a first-hand account from someone who lived in a workhouse and described it as like being buried alive. That is quite something.

For me, the workhouse is one of the clearest examples that show how civilisation is broken. For everyone classified as able-bodied upon entering the workhouse, it was seen by Victorian society as their own doing that they were there. It was seen as their fault that they had succumbed to the workhouse. They were lazy and bone idle, nothing but a disgrace and a burden on the ratepayer. From Catherine's story, we can see that she was carrying guilt and shame that were not hers to bear. This was not her doing. She lived on the brink of destitution and was alone after being torn from her native land. How can anyone point the finger and say it was her fault that she ended up destitute and behind the workhouse walls? She was presented with circumstances that no individual should ever have to endure.

What I see in Catherine's story is an amplification of the impact of an oppressive system of control that still exists to this day. It is one where our government puts the economy before people, and the disparity between the rich and the poor grows. The people of England, Scotland and Ireland were cleared off the land because they were not profitable for the landowners. With no choice other than to move to the cities and seek employment, they were forced to take their chances in a broken place: the slums of Victorian industrial Britain. The landlords deemed it more important to do what they did for power and money, and completely disregarded the Irish people. This view of economics over people is still held in today's government.

Working men and, later, women being given the vote has been instrumental in driving change. Significant advances in democracy were made in the twentieth century. Yet, now we are in the twenty-first century, I find myself living in a world where democracy is on shaky ground. The people are being controlled once again, but this time through the media. The British government has worked out a formula of messaging where they can persuade the poor to either vote for the interests of the very rich, or not vote at all. This formula includes lying and cheating on an unprecedented scale. The media has an incredible grip over people's imaginations and steers people away from the parties who are looking out for the interests of the poor and marginalised. This is why it seems, in many ways, like we are going backwards as a society. The gap between people with positions of power and those who lack money and power is growing. The UK is one of the world's wealthiest countries, and yet with continued austerity, exclusion and marginalisation, poverty is rising each year. Depending on which indicator is used, in terms of total GDP, it is between the fourth and the ninth richest country in the world.[57] Forty-four per cent of the UK's wealth is now owned by just 10 per cent of the population. This is five times the total wealth held by the poorest half. The average household wealth for Britain's richest 10 per cent is 315 times that of the poorest.[58]

The ongoing disparity between the rich and poor, those that hold power and those that are powerless, is vast. Yet, I do believe there is some hope. Many people are waking up and noticing this separation and its scale. When something is amplified, it can be seen more clearly, and this is happening in our world now. It is a chaotic time, but a time when people become aware because of the chaos they see unfolding around them. This period in human history that we are living through is alarming and distressing, but chaos is a prelude to change.

Choices

In Catherine's story, I describe how her life changed when she turned to the drink to forget, be accepted and feel for a moment in time that she was home. I can personally relate to leaning on alcohol for comfort during a period as a young adult. A lot of people I knew did too. For some, it is a phase, and for others, they got stuck there. When I drank, everything felt OK, but it didn't last. Once the effects of alcohol wore off, this feeling would disappear, as it was not the reality of my life back then. I did all the things that I felt society was telling me to do. I got married, bought a lovely house, and embarked on a career that I was passionate about, and yet this wasn't enough. Later in my life, I made more conscious choices about what served me in finding that feeling of contentment and managed to choose something completely different. I chose a life where my work brought me outdoors rather than sitting in an office and where I didn't have a huge mortgage to pay off. I chose a life where I was aligned with my soul's desires, which brought me home. Catherine didn't have the option to choose like this. Her leaving Ireland and emigrating to London wasn't so much a choice as something imposed on her through others' decisions. This had a severe impact on her life and those she loved.

Acceptance and belonging are fundamental in a tribal community. The workhouse was the polar opposite. There was no acceptance of the destitute, and they didn't belong anywhere. This was Catherine's story for much of her life. I am in no doubt that I can relate to Catherine's powerlessness because I have a sense of my own very different kind of powerlessness in the world. A significant part of my spiritual journey has been recognising that I do have a choice and that I am acting from my position of privilege to make these choices. I am not powerless: I can choose how to spend my time and what I do in the world. When I decided to leave my career, I heard a strong voice telling me not to do it, but I followed what felt right over what my mind was telling me. I see putting work over play as staying in my ancestral story of hard graft. It has taken a lot to move away from this pattern. There is something important and healing about breaking away from the old story that has followed through the generations. It isn't easy moving away from that.

A big process for me is rewriting my core language that I am not good enough. If I believe I am something wrong or I have done something wrong, I deprive myself of what gives me joy, beauty and love because I believe I don't deserve it. It is a form of self-sabotage and neglecting myself. I fell into this in the corporate world, working and working and not giving myself time to enjoy the things I loved to do. Sometimes I would be in a position where if I were to stop working for the evening, I would have no idea what to do next. I had forgotten what it was that I loved. When I started my consultancy, I couldn't even blame my boss. This insistent drive for work was coming from within me, rather than from someone pushing me from the outside, and this realisation was a big wake-up call. My compulsion to work hasn't gone away, but I have learned to notice when it arises and address it.

Another theme in Catherine's story is exploitation. I have allowed myself to be exploited in the past, working unpaid overtime, sometimes upwards of twenty hours a week. Saying yes meant that I was saying no to me. I dreamt of this the night after I laid the mandala of heather and ferns outside the workhouse gates in Kensington, the closest point I could get to the spot where Catherine died. I dreamt that I was working and not being paid, then made to be a part of a team to manipulate someone into undertaking something they didn't want to do. In this dream I was reminded of how people will unscrupulously get others to do what they want them to.

Francis Weller writes about ancestral shame and the unspoken grief that surrounds it in his book *Wild Edge of Sorrow*.[59] When he works as a psychotherapist with someone who carries a sadness that is hard to identify, after exploring many possible sources for it, he might ask if there is something in the family history that might be lingering in his client's body. There is often a memory of a loss after some reflection. Perhaps there was a wounding that occurred to a grandparent or some experience of abandonment that resides in the psychic history of the lineage. He goes on to share his reflections relating to tending to this unprocessed grief, which not only frees people to live their own lives but also eases ancestral suffering in the other world:

Ancestral grief also speaks to the grief that remains in our collective soul for the abuses of millions of individuals. It carries the weight of our genocide of the indigenous cultures that were encountered when the European settlers arrived in the new world. It speaks to the shameful legacy of slavery and to the killing fields of the Civil War. This grief carries the shadow of Hiroshima and Nagasaki. It carries the suffering of many cultures across the planet whose paths collided with the march of progress. All this weighs on our psyches. This grief is so immense it is hard to reconcile. We have much work to do here as a culture, and it may take many grief rituals and rituals of reconciliation… to begin to heal this lingering sorrow.[60]

I wonder who grieved for Catherine when she died. I grieve for her now.

***

MOVING BEYOND SHAME

So far, I have shared my reflections on Catherine's life and the shame she held, which has filtered down the ancestral line to me. In the remainder of this chapter, I would like to offer ways in which I have worked through this shame and grief that is residing in my body. This is work I began many years ago. I expect it is work I will still be carrying out in the years to come. I will now share three approaches I have used to work with this: 1. Healing trauma held in the body, 2. Core shamanic healing practices, and 3. Working with ceremony.

Healing trauma in the body

Shifting old patterns and healing ancestral trauma has been the long game for me. Looking back, it makes so much sense to me that the forms of therapy I am instinctively drawn to are body-related therapies as trauma is stored in the body. It felt counter-intuitive when I first discovered this in my thirties, as the thing that was causing problems was my mind. Getting out of my mind and focusing on my body has been incredibly healing and ultimately led to me being trained in one of these therapy models: Embodied Relational Therapy (ERT).[61]

It was my spirit teacher who highlighted that I needed to focus on my body during a shamanic journey. We all have a spirit teacher who resides in the Upperworld and they have a different energy and role to our spirit guides. Think of someone in your physical life to whom you go to learn: to be taught, to sit at their feet and to learn from them. They don't necessarily put their arm around you and sympathise with your challenges in the world. They instruct and are brief with their words. A few minutes with them sharing their wisdom can be life-changing. A person's spirit teacher is like this but resides in the spiritual realm.

When I left the corporate world, I had terrible back pain due to years of bad posture sitting at a desk, not taking care of my core strength, and then pushing too hard lifting stone in an environmental volunteering project. When I came out of that pressurised work environment, it was as if my body stopped holding me up. It needed a rest, and all the pain came through my back. It was so bad that I couldn't carry shopping bags or sit upright in a chair.

At around the same time, I journeyed to my spirit teacher, who is the Greek philosopher Socrates. I asked for his advice about what to focus on as my area of study now that I had left the corporate world. I didn't expect him to say these words: 'Focus on your body, Nicola.' I expected it would be something like earth energies and ley lines, or tree folklore, or ancestral healing medicine. To be told to focus inward and study my body left me a little perplexed, to say the least. I decided to read some of his work, and during my research I read that Socrates spoke of the importance of focusing on the body as the most important thing that a person can do. His reason for this was because if you have problems with your body you are only partly here: partly present and partly focusing on the pain, discomfort and concern. If I am right in my body, then I can give 100 per cent to whatever I decide to focus my energy on.

This is very counter-intuitive within Western culture. I have been encouraged to put everyone and everything else first over myself, including my body. I hadn't looked after my body well for two decades, and so I figured I'd better start now. I had no idea it would lead me further down my spiritual healing path, but it makes sense, looking back. Socrates' guidance led me on a path to make many changes in my life: including taking up regular exercise and eradicating sugar, grains and alcohol from my diet. It is the trauma-body relationship though that I would like to address in particular in this chapter.

As I explained in Chapter 1, when a person suffers a trauma and it is not dealt with effectively, this is stored in the body and passed down in our DNA to future generations. To heal both trauma incurred in this lifetime and that which we inherited from our ancestors, the natural place to look is within our body.

In the ERT model there are seven character types. Each character type is defined according to what happened to a person during birth and up until the age of seven. A person can embody one character type, or multiple combinations of the seven character types, and change predominant character types throughout their life.

A character type is created through energetic 'armouring'. This is caused by holding breath in certain parts of our body. This reflects the world back to us in a way that resonates with our armouring, which we hold in different parts of our bodies through constricting or loosening of the breath. For example, if rage is not allowed in the home when a child is growing up, that child may want to scream and shout, but they are told not to do that. The threat from the parent can be unconscious or conscious, and the child can experience the withdrawal of love and care if they express such forbidden feelings. The child may develop into an adult who has a very strong in-breath, taking things in from the world, but who has developed an energetic armouring so that these feelings are not released on the out-breath. Physical symptoms often follow where the armouring is around the body.

Around the developmental age of two, when a child is being potty-trained, the 'holding' character type emerges. Many people who are drawn to healing work are holding character types, me included. In each of the character types, there are two extreme versions, referenced as the 'yearning' and 'denying' versions. There is also a middle ground, which is the 'creative' version. I can relate to the denying version of the holding character type, which is about needing to stick to the rules, or else I will mess up and be ashamed. Shame is big for the holding character type.

There is something in shame that is hidden, that doesn't get named and that can't be picked up. When you go near it, it disappears like mercury. One way of 'escaping' the shame is by working. If I work then I can climb my way out of the shame, but it is still there hiding in dark corners, keeping me doing more. If shame isn't dealt with by allowing it to come to the surface, then it keeps the whole cycle going. It is the driver behind all my hard work. It is what is happening when I am triggered and feel I have done something wrong, something unforgivable, or I feel I have let someone down. This was a constant feeling while working in the corporations and they thrived off it. This core belief that I am not enough drives me to work very hard and put work above all else, so that I am accepted.

When I think back to Catherine's life, the injustices in the workhouse were astonishing. The poor were humiliated for asking for help. The idea was to shame them into supporting themselves and if they couldn't, then they had to carry the shame of being in the workhouse for the rest of their lives. I have read that families who had to go to the workhouse would walk through woods and fields to get there rather than take the roads and footpaths in case anyone they knew would see them: such was the shame they felt.

This shame resides in me, and so to work with it I have brought it into the light, as shame lives in the shadows. When it comes to light, it doesn't have the same power. I have learnt to recognise how shame feels in my body. It makes me feel small, as though I want to curl up and hide. It ties a knot in my stomach, tightens my chest and gives me a shortness of breath. When I feel this in my body, it reminds me to reflect on what is happening at that moment with my situation. I ask myself who is doing the shaming. Is it something in me or something external making me feel like this? This gives me more choices. This is the privilege I have. I can recognise this and respond to it in a different way.

One antidote to shame is to own who I am. I have worked hard for many years to speak out about who I am and what I believe in. I tried to conform, and it broke me once and nearly a second time. My work now, as hard as it is, is to occupy a position that is seen as alternative, although I don't see it as alternative. For me it is normal. When enough of us occupy this place then what was once alternative becomes mainstream. I am seeing this more and more, as people make the shift and come over to this different position of relating to the world.

Jason and I set up The Way of the Buzzard for this purpose, as a place where those who see the world differently can congregate and come together in community. This is a place where we can go to the Otherworld and the wild places and move our souls that little bit closer to where they want to be. A place where we can travel into a different world and bring back the energies that are most needed at this time.

Shame, if I allowed it to be in the driving seat, would stop me from doing this. It would keep me on the straight

and narrow doing what society wants me to do: what I am
'supposed' to do.

Core shamanic healing practices

I want to explore the word 'soul' before going into detail about
core shamanic healing practices. In Shamanism and some
other belief systems too, such as Christianity, everybody has
a soul. Scientists can't quite explain what it is, but it is the
thing that is there when a person's body, mind and feelings are
stripped away. It is the core essence of an individual, and it is
the part that never dies. It is the eternal self. At the foundation
of many spiritualities is a shared belief in the soul.

Core Shamanism was brought to the Western world by
anthropologist Michael Harner.[62] He studied the spiritual
beliefs of indigenous peoples for over four decades and found a
thread running through them, which he termed Core Shamanism. Each tradition had a way of shifting consciousness to
access other realities, which he called shamanic journeying. He
noted that through shamanic journeying, the medicine men
and women of indigenous tribes would carry out practices to
heal the soul. Two of these soul-healing practices were soul
retrieval and soul exchange.

These core shamanic healing practices are available to work
with any kind of trauma, whether or not it is related to shame.
That said, shame is one of the underlying causes of trauma,
and the practices of soul retrieval and soul exchange are very
effective in the healing process.

Soul retrieval

When a person experiences a trauma, their body goes into a
flight, fight or freeze stage. This is a natural process in order to
protect the body. After the emergency has passed, the energy
should return to the body. But, sometimes this gets interrupted
and the energy or soul part can't find a way back.

In the shamanic tradition, the view is that this energy, or rather the soul part, goes into the Otherworld, away from the personal physical reality. The practice of a soul retrieval brings this soul part back into the person to be integrated. It is usually, although not always, a process that is undertaken or facilitated by a shamanic practitioner. Sometimes soul parts can come back spontaneously during healing work, and at other times a practitioner or the individual will journey into the Otherworld to retrieve it. To read more about this process, I recommend Sandra Ingerman's book *Soul Retrieval: Mending the Fragmented Self*.[63]

When a lost soul part is reintegrated back into an individual, it can be incredibly powerful. I have seen remarkable things happen in the following days and weeks after this process has happened within people. Over the following months, more changes can happen, and these can often be subtle. When looking back on this time, people say to me that the soul retrieval was a turning point, helping them find the strength to change some aspect of their lives and move them closer to contentment.

Soul exchange is somewhat like soul retrieval, in that the person is receiving their soul parts back into them. It differs because the soul parts accessed in soul exchange are residing in someone or something else. In Shamanism there is a belief that when a person is in a relationship with somebody or something, depending on the circumstances, they can give away part of their soul and vice versa. For example, when a person falls in love, they give a little part of themselves to the other person. This is natural, given that we want to share our hearts and souls when we fall in love. When the two people are parted through separation or death these swapped soul parts may stay with the other person, so each soul carries a little piece of that other person's soul. That is unless they go through a process of exchange.

A part of someone's soul can also be taken. This can happen

when there is a relationship of dominance between two people when one person is controlled by the other. This occurs in an unhappy, controlling marriage, and it can also happen between slave and master. What is interesting about this scenario, as I have found in my work, is that the 'master' doesn't need to be an actual person. It can be a 'thing'. For example, in my case, that 'thing' was the 'corporations'.

There are a variety of different ways that soul parts can be given or taken or left to reside in someone else. Soul healing through a soul exchange is a process where a set sequence of activities is carried out between two people or between the person and thing that is holding the person's soul. It involves the two parties who are holding onto each other's soul parts meeting in the spirit realm.

I feel that it is not necessary to ask permission from the other party in order to do this work as the spirit guides of both parties are present and this is happening in the spiritual realm, for the highest good of both individuals. A circle is created where the two parties stand and it is here, with the aid of their spirit guides and the shamanic practitioner's spirit guide, that the soul exchange takes place. After this is complete, any residual work that needs to be done to cut any remaining energetic cords is carried out.

I have undergone the process of soul exchange several times, between myself and ex-partners, and also between myself and the corporations. This was an idea presented to me by my supervisor and shamanic teacher Jayne Johnson. I found it a really interesting and powerful experience to exchange soul parts with a 'thing' rather than a person: the corporations. It certainly helped me in my process of breaking free from them.

I have found the practice of soul retrieval and soul exchange to be helpful when working with others too. What excites me about this work is discovering that these healing techniques can also be applied to our ancestors. An ancestor who was controlled by the oppressive regime into which they were born could have had part of their soul taken, or they could have given it to the 'oppressor'.

When a person dies, they are not automatically reunited with their missing soul parts. The damage happened in this physical reality when they were alive. Therefore, a connection is required with the physical reality for the healing to take place.

If our ancestors suffered traumatic experiences during their lives that they did not have the opportunity to heal, they may have fragmented souls and need soul retrieval. If this is the case, it is entirely possible for soul retrieval to be carried out for them during the ancestral healing work. Likewise, if they gave part of their soul to another person or thing, or had part of their soul taken, it is possible to facilitate a soul exchange for them.

These practices can be undertaken solely by the shamanic practitioner journeying by themselves, or it is possible to do this process with the person who is seeking the healing of their ancestor in a three-way process. If the opportunity presents itself as you progress with your ancestral healing work, I would recommend this three-way engagement. You are part of this story, and this will support you in your experience of ancestral healing so that all the family line heals. As with any work that you undertake in the spiritual realm, always seek the advice of your ancestor ally guide to find out what you need to do every step of the way. To find a shamanic practitioner, the Indie Shaman website is a good place to start as they hold a list of accredited practitioners.[64]

I will share an example of a soul exchange I carried out with Catherine and her family in Chapter 6. The final step I would like to discuss before we move on to the next chapter is ceremony, and how this can help in our personal process to move through things we are dealing with.

Creating ceremonies

An ancestral healing ceremony might sound quite formal, but we can create ceremonies about anything at any time. Ceremony is incredibly powerful. Think of the times when ceremonies are held in our modern Western culture. They are at moments in our lives that are significant and at times of change that we want to mark somehow: the naming of a new baby, the joining of a couple in union, and honouring the life of a loved one after they die. We carry out a ceremony for something significant. Ceremony puts a marker in the sand to tell ourselves, and anyone who is listening in this reality and all the Otherworld realities, that there is something that we want to be acknowledged. We hold a ceremony to announce that this is a point in time where there is a change.

It stands to reason that ceremony and ancestral healing go hand in hand. For example, we can hold a ceremony to honour an ancestor and the life that they led. Isn't it nice when we achieve something in our lives and are recognised for it? When we are seen, something shifts in us, and we can do this for our ancestors. Knowing the lives that they lived, and the things they endured, we can be a witness to this, and say thank you to them for giving us life. If they hadn't gone through what they went through, then we probably wouldn't be here.

This is also an opportunity to acknowledge our ancestors' deeper wounding and the choices they had to make that are still impacting many generations down the line. I feel it is wise to remember that times were very different in the past. During the Industrial Revolution, as people moved into the cities to seek work, communities were ripped apart. It was likely that as the fabric of society changed so rapidly, many people no longer had elders around them to help them with their challenges. To endure the hardships of the eighteenth, nineteenth and early twentieth century, poor people had to shut down to survive. In doing this, they chose not to speak about the things that were causing them pain.

But that said, this was back then, and for many, this level of dissociation was necessary for their survival. Depending on our individual circumstances, it isn't necessarily helpful for us to be like this now. Yet as I have already discussed, these ways of coping get passed down our ancestral line in our genes, and we may continue to react unconsciously in various situations to our detriment.

We can use ceremony to request a change that we would like to happen: the ending of a pattern. Taking the example of some of the ancestral patterns I have discussed in this chapter, I could create a ceremony to end the feeling of shame and fear of lack that underlies my need to work. We can put a call out that we want to end an undesirable inherited ancestral pattern. We can ask our spirit guides to help us, and through this process, our friends in this reality and the Otherworld can witness that this is our intention.

Let me give you a few examples to illustrate what an ancestral healing ceremony might look like. I have taken part in them intentionally, and also in one that kind of sprung up on me, so I seized the opportunity.

The planned ceremony was to celebrate the gifts that have been passed down my family line. With Samhain being the festival of the ancestors, this is a good time to do this. I might cook them a meal or create an altar to my ancestors and light a candle that I leave burning all night. The yew tree is the tree of the ancestors, which is why very old yew trees are found in church graveyards, often pre-dating the Norman church that stands there on the old ancestral ground. I might bring a yew branch into my home and lay it on the altar in remembrance of all of those who have walked before me. These are practices that I do alone or with Jason or as a group with others. One year at Samhain, Jason and I held a ceremony at the Monastery in Manchester. This was a ceremony to celebrate the gifts that have been passed down my family line. Often in our ancestral healing work, we are drawn to focusing on the patterns that have been passed down the ancestral line that are no longer helpful to us. In my case, this is the drive to put work above all else, yet there are qualities that have been passed down the family line that are incredibly beneficial to us, and that have undoubtedly ensured our survival and continuation of the bloodline. In this ceremony, I spent time reflecting on what these positive qualities were. I reflected that this includes having determination and drive. These qualities have brought me to where I am now, and I am grateful for them.

As well as marking the festival of Samhain, I have honoured my ancestors at other times throughout the year. Sometimes this has been through planned ceremonies. However, unplanned ceremonies have also happened quite spontaneously when the moment presented itself. At our annual Space to Emerge micro-festival gathering that we run in Cumbria in the northwest of England, I partook in a powerful process in the Women of the Three Rivers Red Tent. This took me by surprise, and I seized the moment. A group of women gathered inside the tent, and we shared stories. I had been working on gathering Catherine's story all through the winter and was holding it within me. At the end of the session, we were invited to light a candle for a woman who had touched our lives, and I spoke of Catherine. I acknowledged her hardships and thanked her for her sacrifices. At that moment, something shifted in me that is very hard to put into words: the deepest things often are. It was a feeling that I had finally brought her completely into the light. Her life was being witnessed not just by me but also by other women sympathetic to her struggles.

It is important to check in with your ancestor ally in creating a ceremony to honour ancestors when it comes to deciding what kind of ceremony to hold, just as with the process of visiting ancestral land. I do this by going on a shamanic journey to my ancestor ally to meet with her and explain what I intend to do. I ask her if there is anything that she recommends for me to do.

When it comes to designing the ceremony, there is a set formula that I follow in my shamanic practice. This involves opening up the space by welcoming in the elements of life along with the beings of the Upperworld and the Lowerworld, and then closing down the space at the end. By doing this I am following an ancient practice of creating sacred space, where each of the four directions, north, south, east and west are acknowledged along with the elements that reside there. This puts a signal out there to Spirit, the universal energies, that something different is happening away from the everyday mundane, and our spirit guides know to come and listen. Opening sacred space and holding a ceremony might seem a lot to undertake at first, but like most things, I find that over time it becomes second nature. If there are three things I recommend to do as part of your spiritual practice, it is ceremony, shamanic journeying and nature connection. It is well worth mastering and these are all things that we teach in our Mystery School.

Traumatised through separation

If I were to draw a circle and write the word trauma in the middle, all the themes I have discussed in this chapter come from this. The core theme is trauma, and this is transgenerational for many people. So many of us are traumatised as we are living in a society that is not allowing us to be authentic and real.

One of the ways this can be changed is by understanding, feeling and exploring how we got here, asking ourselves the question: 'Why am I in the position I am in now?' I believe that we cannot do this without checking in with our ancestors.

The way our Western world operates is very different from the natural way of life for human beings. Until the birth of civilisation, people lived in tribes. This is how it always was throughout evolution. Daniel Quinn speaks of this in his book *Beyond Civilization: Humanity's Next Great Adventure.*[65] He shares how living in tribes is an important aspect of being human. Humans evolved for hundreds of thousands of years living in tribes, and it is our natural way to live in a community, taking care of each other and the environment that we live in. Quinn says: 'Tribes exist for their members – and for all their members, because all are perceived as involved in the success of the tribe.' Civilisation has led us to a place where tribes no longer exist, and this valuing of all people no longer happens.

In this modern world, I believe that the way we live in the Western world also keeps us separate from another thing that is most important to humans: it keeps us separate from the Earth. During my time working in the mainstream world, I was separate from nature and the way my true being wanted to live. My introduction to Shamanism and shamanic training was a coming home to what I knew intuitively as a child but from which I had drifted away. Deep down, I wanted to reclaim that part of me.

I will speak more about this in the next chapter. It is time now to go back to the nineteenth century and to see what has become of Catherine's son, George, my great-great-grandfather. Torn from his mother's arms as a small child, he grew up with the definitive experience of separation, away from the love of his parents, and grew up inside the walls of an institution designed to breed out insolence and create the ultimate worker.

This will be the last chapter of exploring my ancestral story, and through it, I will continue with the narratives of separation, dissociation and work.

CHAPTER 5

The Next Generation

George was just 3 years old when he was was sent to the industrial school. These were workhouses that were purpose-built to accommodate children from 3 to 16 years old. Battersea Industrial School was a five-mile journey south across the River Thames.

It was a huge ornate building on the edge of Battersea Common, home to around fifty children. These were boys and girls of all ages who had been forcibly separated from their parents, or who had been orphaned, their mother and father having died of any manner of diseases or dangers that afflicted the poor.

George's memory of his mother quickly faded until all he could remember were her soft dark eyes and the safety he felt when she held him in her arms. He knew that she was alive and living elsewhere but would never dare ask after her. She brought shame on him, and they were kept apart for a good reason.

He was born illegitimate, as his mother was out of wedlock, which came with its own curse and humiliation. His very existence was a disgrace, an embarrassment to Victorian society. He lived every day with this reminder.

Although he understood why he and his mother were kept apart in one sense, he also spent his childhood confused as to why she had deserted him. Why did she not try harder so they could be together? Why had he been abandoned? George was not to leave the walls of his new home again until he turned sixteen. He was to spend his childhood growing up within the confines of an institution.

Industrial schools were a recent addition to Victorian Britain. They were built to house vagrant, destitute and disorderly children who were considered at risk of becoming criminals. When George first arrived, there were only a few such places in the country. By the time he was 10 years old, there were thirty. Some of the industrial school buildings were dubbed 'pauper palaces' because of their magnificent architecture. They were an awe-inspiring sight to boys and girls coming from the streets or lodging houses of Britain.

These establishments were built to turn pauper children into able and employable citizens. Consensus in society was that pauperism was in the blood: insolence breeds insolence. To end this perpetual cycle, these children needed to be separated from their parents and brought up in such a manner as to make them God-fearing, useful and healthy members of society. It was considered that the ingrained immorality of the workhouses' older residents would rub off on young paupers and turn them into criminals, and so they were removed from their influence entirely and given an education to eradicate the germs of pauperism and make them fit for a productive life.

At the industrial school, the children studied the Bible, reading and writing, dictation, multiplication tables, arithmetic and geography, as well as having vocational training in their teenage years. This included tailoring, carpentry, shoemaking and blacksmithing.

The overseers of these workhouse establishments often came from a military background and brought regimental authority into the workhouse. There were strict rules: never tell lies and only speak when you are spoken to as children were to be seen and not heard. Whipping was common and brutal. As a consequence, the children had a sullen, cautious glance, and when they spoke, it was in whispers.

Time served

George was dressed in a uniform, as were all the other boys, and he was given a number. Here he would no longer be called by his first name, just his number – sixteen.

His days were monotonous. They began at 7 am in the winter and 6 am in the summer, where he was woken up by the ringing of the bell that would punctuate the order of the day. The boys would dress, strip their beds and go for prayers on the landing before starting the housework. The children were expected to perform almost all of the domestic labour at the institution. This included working in the kitchen and laundry and doing general household tasks such as making and changing beds and cleaning the rooms.

After the morning chores were complete, they would all file in line into the dining room for breakfast. Most days it was simply watered-down oats and dry bread known as gruel. There was very little given out to them and George was constantly hungry.

After breakfast, the children would spend the morning in school. The teaching method used was repetition and George would spend hours each day literally repeating what the teacher was saying again and again. The boys were kept separate from the girls and taught differently as it was considered that the boys had bigger brains than the girls. So, they had harder arithmetic and were taught geography and history.

They spent the afternoons labouring to earn their keep, while the younger boys were given menial tasks such as making matchboxes or paper bags. One of the worst jobs was picking oakum. This involved pulling apart the old ropes used in ships. The coarse fibres wore away the skin on George's fingertips, so they were red and sore. It was mind-numbing sitting still on a chair next to the other boys for hours on end, not being allowed to speak while doing this.

The industrial school was a place of routine and discipline, and there was no warmth or comfort here. It was no place for a child to grow up. There were not even any toys. Later in the nineteenth century, toys were provided, along with occasional outings to the countryside or seaside as conditions were improved. But in George's time there were none of these things. It was a tough childhood. At times the boys had to work in complete silence. If anyone was caught out so much as smiling, they would be punished.

George found night times the hardest. The boys would be shut up in their dormitory with no candles for light. They had to stay locked in here in the dark for twelve hours. George felt so alone, with no one to hold and comfort him through the night. There was no love growing up in an institution like this. There was no one to wipe away his tears. In the first few years of his life, George had, for a fleeting moment, known what it was like to be held in the embrace of loving arms. But this time was brief and had soon been taken from him. As he grew older, memories of his mother faded altogether until she was just a name and a feeling: a feeling of someone who had once wanted him, but not enough to want to be with him now. He had been abandoned just like the other children here. Lost and miserable, his mother felt so far away. He thought of her every night and wondered if she ever thought of him. Every day he hoped that she would arrive at the workhouse door and take him away. She never came.

On Saturdays, the children stopped working at 1.30 pm. Saturday afternoons and evenings were spent preparing for Sunday by bathing, changing linen, reading scriptures, and learning Gospels for the Sunday church service.

Exercise and sport were considered an important part of the school's regime with a good-sized playground and playing field for football and cricket. On Sunday afternoons, the children were given time in the playground. This was a square yard approximately one acre in size and made of concrete paving slabs. The one-storey brick buildings that surrounded it were used for offices and storerooms. In the darkest corner of the yard, there was an empty room. This was used to confine disobedient boys.

George lived under constant fear of punishment or of doing something to upset the schoolmaster. When it came to discipline, the rules regarding the punishment of workhouse children were extensive, in line with the popular expression at the time: spare the rod and spoil the child. Punishments were administered in the gymnasium on a Friday afternoon. It was a gloomy room with a high ceiling, and all the boys would file in and form three sides of a square. In front of them was a long desk where the boys who were to be reprimanded awaited their trial and punishment. For minor offences, a boy was laid across the long desk, face downwards, feet strapped and held by a Sergeant. A cane, as thick as a man's thumb, was lifted up slowly and dramatically and then, with a swish brought down across the boy's bottom. The spectacle was terrifying, and invariably, a child would fall out of rank in a faint. Recipients would cry loudly and have to be carried away afterwards to recover. For more serious offences, a birch rod was used. Sometimes the caning would be so bad that the boy would need to be taken away to the surgery for treatment. This would depend on the level of the offence committed and the mood of the teacher inflicting the punishment. Some boys would try to escape the industrial school and climb over the walls. When this happened, and they were caught, a boy could receive up to twelve strokes with the birch rod. There were instances across the country where the whipping was so severe the boy never recovered and would die from his injuries.

Another punishment that would be administered for bad behaviour was a reduction in the quality or quantity of food. George learned quickly that he needed to hide his vulnerability and disown feelings and thoughts that were not permitted in the institution. He learnt to survive the trauma of growing up in such a place by shutting down emotionally and freezing in the face of something sad, frightening or infuriating.

As George grew older, he was taught skills for the work-place. By the age of eleven, he had learned to make and mend his clothes and by the age of thirteen, he learned the same for his shoes. As he grew older still, George was trained in carpentry, joinery, bricklaying and agricultural work.

In other workhouses that were less well equipped to educate pauper children, a rudimentary education was given. Unscru-pulous workhouse masters would take backhanders to sell the children as apprentices. It was effectively a slave trade: each child was sold for £5 by the workhouse master who kept the money for himself. Some boys were bought to work in the army and navy, again through backhanders with the work-house master. Others were sold to the mills of the industrial north. Fortunately, George was not sold to these places as he was better trained in skills that later enabled him to set up as a tradesman.

George's path to redemption from his disgraceful origins was through work. Everything about that school geared him up for working and this was his identity. It became his ticket out of poverty and to finally matter within society.

Beyond the workhouse

When George turned 16 years old, the school found him an apprenticeship as a carpenter and provided him with the clothes he needed. He had a trade, he could read and write, and he had been taught to be careful with his money.

Conversely, there were thousands of young men his age roaming the streets of London who had lived a very different life. They were unkempt and made their way in life through crime and deprivation. These were the ones who had survived life on the streets. In London, a child's life was nothing; they lay in the street in their thousands, dead and treated like dirt. Every day George had spent in that school was burnt into his soul, and yet he had emerged from there with an opportunity to rise above the life of a pauper. He felt hopeful when he left, though it took some time adjusting to his new-found freedoms beyond the walls of the workhouse.

George became a carpenter, initially as a journeyman or day labourer. He worked on construction projects that were building Victorian London. By the time he turned twenty, he was living in Sydenham, an up-and-coming, desirable part of London. This was just a mile or so from the newly relocated Crystal Palace, a giant glass exhibition hall that was originally located in Hyde Park in central London.

After completing his apprenticeship, George married Mary Ann Dupoy. She was a tall lady from noble stock. Her father was a French revolutionary. He had fled France after the restoration of the monarchy and made a life for himself in London. Mary Ann had been schooled at home and was quite the eloquent lady, although very poor. She had grown up in St Giles, Cripplegate, a district not far from Westminster that was known for having one of the worst slums in London as well as the crime that came with it.

George and Mary Ann married in October 1876, four months after George's mother Catherine passed away. He was not aware that she had died. George met with his mother once after he left the industrial school. He felt detached from her when they met. Catherine was an old Irish lady, and George was London-born Irish and keen to forget his foreign roots.

He lived in the constant shadow of the stigma of spending his childhood in a workhouse. He wanted to distance himself from that sad entry into the world and all the shame associated with it. It was everything to him to ensure he was an integrated member of Victorian society. The Irish were a disgrace, and bastard children were forever tarnished with the shame they brought to the world. He wanted to leave all that behind him so he would be accepted into society. When George had visited her in the workhouse, there was a heavy sadness between them. There was no life for them together now. He was a grown man with his dreams to chase.

George and Mary Ann's first home was a terraced house in Peckham, six miles to the east of Battersea. It was a comfort to them both. They were wealthy enough to have a 'best room', the parlour that was located at the front of the house. Behind this, at the back of the house, they had the kitchen where they would spend all their time. They named their first daughter Rosina. Their second daughter was named Mary Ann Catherine Riley after their mothers. She was a bonny girl who was to go by her middle name, Catherine, throughout her life.

Mary Ann Catherine was born on 12 February 1879. This was thirty years to the day that her aunt, Emily Charlotte, had been baptised during those first few months Catherine had fled the Great Famine and arrived in London.

Throughout his life, George hid his past and his humble and disgraceful beginnings. He and his wife, Mary Ann, went on to have twelve children: four boys and eight girls. George passed his trade down to several of his sons who also became carpenters. He brought them up to embrace his philosophy of the utmost importance of work. Through work, he became someone, and so his children never had to endure what he had to do in the workhouse. His mother's sacrifice meant that he didn't have to live a life on the streets. He had had a terribly lonely childhood, but he was someone in society now, and future generations would benefit. He had moved away from the poverty of the slums that the poorest people on the lowest rung of society would have to endure for generations to come.

Catherine had died alone on the other side of London, not knowing if her sons would succeed or what lay ahead of them in their lives. She did not know of the happiness that they and the future generations of her family would experience. Her story went unspoken, and her grief and sadness were left to linger in the shadows for two centuries. Then, after a decade of searching by one of her descendants, who turned over the dust-laden stones, sifting through page after page of old papers, her story was to be brought back into the light.

The generations who came after her would not know of the injustices she had endured and survived. They would know nothing about how she was denied the right to sit peacefully in her croft with her husband and children, eating steaming potatoes they had grown themselves and cooked over the open fire. Nor how she had to say goodbye to the robin who would come onto her doorstep and feed from her hand. Or how she had to leave her homeland forever, never to return. They would not know how she had longed to see her children playing together on the mossy knoll just as she did as a little girl. Or how they would no longer gather at her mother and father's home on the eve of winter and listen to the old stories spoken into the flames of the peat fire. Or how they would bed down, the whole family together head-to-toe on the floor, bellies full of stew. Her son George was to know her as a fallen woman who brought shame and burden on society – someone that Victorians despised. Through sacrifice and hard work, George had redeemed himself and become someone who mattered in the world. Their secrets would be buried away.

***

WORK NEMESIS

When I was a child, I would lose track of time on a daily basis whilst playing out in the orchard and back fields. I had sheds and haystacks I could create dens in, trees to climb and my vegetable and flower garden to tend. I would walk my nan and grandad's dog, Carla, and build an obstacle course out of boxes and garden canes for her to jump over. I created a club with my best friend, Helen, and my chicken, Elsa. We called ourselves 'The Investigating Three'. We had our own branded notebooks and badges and would prowl around looking for interesting things to examine and places to explore. When it rained, I would be indoors making all kinds of things out of cardboard boxes. I made a castle for a gummy bear with a working drawbridge, and a three-bedroom house for a miniature teddy out of a shoebox, which was lined with real carpet and wallpaper. On windy days I would try to make a kite out of bin liners and sticks. As a teenager, I continued my childhood obsession with horses and spent my weekends riding friends' ponies. Where other girls in my school started to hang out in town centres, I would spend my time revelling in anything horse-related. My friend and I would dress ourselves and the pony in elaborate outfits and enter fancy dress competitions at the local horse show.

This all stopped when I left school and entered the world of work. I stopped being creative, and I didn't even notice it happening. In my free time, I replaced creative pursuits with drinking with friends and that was how I spent my downtime. Alcohol led me into the spaciousness, rest and laughter I so desperately craved away from the workplace. Alcohol softened, moved and blurred the edges, and enabled me to party hard. It is interesting to reflect that when I started work, I stopped being creative in my personal life. My creativity was kept within the confines of the workplace. As the pressure of work built up over time, I stopped playing altogether.

I have really struggled with overworking. It is my nemesis: the thing to overcome. I didn't realise it was an issue when I had a career as I thought that putting work above all else was what people did. But I became ill because of it. When I left work inside the corporations and set up my sustainability consultancy, I have mentioned that I was surprised to see I was still overworking. I was in control of my time in theory. This was the reason I decided to go out on my own in the first place. Yet, I wasn't any more in control of my time than when I worked for someone else. It has been the thing I have been grappling with in recent years as I moved fully into working in the field of personal and spiritual development.

When I uncovered the story of George Riley and his childhood spent in the industrial school, it was a revelation to me. I began to understand why, after years of therapy trying to overcome my incessant need to work, I hadn't been able to beat it. This need to work has been ingrained in my family for generations, installed by the experiences of my ancestors growing up in the workhouse. It came down both my maternal and paternal lines, as my great-great-grandfather up my maternal line also spent his childhood alone in a workhouse.

At the beginning of this chapter, I wrote the last of Catherine's story by writing about her son George's life, which is the legacy she left behind. It was a significant moment for me when I discovered that I had an ancestor brought up as an orphan in the workhouse.

George was conditioned from a young boy to be a worker, and knowledge of this has helped me unpick my relationship to work. In this chapter, I will reflect on my challenge with overworking and how I have made steps to overcome this. I will provide some context as to how the Western cultural work ethic has arisen and then explain my antidote: be happy, play more, be creative and dream courageously. I will finish with my five steps to moving into a different way of being and working in the world.

Trained to be a worker

The industrial school was an institution established with one single objective: to take children off the streets and train them to be workers. To that end, it was a success.

George Riley and his wife Mary Ann were my only ancestors from the eighteenth and nineteenth centuries who could write. I know this because I have studied the marriage certificates of all my ancestors during that period. On a marriage certificate, the person needs to write their name, and if they aren't able to write, they draw a cross, as 'their mark'. George wrote his full name on the marriage certificate, and Mary Ann wrote hers underneath.

George was educated and left the industrial school with an apprenticeship as a carpenter, but this came at a great cost. He grew up away from his family and did not know love. He entered the outside world as an adult believing that the only way to redeem himself from the shame of being born illegitimate was to work. Only this would earn him a place in society, nothing else.

I have mentioned that illegitimate children were judged as being born to parents of a low moral standard, with the woman considered responsible for this sin. Society then attached that stigma to the child. Layered on top of this was the humiliation of having lived in the workhouse. Had George revealed the truth about his past, it would have meant limiting his job opportunities. I wonder whether he even revealed his humble beginnings to his wife.

When I was sitting by the fireside in an old Irish cottage in the County Down Folk Museum, a man in traditional nine-teenth-century Irish costume walked in. He was a member of staff, and as we chatted, he told me that his father was illegit-imate but had lied about it throughout his life because of the shame. Being illegitimate had stopped his father from becom-ing an officer in the army. It was very telling for me to hear first-hand exactly how much shame stayed with a person for being born out of wedlock, even when this was well into the twentieth century.

Stigmatised and unwanted, George did however have an advantage over other pauper children because of his training at the industrial school. George came from nothing and made himself a respectable and accepted citizen of society, but he had to hide his low origins. Growing up in an industrial school must have been terrible, and so when he had a family of his own, George would not have wanted his children to experience the same fate. He had twelve children, which is a lot even in the nineteenth century, especially considering he was a Protestant. He would have had to work very hard to keep them all.

I don't know what the conditions were like in Battersea Industrial School, but I do know that George was a small man. I know this because of information that was passed down from my great-grandfather to his father, my grandad. The story was that George was a small Irish man who married a tall French woman, and they had twelve children and lived in Tottenham. On researching my family tree, I found the information to be correct about who he married, where he lived and how many children he had. So, it stands to reason that the story around him being short would be true too. All the men in our family are very tall, so it suggests that George was underfed at the industrial school and went hungry through his childhood. The workhouses were renowned for feeding children poorly: think back to the famous story of Oliver Twist. George was a child just twenty years after that novel was written.

To get an insight into what it is like to grow up in an institution away from family, I have read the book *Trauma, Abandonment and Privilege: A guide to therapeutic work with boarding school survivors* by Nick Duffell and Thurstine Basset.[66] It explores the impact of boarding schools on children when they are sent away to these establishments aged seven. There is a particular way the children need to adapt to being away from their families. In many cases, it has alarming and sad consequences. Behaviours that emerge include the following: freezing through trauma; disowning feelings and thoughts that are not permitted by the institution; adopting a survival personality; employing disassociation; learned high functioning and the imposed ethos at the boarding school of self-sufficiency; fear of abandonment; a tendency to shut down emotionally and freeze in the face of something sad, frightening or infuriating; the need for there always to be a plan or a task; the preoccupation with rules; the imperative not to be wrong, and disowning vulnerability.

That is quite a list, and I can relate to many of these. These themes have been present throughout my life and have come into my awareness during therapy over the years. I am a master at disassociation in situations where I perceive conflict. It is as though a big part of me leaves the room as my body freezes in one spot. Also, I have strived for independence and self-sufficiency throughout my adult life and feel greatly wobbled if I don't have a plan to follow. I found it fascinating to read this list of traits of people who had grown up within an institution and how I can relate to so many of them.

Undoubtedly the decision Catherine made to be in the workhouse, and the resulting impact of George going to the industrial school, changed the course of my family line. Generation upon generation of Irish descendants remained in slums in the port cities of London, Bristol, Liverpool and Glasgow. These are areas that are still among the poorest in the UK today. Catherine made a sacrifice that led to relative prosperity compared with what the outcome could have been. George had a good life with a very large family, and all twelve of his children survived into adulthood. What he had lacked as a child, he made sure his children enjoyed, and he lived his life with his family around him.

However, the extreme work ethic has also been passed down the ancestral line. Sometimes, when I am at my worst, I have no idea what to do other than work. To put this another way, I don't know what to do if I am not working. In Duffell and Basset's book, there is a quote from ex-boarder and author George Orwell that particularly stands out to me. This poignant passage was taken from a notebook found by his bed at his death:

> It is now 16 years since my first book was published, and about 21 years since I started publishing articles in the magazines. There has literally not been one day in which I did not feel I was idling, that I was behind with the current job, and that my total output was miserably

small. Even at the periods I was working ten hours a
day on a book or writing five articles a week, I have
never been able to get away from this neurotic feeling
that I was wasting time.[67]

Reading George Orwell's experience here struck me. Here is
someone who has vocalised that they feel that they are under-
performing no matter how hard they work. I can relate to this.
No matter how much I work, I often feel like I haven't done
enough. There is always more to do. If I am not using my time
productively, then I am wasting time, and there is a part of me
that feels this is unacceptable. A part of me doesn't know what
else to do other than to work and that I am only of value if I am
working: that I cannot be alive if I do not work. I feel I must
be doing something productive; otherwise, I am wasting time.

Overworking is a disorder, and it has a name: workaholism.
The term comes from alcoholism and is used to describe the
addiction to work. A workaholic has a compulsive drive to work:
an obsession with work that is all-consuming. This prevents
them from maintaining relationships, pursuing interests outside
of work, and taking steps to maintain their health. As with other
addictions, the individual works to suppress underlying feelings
that are causing them distress, such as anxiety and shame. At
the height of my career as a sustainability manager, I certainly
fell under this definition. However, it wasn't named at the
time. I was working in a culture where these attributes were
rewarded. Now I have ended that line of work and am looking
from the other side, I can see that I do have a tendency towards
workaholism, and it is something I am continually monitoring.

One of the ways I am freeing myself from this is through
telling this story – to be mindful of this tendency in the
conscious part of my brain. If it is left in the unconscious,
the old patterns will continue. I keep this awareness in my
conscious mind and notice relevant thoughts, behaviours
and actions as they arise day to day that are connected to
overworking.

Needing to be busy

One thought process I have followed is to reflect on what George and Catherine might like to tell me about my compulsion to work. I sense they would say: 'Don't overwork because of the situation we were in.' The privileged few created the circumstances that the workers endured. Catherine and George were made to feel shame and for them to work and work, as it suited the privileged, those with power. This dynamic is still in play today, where the worker is kept in check to earn money for the rich. This need to overwork is ingrained in me as well as being prevalent in the world. Yet when I observe indigenous communities and how they live, I don't see them working all hours. Watching all three series of *Tribe*, featuring expedition leader Bruce Parry living alongside indigenous peoples across the world, has taught me this.[68] Parry spent extended periods living with the tribal people of the Amazon, Africa and Asia, and hunted, cooked and ate with them and tried their recreational and ceremonial practices. By watching the series, I got a real sense of the value tribal peoples place on the natural world, their customs, and upon the community. I understand their sensitivities and vulnerabilities to the impacts of encroaching Western culture. As I was growing up, the narrative I learned was that indigenous people are poor and have nothing, and yet I see them holding onto important things that our modern-day culture has lost.

The circumstances Catherine and George were in is at the extreme end of the scale to my situation, and yet the underlying energy feels like it is the same. I am still dependent on a system that is broken and does not work for me.

I can reduce emotions I feel in response to this as fear and detachment. The antidote to this is to look at why I have this fear. What am I afraid of? For me it is a fear of eviction, of losing everything that I have and being alone in the world, metaphorically being kicked out of the tribe. I believe this is the underlying reason for my breakdown when I was twenty-one.

My fear of eviction keeps me working. I need to rewrite this story so that it does not have power over me, but instead, I will have power over the story. This has been one of the outcomes of going on an ancestral pilgrimage, leaving home, and sleeping in places where my ancestors lived. I bought a little red van for this purpose and enjoy nothing more than heading off in it, gathering stories and bringing them back. This isn't reliant on money being available. I just need to trust that there will be enough, and there always is. This is what happened with my trip to London and my trips to Northern Ireland: just going and trusting, knowing that I will survive okay as I am doing absolutely the right thing for my being. I am jumping off the cliff and not knowing what will happen, and that is okay.

My soul is guiding me to carry out these steps. By following this breadcrumb trail, I am connecting with my ancestors and healing my ancestral line. If Catherine had the freedom to do this, I am sure she would have done it too, if she had the choice. But she didn't have a choice. Her choices were taken away from her when she had to leave her homeland in order to stay alive.

My need to be busy, to be achieving, was particularly apparent during one of my ancestral trips to Northern Ireland. I tired myself out driving from here to there, always feeling like I needed to keep moving. One Sunday, I was camping close to the beautiful heather-clad Sperrin Mountains in County Tyrone, one hour west of Belfast. I woke up and decided that I needed to drive to the coast, to a place where Catherine might have lived. I had found a birth certificate in the archives for a Catherine that lived there, and there was a possibility it could have been hers. So, I got up early and drove for two hours. When I arrived, I didn't get the inspiration I had hoped for as it was a developed area. The Victorians developed the north coast of County Down, and so it is quite different to other parts of Northern Ireland and the Republic of Ireland. I regretted my decision. I could have played out in the mountains and had a very different day. This is a pattern in my life: I do what I feel I need to do rather than what I want to do.

The farmers of nineteenth-century Ireland had a different life to us, and were driven by different things. I have read that they didn't work, work, work all the time. Creativity was key in their culture, which was rich in music and storytelling. This is a legacy that still prevails to this day: the Irish are known for folklore, music, language, art and storytelling. Catherine and William would have invested time in their land, but they would also have had a lot of downtime. They wouldn't have been in servitude to the system, earning money so they could spend it on material things. I drove to the coast because I felt I ought to do it, and yet it was only me who had set the task. I could have easily reneged on it. I called home, and Jason reminded me I was on holiday and that I wasn't allowing myself this joy. I find that my working patterns are amplified when I take myself off on ancestral trips such as these.

The wild edge

One of the practices I have used to free myself from these ancestral shackles of a life full of work and to find my way to freedom is through Wild Therapy. Humans have been domesticated: this is the purpose of civilisation, taming the world and putting it to work to meet someone else's desires and needs. Wild Therapy is a stripping away of these layers of conditioning by being in and engaging with the wild: going out into nature to let it roughen up my smooth edges, to untame that part of me that has been told what I must be and do to fit in.

Rewilding is gaining more and more momentum in the spiritual and personal development field. It means a return to nature, re-establishing our connection with the wild. Nature is a place to heal. Rewilding is about getting to that raw wild part within us, the part that got disregarded by society when we were born: our wild twin. There are a number of old stories that speak to this, of the abandonment of our wild twin at birth. It is a concept taught to me by Dr Martin Shaw of the Westcountry School of Myth, and he has published a book about this called *Courting the Wild Twin*.[69] Lining a room inside our hearts with crow feathers and welcoming back our wild twin is spiritual work. This is leaving the domesticated, tame, and familiar to be brave enough to rediscover our wild edges.

Jason and I run a retreat on the wild peninsular of Humphrey Head on the Cumbrian coast where, according to legend, the last wolf of England was killed. This holds great symbology as something in our landscape was tamed when the last wolf drew her final breath eight hundred years ago. The wild was banished by the Normans at this time, with field boundaries created and woodlands cleared. Both nature and humanity were pinned down and tamed. By honouring and working with the energy of the last wolf, I feel we are rekindling the wild within us.

During our last trip there, I had a dream of the space where the wild met the domesticated. There is a perception that the wild is dangerous and the domesticated is safe. This view traps and keeps me from taking risks and facing those dark places where the soul so often hungers to go. The main feature of the dream was wild gibbons running uncontrollably around Chorley town centre, which is my local town. At the end of the dream, I saw two monkeys sitting in a shop doorway dressed in Victorian period costume. The female monkey had a purple silk dress on with puff sleeves, and the male monkey wore a black suit. They had a baby monkey in an old pram on the floor. They looked right at me and placed a finger up to their lips gesturing me to be quiet. They whispered to me that they were hiding.

I interpret this as the wild part of me wanting to blend in. There was something raw and unbridled about the gibbons tearing uncontrollably around the town, and there was something terribly sad about the monkeys trying to conform to an environment that was completely ridiculous and unnatural.

As I approached Samhain in the year of my wilderness vigil in 2018, I journeyed to my ancestor guide Elder to ask her for advice about Catherine Riley. I wanted to know how to use this time. She told me I would see Catherine if I looked down the tunnel. I turned to look down the tunnel that was to my right, and sure enough, I saw her standing there with her two children. This was the last time that they were all together. I had seen this image before in the weeks running up to my vigil when we undertook a day's walk, from sunrise to sunset, as part of the preparation process. I was given two words: fear and detachment.

Rewilding is helping me move through the fear that has been passed down my ancestral line through my DNA. It has also helped me come back into my body, along with the Embodied Relational Therapy process to reattach that I explained in Chapter 4. This has helped me come home.

I still fear that I am not enough and that I will not have enough. It means that I don't allow myself to do the things that I am passionate about because of this. At my most extreme, at times working in and for the corporations, it was as though I was ground down and became a walking dead person. I forgot who Nicola was, I forgot who I was. Over the years, I have taken steps to address this fear within me, and it was my drive to undertake the wilderness vigil: I decided I needed to look fear right in the eyes.

Ancestral fear

There were seven hundred workhouses in Britain at its peak, which were home to one-quarter of people in Britain. The largest workhouses, such as St James in Piccadilly, housed up to one thousand people. Abusive behaviour from workhouse staff towards inmates wasn't allowed officially, although it did happen. The inmates were overworked and underfed, forced to live in confined spaces and locked in at night. They were tormented physically as well as psychologically, beginning with them being stripped naked, washed and given a workhouse uniform. Family members were separated and only allowed to see each other for one hour every Sunday, and only if they had all been well behaved. If the children were sent to the industrial school, they would never see their parents again until they were adults. The workhouse was so feared that families stuck together through thick and thin to avoid them.

Segregation was at the heart of the workhouse. By isolating poor people, it was believed that the toxic influence of poverty could be contained, and the spread of degenerate behaviour stopped. By threatening to break up families, the workhouse played into people's worst fears. It was meant to be terrifying so that the poor would do anything to avoid it. Life on the inside was worse than earning a pittance on the outside. Emotional detachment and shutting down was the only way to cope with the trauma in these institutions and this has come through to me. I believe that two traits have been passed down through the DNA in my family line. These are the fear of poverty and the need to dissociate in difficult situations.

The day I walked out of the forest from my wilderness vigil was the one hundred and forty-second anniversary of Catherine's death. I researched online for the numerological meaning of this number and discovered this is linked to self-reliance, building a secure foundation for the future, new beginnings, self-sufficiency, determination, independence and focus. It is revelations such as this that helped me know that I am on the right path and going in the right direction.

What I have learned is that I need to trust myself and trust that there will be enough. I saw this in a dream. I was walking through a university building where they were teaching the arts. There was painting, writing and all kinds of art. I overheard a lesson as I was walking past about freely expressing oneself and trusting that you would always have enough at your disposal to have a good life. The last teacher I saw had three students. She told them that people work until they drop because they are afraid that they aren't enough – that they will run out of the things they need to survive. But she said that simply isn't the case and that you need to have the confidence that there will be enough to survive easily. You need to believe that you can find this at your feet. By the time I walked out of the building, I was crying. Why hadn't I been taught that? Why were there only three people in that class? The grace of that whole series of lessons was so beautiful and uplifting.

I am learning to rewrite my core language, which states that I am the only one who can look after myself, and it is all down to me: that I have to do it as no one else will. Underlying this is a need to trust there is enough. I need to trust that everything can be found at my feet. The Earth will provide.

Two hundred years of toil

I have mentioned already that I was taught at school that the Industrial Revolution was a good thing. Don't get me wrong, I enjoy many of the things the modern world has to offer: my washing machine, for starters. But something happened during the period of the Industrial Revolution: a work culture was born that enslaved, demoralised and depressed the working classes. We are conditioned in Western culture from a very early age to think that life needs to be this way. I was brought up with the belief that the correct way to start each day was to leap out of bed in the morning and set to work as quickly as possible.

Tom Hodgkinson, in his book *How to be Idle*, explains what happened during the Industrial Revolution in those two hundred and fifty years of human history.[70] Hodgkinson refers to the English historian E.P. Thompson's classic book *The Making of the English Working Class*, where it is argued that the creation of the job is a relatively recent phenomenon, born out of the Industrial Revolution.[71] Thompson states that work was a much more haphazard and unstructured affair before the factories of the eighteenth century. People worked and had 'jobs' but the idea of being chained to one particular employer to the exclusion of all other money-making activity was unknown. The average person enjoyed a much greater degree of independence than today.

In his book, *The Protestant Ethic and the Spirit of Capitalism*, sociologist and historian Max Weber wrote that during the eighteenth century a new Protestant work ethic emerged based on the idea of work and earning a lot of money.[72] This replaced the old mediaeval ethic, which was based on mutual aid. The Industrial Revolution saw the dawn of employment, with families becoming entirely dependent on earning a wage rather than being able to feed themselves by growing their food. They might have been earning more money, but at a great cost to their quality of life. The job was created to make things easier for those at the top. People were stripped of their independence in order to service the dreams of a socially aspirational mill owner, for example. Such a person believed the working class should work hard.

The poor were forced into factories and modern wage slavery, doing manual work, whilst the rich assured them that this was the only way to wealth and civilisation. As Hodgkinson eloquently states: 'The ascendancy of the dock and the machine tore us from nature.' Once working, the people were no longer able to organise their day according to their mood. Instead, they had to obey an externally imposed regime completely removed from their previous way of life.

Hodgkinson wrote about philosopher Andrew Ure, who produced an article in 1835 called *Philosophy of Manufacturers*.[73] It was aimed at the new factory owners who had to deal with the difficulty of 'idlers' by creating an environment where people were driven by the need to work. Ure wrote a passionate and persuasive argument for the factory system in England,

spoke of the challenges of coping with a nation of idlers, and
shared advice on brainwashing:

> It is found nearly impossible to convert persons past
> the age of puberty, whether drawn from rural or from
> handicraft occupations, into useful factory hands. After
> struggling for a while to conquer their listless or restive
> habits, they either renounce their employment sponta-
> neously, or are dismissed by the overlookers on account
> of inattention … [there is] a need to subdue the refrac-
> tory tempers of work-people accustomed to irregular
> paroxysms of diligence … it is excessively in the interest
> of every mill-owner to organise his moral machinery on
> equally sound principles with his mechanical, for other-
> wise he will never command the steady hands, watchful
> eyes, and prompt cooperation, essential to the excel-
> lence of product … there is, in fact, no case to which the
> Gospel truth, 'godliness is great gain,' is more applicable
> than to the administration of an extensive factory.[74]

The industrialists used religion as one way to create this
message and manipulate the masses. It was God's will that
you worked hard. Thompson wrote that 'not only the "sack";
but the flames of Hell might be the consequence of indisci-
pline at work'.[75] The other way of converting the rural idlers
into industrious workers was hunger. Keeping people hungry
ensured they would work and work to earn more money. Then
to make them work even harder, pay them less so that they
need to work longer hours to earn enough money to survive.

All these factors led to the delusion of a love of and an
intense desire to work, well beyond the point at which an
individual is exhausted. This has parallels with the experiences
of Catherine and her family. This belief is still ingrained in me
now, and my spiritual path is to find ways to overcome this.

***

ANTIDOTE TO WORK

This brings me on to the final part of this chapter, where I will elaborate more on four of the ways I have found my antidote to work: 1. Being happy with less, 2. Play, 3. Creativity, and 4. Creating the vision.

Happy with less

The Happy Planet Index is a global measurement methodology used to compare the happiness of nations.[76] It shows how well governments are doing at helping people achieve long, happy, sustainable lives. It is interesting to note that getting richer does not make a country happier in the long run, according to research. In the long term, the sense of well-being in a country's citizens does not go up with income.[77] In the Happy Planet Index, the United Kingdom scores 31.9 and ranks at number 34 despite being one of the richest countries in the world. Nicaragua is one of the poorest countries in Central America and the second poorest in the Western Hemisphere. Yet, it ranks number 7 with a score of 38 on the Happy Planet Index.[78] This suggests that to a certain point, the amount of money a person has correlates with how happy they are. However, after all a person's basic needs are met, the trend changes and having double the money doesn't make a person twice as happy. Or, to put it differently, there is a plateau.

Over the years, I have grown to learn that money does not bring happiness. It is counter to what I was taught at school, so I left there and launched myself into the adult world with the understanding that having more money meant that I would be happier. I had my doubts that this was true. It didn't take me long to realise that my goal in life wasn't about being rich.

Several years ago, I heard a quote that really spoke to me about this relationship between money and happiness. José Mujica was the President of Uruguay from 2010 to 2015 and was considered to be the world's poorest president for his lack of interest in personal material wealth. He spoke these words during an interview for the film *Human*:

> Either you are happy with very little, free from all that extra luggage, because you have happiness inside, or you don't get anywhere. I am not advocating poverty. I am advocating society. But since we have invented a consumer society, the economy must constantly grow. We have invented a mountain of superfluous needs, shopping for the new and discarding the old. That is a waste of our lives. When you shop for something new, when you buy something new, you are not paying money for it, you are paying with the hours of your life you had to spend earning that money. The difference is that life is one thing money can't buy. Life only gets shorter, and it is pitiful to waste one's life and freedom in that way. [79]

José Mujica makes a striking point here, in that being caught in the cycle of consumerism is costing us our time. I need to work to earn money to buy the things that I 'want'. If I buy less, I need less money, and therefore I can afford to work less. This is the first of my antidotes to work – that it is important to be happy with having less. If I were to aspire to several foreign holidays each year, a nice car and a large house full of cutting-edge possessions, I would have to earn much more money to maintain that kind of lifestyle. By having less, I have more freedom, as I don't need to spend as much time earning money to pay for things.

In his book *How to be Idle*, Hodgkinson refers to consumerism as a driver to encourage people to work hard:

> The claim that capitalism has delivered us from excessive toil can be sustained only if we take as our point of comparison eighteenth- and nineteenth-century Europe and America, a period that has witnessed what were probably the longest and most arduous work schedules in the history of mankind. And there are new enemies

of leisure today. Hunger and God have been replaced in the consumer age by possessions and status. The advertising industry leads us to believe that life will be improved by the purchase of a product. The purchase of a product requires money. Money requires hard work. Or debt. We go into debt to chase our desires and then keep working to pay the debt.[80]

It is an interesting theory that hunger and God, two of the things that drove George to work in the way he did, have been replaced by possessions and status. I am very happy to let both possessions and status go in pursuit of a life of greater freedom.

Play

One of the things I am very aware of is feeling guilty when I am not working. As Oscar Wilde wrote: 'It is awfully hard work doing nothing.'[81] There has been two hundred and fifty years of indoctrination in the work ethic and the guilt is hard to shift.

I was guided to play more in the first few months after leaving work for the corporations and closing down my sustainability consultancy in the autumn of 2015. It was approaching the time of the Harvest Moon, and in preparation for tuning in to these energies, I went on a shamanic journey to ask what I should welcome into my life. I was taken to the orchard where I spent my childhood playing. My pet chicken Elsa was there. Elsa was a very special chicken. She was one of those chickens that I could do anything with, and we used to spend much of our time together. She would ride in my go-kart and the basket of my bicycle. I would push her around the village in a pram and build a den for her in amongst the haybales at harvest time. She was always very obliging and enjoyed human company immensely. I named Elsa after the rescued lion cub in the film *Born Free*, which was one of my favourite films as a child.[82]

During my journey, Elsa told me that I needed to focus on play, adventure, and fun. These were the club's attributes that I formed with my friend, 'The Investigating Three'. She reminded me of this club, which I had forgotten about, and how I embodied the qualities of play, adventure, and fun as a child.

On the night of the full moon, Jason and I held a ceremony at a stone circle that is special to us, Arbor Low in the Derbyshire hills. We gathered our The Way of the Buzzard community together and in a circle of around fifty people set our intentions for what we wanted to welcome into our lives. I firmly spoke the intention that I would like to invite those three qualities into my life.

I am still exploring and unravelling the layers as to why I find putting play over work so hard. No doubt, it was a factor in leading me to uncover my ancestral lineage back to the time of the workhouse. In the days soon after the ceremony, something incredible happened – or I should say someone incredible trotted into my life – that enabled me to immediately bring these qualities into my day-to-day living. It began when I was taking a walk up on Anglezarke Moor. A horse and rider approached and I offered to open the gate for them. Our ensuing conversation led me to have access to a beautiful chestnut horse named Colonel. This reignited a distant childhood passion for horse riding. I looked after Colonel two days each week, which worked well as I could only commit to looking after a horse part-time. He got me out of the house and away from working on the computer, but I often felt challenged enjoying myself so much when I thought I ought to be working. When I was riding out around the bridle paths on the edge of the West Pennine Moors, having the best time, I would often call Jason to check that it was alright to be out having fun. I needed external reassurance as I wasn't able to give it to myself. I still catch myself doing this sometimes, even now.

Being happy is an act of radical activism. Doing my own

thing, knowing I am in the place where I want to be, is a radical act. I am making choices about the things I want and don't want to do. By doing this, I own my privilege. Privilege is about owning it and using it for the benefit of everybody.

Returning to the topic of idling briefly, Hodgkinson interviewed the philosopher Terence McKenna. He asked him why society doesn't allow us to be more idle. McKenna replied with this response:

> Idle hands are the devil's tool. In other words, institutions fear idle populations because an idler is a thinker, and thinkers are not a welcome addition to most social situations. If we are all kept very busy, under no circumstances are you to quietly inspect the contents of your own mind. Freud called introspection 'morbid' – unhealthy, introverted, antisocial, possibly neurotic, potentially pathological. Introspection could lead to that terrible thing: a vision of the truth, a clear image of the horror of our fractured, dissonant world.[83]

Hodgkinson goes on to respond: 'This prejudice is well established in the Western world. Governments do not like the idle. The idle worry them. They do not manufacture useless objects, and they do not consume the useless products of labour. They cannot be monitored. They are out of control. They do not want to live like their leaders. They do not want to be helped.'

Idling and play do not come naturally to me as an adult. They have been conditioned out of me. However, I have ways to trick myself into both idling and playing, and one of these is through being creative.

Creativity

Creativity and spirituality are one and the same thing. To be creative is to express our true selves. When I am not in the flow, creativity doesn't come easy to me. Elizabeth Gilbert has written a fantastic book about creativity called *Big Magic: How to live a creative life and let go of your fear.*[84] She taught me that I need to let go of perfection and reason. Creativity doesn't need to have a purpose or an end goal. It is the act of being creative that is important.

I am dyslexic. My brain is wired slightly differently from a person who, these days, would be considered 'neurotypical'. It meant that I struggled in the education system, as during my years at school my dyslexia was not diagnosed. Everything was difficult for me, and so I needed to work harder than my peers to keep up. This is the downside of dyslexia but there is a huge upside in that my mind is very creative. I learnt this from a book by Ronald Davis, *The Gift of Dyslexia: Why Some of the Brightest People Can't Read and How They Can Learn.*[85] Dyslexic people have a particular way of looking at the world and how they set their mind to things. When I was growing up, the qualities I gained from my dyslexia were not recognised, but they have been in the wider world. In an extensive survey of self-made millionaires, 40 per cent of entrepreneurs were found to show signs of dyslexia.[86] One of the gifts of my dyslexia is my creativity. Creativity comes easily to me when I give it the space.

When I drop into a creative space, time disappears. When I am crafting or drawing, I can happily skip meals and lose track of time. I go back to that Nicola who would play in the fields, and nothing else was important at that moment. I believe my creativity is a true expression of my soul. In the workplace, I gave my creative self to someone else, to fulfil someone else's mission. Out of the workplace, creativity is mine to enjoy once again. It has been an important part of my spiritual work to find my way back to my creative self. Being creative makes me happy.

Creating the vision

The final antidote to work is creating the vision. One of the things that happened to me during my early adulthood was that I realised I wanted to live in a different world. Seeing the foibles of civilisation showed me a world that I did not want to be a part of. How could I envision what a different world would look like?

When I limit myself to my conscious mind, I am limiting myself to considering what I already know to be possible. To contemplate a different world, I need to go into the unconscious. My aim in life is to make my dream a reality: I need to be the future.

I came to this realisation early on in my spiritual awakening back in 2009. I was drawn to celebrating the Winter Solstice at Stonehenge. I asked my friends, but no one wanted to come with me, and so I went alone: just me and a few thousand strangers. I found a spot to meditate amongst the crowds, and as I closed my eyes, I became a tourist attraction with people taking photos. I could hear the clicking of the camera shutters as it was back in the day before mobile phones with cameras were more commonplace. Despite this disruption, I got a message from my spirit guide. The only guide I knew back then was Titan. He said to me: 'Be the future.' This chimes in with the famous Mahatma Gandhi quote: 'Be the change you want to see in the world.' Although, I think my message was punchier!

To follow the breadcrumb trail to the future that I wanted, I needed to create a vision of this future. I needed to move from the paralysis I felt when I could only see things wrong with the world. How do we change the course of destruction humanity is heading towards? As Charles Eisenstein says: 'Be clear on the destination of where it is that we want to get to and then watch out for signs on our role to get there.'[87]

When I worked as a sustainability manager within the corporations, we would carry out visioning exercises as part of the sustainability training courses I delivered. I would give out colouring pens and pencils and sheets of paper and ask the managers to draw what they saw as a sustainable world where we were kind to the Earth and each other. I would then ask them to speak about what they had drawn, and we would build a picture in our minds together. It was a great exercise and yet what I have come to realise over recent years is that we were limiting our ideas to what our conscious minds could see.

When I drop into the unconscious, I am tuning in with the infinite. Anything is possible. I mentioned earlier that the role of the Shaman is to go to the other realities and bring back the energies that are most needed at the time by shifting their consciousness through journeying. Connecting in with other realities was carried out for tens of thousands of years by our distant ancestors during the Palaeolithic and Neolithic periods. It is still carried out by nature-based indigenous cultures today. So how can this shift in consciousness help us now? Well, we can literally journey to the Otherworld to dream a new world into being.

Alberto Villoldo speaks about this in his book *Courageous Dreaming,* and it is one of my go-to shamanic books. Here is what Villoldo says in the first few pages about courageously dreaming:

> The nature of the cosmos is such that whatever vision you have about yourself and the world will become reality. As soon as you awaken to the power you have, you begin to flex the muscles of your courage. You can then dream bravely: letting go of your limiting beliefs and pushing past your fear. You can start to come up with a truly original dream that germinates in your soul and bears fruit in your life. [88]

Courageous dreaming is the process of adopting an eagle's view. The eagle flies high into the sky and looks down on the landscape from a different perspective to us. From here, the eagle can see the bigger picture. It can scan the horizon and also zoom in and see the details below. It is a gift to be able to see things from both these viewpoints. Courageous dreaming is an important antidote to work. Instead of working to a vision that civilisation teaches, I can travel to the Otherworld and dream a different world into being. Building this world is fun as it involves play, investigating and creativity. These are the three qualities I was guided to focus on by Elsa at the time of the Harvest Moon.

THE GREAT ESCAPE

In the remainder of this chapter, I would like to share how I broke free from the work system and left one world behind so I could dream another into being. I have successfully moved away from needing to work for anyone and having to survive a career in the corporations. I often get asked the question: 'How did you do it?' I know that some people want to move out of their current work into something that is more in line with their ethics and is more fulfilling, and that gives them the luxury of their time back. How did I manage the great escape?

The truth is it took a long time to gear myself up to leave working for the corporations, and it took a lot of guts. I was unhappy in my job for a large part of my career. I enjoyed what I did, I just didn't enjoy the corporate culture. I loved being creative, and I loved the variety. I felt I was making a difference to the Earth, and I made lots of friends among my colleagues. I struggled with some of the people and group dynamics, and the slow pace of being able to change anything in large businesses. Most of all, I found the pressure I was under the hardest to cope with. We were a tiny team in a large organisation. With the onset of the financial recession in 2008, things got a lot worse quite quickly. As I awakened spiritually, I began to resent the ethos that corporations held around reducing their impact on the Earth. The fact that any change they made had to fit in with a business case, meant that for much of the time it felt like all that we were doing was rearranging the furniture on the Titanic. We won awards for our work and we were seen as at the leading edge of corporate sustainability, but it wasn't enough in terms of what was needed to stem climate change and live sustainably on the Earth.

So, what did I do? How did I leave the machine? Well, I procrastinated for a long time: years in fact. I am not alone in this, some of the greatest thinkers in the world were also procrastinators. Author Adam Grant talks about this in his book *Originals: How Non-conformists Change the World.*[89] Martin Luther King Jr, for example, was apprehensive about leading the Civil Rights Movement (1954–1968). Keen to spend time with his family and do his church work after completing his PhD, King was nominated by a group of civil rights activists for the presidency. He reflected later that, after the incident of Rosa Parks refusing to give up her seat on the bus, it all happened so fast. He didn't have time to think. He said that had he had time to think about it, he almost certainly would have turned it down. Yet, he overcame his trepidation and went on to deliver one of the most memorable and impactful speeches of all time about his electrifying vision of freedom.[90]

During the Renaissance, astronomy stagnated for decades because Nicolaus Copernicus refused to publish his original discovery that the Earth revolves around the sun. Fearing rejection and ridicule, he stayed silent for twenty-two years, circulating his findings only to friends. A major Cardinal learned of his work and wrote a letter encouraging Copernicus to publish. Copernicus stalled for four more years. His theory only saw the light of day when a young mathematics professor took matters into his own hands and submitted it for publication in 1543.[91] Grant reflects procrastination is a common habit of creative thinkers and great problem-solvers:

> The drive to succeed accompanied by the fear of failure have held back some of the greatest creators and change agents in history. Concerned with maintaining stability and attaining conventional achievements, they have

been reluctant to pursue originality. Instead of charging full steam ahead with assurance, they have been coaxed, convinced or coerced to take a stand.[92]

I find it reassuring hearing Grant reflect that procrastination is common among creative thinkers. It helps me appreciate that I am not alone when it comes to delaying making a decision.

My long and arduous procrastination period before leaving the corporations was a sticky phase. This is what Charles Eisenstein calls 'the space between stories'.[93] As one story falls away, another is yet to form. I liken this phase to the pupa stage of the lifecycle of a butterfly. To expand a little on this story, the caterpillar eats and eats to grow bigger until it can no longer eat or grow any more, and at this point, it forms a chrysalis. Then, after some time, the butterfly emerges from the chrysalis with wings and flies away in all its beauty, adding grace to the world wherever it chooses to fly. But what happens in the phase between caterpillar and butterfly, inside the chrysalis? What happens in the darkness hidden from our eyes?

The caterpillar forms the chrysalis right after it has gorged itself, and inside the hard casing, it dissolves into a gooey liquid mess. It has no form. The caterpillar essentially turns itself into a soup. This sounds very much to me like the 'space in between stories' stage Eisenstein suggested. I was preparing to leave the corporations, but I didn't know how to, nor what I would do to survive once I was on the other side. My life was a gooey liquid mess.

From the outside looking in, it might seem as though the game is over for the caterpillar when it forms the chrysalis. However, what is actually happening inside that hardened case is an incredible process of transformation. Within this caterpillar liquid are what are called imaginal cells. These cells have ideas about what comes next, and they inform the other cells around them. Through this process, new cells form in the shape of a butterfly. They move through the goo to where they need to be, and over time, eventually something new and beautiful is created. It can be a quicker process and take only a few weeks, or it can be a long process, taking up to two years with some species of caterpillar.

I was in the chrysalis stage for many years. I survived and made it through the transformation by doing five things: following what I love, being supported by an elder, accessing inner guidance, investing in myself and being okay with not knowing. These are all focused on recognising and taking care of those new and tender imaginal cells. I will explain them now.

Following what I love

Firstly, I followed what I loved, and this might sound clichéd. However, it took me several years to even figure out what it was that I loved, and then several more to allow myself the time to do it. I will tell you more about this in a moment. However, advice to anyone looking to move into more fulfilling work is to work out what you enjoy doing, no matter how random it sounds and feels. Give yourself the time and space for things to unravel.

Corporate training taught me that I must always have a plan and be busy, and I must always be doing something that has a point to it. I got so good at this that the 'real me' didn't get a look in. I have already mentioned that at its most extreme, I forgot what I loved to do. I forgot the things I enjoyed as a child. At best, I knew what I loved doing, but I couldn't find the time to do it. This is what I call the business of being busy. With so many responsibilities, never-ending to-do lists, and seemingly diminishing time in the day with every year I grew older, there was less and less time to do what I enjoyed doing. I am reminded of the words of Rumi when thinking about this idea: 'Let yourself be silently drawn by the strange pull of what you really love. It will not lead you astray.'[94]

Rumi speaks of the importance of creating time to do the things that you love. For my creativity to be unleashed, I needed to still myself and get creative in changing the direction my life was taking. I had to find a way to get in touch with my creative self. It wasn't an easy road, and there were sacrifices, but it did lead to incredible things.

I love going on adventures to different landscapes in the British Isles, whether hiking in the fells or camping out. Hodgkinson speaks in his book *How to be Idle* of camping 'as a way of reconnecting with our primitive selves: we enjoy it because it lights a dormant memory of how we once lived.'[95] I have always advocated this, and I now live a life where I can do this for much of the year, should I choose to. My record is sixty days away camping around the UK and Ireland over ten months. I love to camp out in beautiful places that feed my soul. I like swinging in my hammock suspended between two trees in a woodland or waking up in my bivvy bag on top of a mountain. I enjoy pitching my expedition tent on the side of a cliff or lounging around in my bell tent, complete with a wood burner. I relish stealth camping in my little red van or going on adventures with Jason in our black VW campervan. I love the simplicity and variety that camping gives me. It takes me one step closer to a feeling of freedom. Allowing myself more and more space to do this has undoubtedly become one of the factors that led me to where I am today.

What might 'following what you love' look like? If someone tells you about something that sounds good, and you have never done it before, but fancy it, turn off the chattering mind and follow your gut. If an idea pops into your head about something you would like to do, seek it out and do it. If you remember something you loved doing as a child but that you stopped doing because of work or some other reason, do that thing. One thing leads to another, and before you know it, you look back and get a clearer picture of what just happened to take you to the thing that you love doing. This isn't about having a vision of where you want to get to. It is about simply following what you love, knowing that there is a destination, but you just don't know where that is yet. It will unfold over time as it did for me.

Supported by an elder

The second action I took to change my world was to find myself an elder: a mentor. I have already talked a lot about this in Chapter 3. Mentors present themselves in different guises, but I am a firm believer that if a person wants to effect real change in their life, then having a regular go-to person is a must to help them forge a new path and address old patterns that are blocking them from walking it. I also believe that if a person puts a request to the universe that they need help, then help will follow. Having a person to go to every week ultimately helped me understand what it was that I wanted from life. This was the foundation of my great escape. I needed someone to help me break through old patterns like not being able to say no, not having the ability to figure out what it was that I really wanted to do, feeling as if I did not have a voice, and that I ought to be doing things all the time. I felt anxious, afraid, and lacked confidence and trust that I was enough. Having ongoing support from a mentor helped me address these things that held me back from achieving what I wanted from life.

Accessing inner guidance

The third step that I took was to learn how to listen to the quiet voice inside. I learnt to find a way to hear my inner guidance. This is my soul guiding me to where the real Nicola, deep inside, truly wants to be. Hearing this voice is no easy feat, given the busyness of the modern world. It often seems that our world is set up in such a way to distract us from being able to hear that quiet voice within.

There are many different ways to tune into your inner guidance. Shamanic journeying on the drum and nature connection work incredibly well for me as ways to shift from my conscious mind into my unconscious mind. What is key is finding a way to connect with something greater than myself. I love shamanic journeying as it is a quick way to meet my spirit guides and seek answers to the questions I have. In fifteen minutes or so, I can have an answer, although I admit interpreting the full meaning of the response takes longer at times.

I also love seeking guidance from nature as it is right there outside my window. I have found deep meaning in the hop of a blackbird across our front lawn, the call of a crow just before dawn, the leap of a roe deer over a dry-stone wall, and the golden eagle soaring the thermals above me. Nature has guided me in different ways in recent years. I have gained lessons from trees, such as how the oak has unwavering strength, the birch shows the joy of new beginnings, the rowan shows me determination, and the yew demonstrates acceptance of endings that are necessary to make way for the new.

What has become clear to me over the years is that my everyday way of thinking isn't enough. My conscious mind does not have all the answers that I need to take me to the places that my soul wants me to go. As Albert Einstein said: 'We cannot solve our problems with the same level of thinking that created them.'[96]

Learning to listen enabled me to find out my soul's purpose. In 2010 I didn't know it would be my final few years working in the corporations and having a 'mainstream job'. I thought I would be in that career forever, and although I was unsettled and wondering if I was in the right place, I did feel resigned to the life I had chosen.

I was one of a small number of people selected to attend a six-month leadership development training programme. We were on a short residential course in Cornwall, in a beautiful place called Embercombe. Interspersed with the usual corporate training activities, we slept in yurts, ate home-grown food, spent time working in the fields, weeding runner beans and digging potatoes. At night we gathered around the camp-fire to drink beer. We had a great time, and I felt like I was home. I loved the energy at Embercombe and everything it stood for.

A few others on the course really didn't take to the place and found it too alternative. They were used to plush hotel venues with hot showers and stylish dining. This was, for some of them, their first taste of the alternative way of life. It was new to them but normal to me. I was in my element. One of the course participants, who was not particularly enamoured with Embercombe, did not hold back on giving his opinions. We were at the opposite end of all the psychological profile models, which meant we were often paired up in exercises to explore our differences and see where each other was coming from. We developed a good working relationship while in Embercombe, but I was disappointed and a little perplexed that he didn't love the place like I did. For me, this was the most amazing place. It was all about the land: living from the land and learning from the land. It was so beautiful there, with such an incredible community.

I was sitting on the minibus waiting to go back to the train station at the end of the four days together when I saw him waiting in the queue to climb on the bus. I can see him as clearly now as I saw him then. He was standing with his hands in his pockets, looking around, a far-gazing stare in his eyes. I watched him mutter to himself the words: 'I am really going to miss this place.'

There it was, a life-changing moment for me. I saw some-thing shift in that person that changed my life. I realised that if we are to change the way we live on Earth and live sustainably, we need to do just one thing: we need to fall back in love with the Earth again. To do this, we need to get outside and rekindle our relationship with her. It was a ground-shaking realisation.

For my career, I had been trying to help people understand that the way we are living on Earth right now will be the end of us, and that we need to change. Through this exploration, I had become a qualified trainer, accredited auditor and Chartered Environmentalist, and I tried so many different techniques. But the shift in people that I was seeking just wasn't there. At that moment, I realised that the work wasn't about procedures, policies, auditing and programmes: it wasn't about that at all. It was about helping people fall back in love with the Earth. This realisation caused me to change my whole line of work and over time led to me meeting Jason and setting up The Way of the Buzzard and The Mystery School together.

Messages can come to us from Spirit in many different ways. After my spiritual awakening, I needed to be open to messages so that I could find the core thread that would under-pin all my future work. Receiving the message 'find ways to help people fall back in love with the Earth' was pivotal for me. Had I not been in long-term psychotherapy, had I not learnt how to listen to the quiet voice, I would not have made the changes to my life that I am now enjoying.

Investing in myself

The fourth step I took in transforming my life was to invest in myself, both in terms of time and money. When I worked in the corporations, I jumped at any opportunity to go on train-ing courses. When I left the corporations, this continued, only they were different kinds of courses and I had to pay for them myself. I chose courses that I loved without thinking about the end goal other than learning about a particular subject or practice.

To give myself time when I left my 'proper' job, I have mentioned already that rather than taking up a position in another firm, I decided to set up a consultancy and work for myself. This meant I wasn't bound to someone else from 9 am to 5 pm every weekday and constrained to five weeks annual holiday. I have seen other people do this, reducing their hours to free up one or two days a week to focus on something else. When I was made redundant from the construction firm, I just wanted out and never to work in that field again. But I endured it part-time for another four years while I retrained to do what I loved doing the most, all the while trusting that it would all turn out alright, which it did.

It was tough doing two jobs at the same time, treading water with one while working hard to grow the other to a level where it was bringing in enough money to support me. I knew it wasn't forever and that it was a means to an end, so I just knuckled down and did it, reaching out for support along the way as I broke down old patterns and prepared myself for a new line of work.

When I started on my career path as a young adult, I underwent three years of training at university. As I took steps to leave working for the corporations, I saw this new stage in my life through the same lens. I needed to invest time and money into retraining during my thirties if I was to change my work in the world. To get to the place I am today, I have invested a lot of time and money in workshops and courses over the years. I have foregone holidays and other luxuries, and invested in countless weekends attending courses, and it has all been worth it. Investing in myself is an important step.

If this strikes a chord with you and you are left wondering which courses to take, my recommendation would be to go back to my advice to follow what you love. If you don't feel you have the time, find a mentor who can help you understand how you can create time.

Not knowing

The fifth and final step I took was that I learnt to be okay with not knowing exactly where I was going in life. I learned to trust my gut. I believe that if I am on the right path, the universe will unfold so that I get to where my soul wants me to be.

One of the things that has helped me to go with the flow is following the natural cycles of the year, which I talked about in Chapter 2 as I described the Wheel of the Year. When the pace of life seems to be getting faster and faster, I just need to look outside and see the huge transformation taking place out in nature but at a slower pace. When winter turns to spring, I see the emergence of new shoots to the soundtrack of the changing birdsong. Yet it is three months until new growth really reveals itself in May, when the leaves in the trees explode into the world and baby animals emerge from their mothers' bellies. Come August, we see the farmers gathering in the first harvest, and I can taste the approach of autumn in the air. Yet it is another three months until the cold days and long nights start to set in at the end of October.

With each of these turns in the Wheel of the Year, there is an opportunity to pause and reflect on what has passed and what to welcome into my life. A tree doesn't grow to its great height in a few months. Each year it grows a little more during the warm days and then retreats in the winter to gather itself ready for another burst the following year. I find that combining this awareness with the power of ceremony has been a great practice for marking the Wheel of the Year and tuning in with nature's transformational energies. I have been following the natural cycles of the year for approaching fifteen years now and having this natural structure to the way I approach my goals has been invaluable.

Following what I love, finding a mentor, learning how to listen to my inner voice, investing in myself and being okay with going with the flow has led me to a very different life, beyond the soupy chrysalis phase. Transitioning from one way of working in the world to another takes time, and I didn't find it easy.

My final advice for anyone embarking on or in the midst of this process of changing their life is, just like the caterpillar who creates a cocoon, create a safe space for the deep inner work to take place. Put up your boundaries. Reach out to find support, and rest. This can be a difficult time and you need to allow yourself space to be still, and alone. In our busy lives, this might seem impossible, but growth needs space to happen, and whatever time you create for yourself will pay back dividends.

For change to happen, a really fulfilling, profound change, I needed to let the old story fall away. This is part of the process that Charles Eisenstein speaks of when he describes the space between stories. It was painful letting go of my old story. It left me with a big gap and inertia in my life, as I felt that nothing was happening and that I needed a clear plan in front of me. In this sticky moment between stories, which at the time felt like a lifetime, I needed to reach out and find whatever felt like a balm. I also needed to spend time with other open-minded awake people who 'got it'. Often these were not people I had regular day-to-day contact with, but they offered me a real cushion.

Making choices

In this final chapter of Catherine's story, I have focused on her son George, my great-great-grandfather. The choices Catherine made must have been terrifying and incredibly hard to live with. Her sacrifice meant that her son had a chance at life. Left to the fate of living on the streets of London, George may not have survived. He almost certainly wouldn't have thrived in the way he did after receiving an education in the industrial school. He had a profession that he could pass on to his sons. He fathered twelve children and lived well into his seventies, a good age even by today's standards.

What strikes me about George's story, however, is how hard his childhood must have been. I can't imagine how lonely he must have felt growing up inside the walls of an institution without knowing the love of a parent. Throughout his whole childhood, he was conditioned to work. When George walked out of the workhouse gates when he was sixteen years old, he would have little knowledge of the world. He would only have known what he was taught in the industrial school: that he was born in disgrace, and his only salvation was to work.

This ingrained work ethic has been passed down the ancestral line from generation to generation to me. I am the lucky one as I have the opportunity to rewrite this story. Gaining awareness of my ancestry has enabled me to see the story and decide what part I want to play in it. I am fortunate in that I have learnt how to seek the support I need to overcome unhelpful patterns holding me back from where my soul wants me to be. My ancestors didn't have this choice available to them. If they had, I believe they would have done the same as me: I sense they would have taken back their freedom.

This is my personal story in a much bigger story, the world story. I can see there are two worlds, two scenarios playing out here on Earth. There is the old world, the only world that many people can relate to. This world is built on inequality, with the powerful elite minority controlling the majority. This world has been set up so that most people feel powerless and that they do not have a choice to live in any other way. They believe that this is the only way life can be.

I realised that I did have a choice, and I managed to find it in me to break away. Now I feel I am helping to create another world. As I look back from this position, I see the old world crumbling away. The old-world system is at breaking point. Although the move across was difficult, I find life very easy now in comparison. It was worth the effort and struggles.

When I worked in the corporations, it was exhausting. I was in the old world, and it was a challenging place to be, working within the old structures. At the same time, when I was starting a new shamanic offering in the world with Jason, The Way of the Buzzard, I seemed to have unlimited energy for my work. I see this now in two different ways in terms of living in a changing world. One way is to hold onto the past systems, structures and values. I grew up believing that this was the only way things could be. The other way is to challenge this viewpoint and courageously dream a new world into being. I do this by holding on to a vision of where I want to get to and then stilling myself to hear the role I have to play in building this. When I am in the new world, I see opportunity and hope, as we have a chance to create something new. Some might say this is blind optimism, but it is a place I am very happy to be in. It lifts my spirits through the day no end.

Through The Way of the Buzzard work, we offer a place for those imaginal cells – the cells that take the lead in the pupa phase – to grow in the new world. For me, this is not about fighting. If we fight, we are going to lose. I learned this in my career as a sustainability manager. Fighting only leads to one thing, and that is burnout. We can never win a direct fight to change the old system that we have been born into. I believe that the way to change the old system, the old world, is to stop and listen: the solutions can be found in the silence. This takes dropping down to another level, far away from the energy that is needed to fight. We need to stop, listen and find another way. My place to listen is out in nature and by shifting consciousness and journeying into the Otherworld.

Now is the time to develop ways to feel more connected to the world, the real world, the Earth. It is time to learn ways to connect with nature and the spirit realm. I believe this is where the answers lie, for every one of us.

When someone tunes into their inner knowing and the wisdom of the Otherworld, they are taking their first step towards moving away from the old system. As they do this, they simultaneously move one step closer to the world their soul wants them to create. When someone spends less time in unfulfilling work and more time doing what they really want to do, this is a direct action to creating a new world, a new way of being on Earth. This feels like a revolutionary act to me.

In my experience, one of the most important things that a person can do in these times is to honour those that came before us. Our ancestors have so much wisdom to share. There is also much healing that needs to take place; healing wounds passed down the ancestral line. Through this book, I have shared just one story: one I was fortunate enough to be able to uncover. In the final chapter, I will share the steps I took to find Catherine's story and share a pathway for readers who want to embark on their ancestral healing journey. It is a privilege to be in the position to be able to do this, and I am delighted to be sharing this adventure with you.

CHAPTER 6

REFLECTIONS & PATHWAYS

We have come to the final chapter of this book, and I would like to take a moment to reflect on the journey we have been on together following Catherine's life and the themes that have arisen. Then I will share some thoughts on my ancestral healing journey and offer the reader a pathway to begin their own.

Together we have followed Catherine's story from her growing up in Ireland and making the trip across the Irish Sea to England to escape the Great Famine. We have seen her struggles during the decades that she lived in London and looked at the legacy she left behind. In each chapter, I have pulled out themes from Catherine's life that I can relate to in my life, and shared ways in which I have rewritten the core language I have inherited.

In Chapter 2, I began Catherine's story with the first half of her life when she lived in Ireland. I explained the history around the time of the Great Famine of Ireland, and how my ancestors were cleared from their land in England in the period leading up to and during the Industrial Revolution. I shared practices that I have adopted in my life to address the inherited wounds that might be passed down when an ancestor is removed from their land: reconnecting with the Earth and healing through nature, including time out in nature, creating a relationship with place, learning to flow with the seasons and growing my own food.

I picked up on Catherine's story again at the beginning of Chapter 3, where I described events that happened during her first few years as she arrived in the slums of London. In this chapter, I addressed the theme of oppression and control, building on the dynamic between power and powerlessness and the privileged and underprivileged. I explained how this paradigm originated from the dawn of civilisation and shared how oppression has played out in my life. I focused in particular on my time working within corporations and how this led to the beginning of my waking-up process, finding my voice and making my escape. I also described ways in which I have overcome oppression and control in my life: finding an elder; choosing my response; seeking guidance by shamanic journeying to the Otherworld, including meeting an ancestor ally; and trusting my gut.

In Chapter 4, I addressed the remaining period of Catherine's life in London, and painted a picture of the conditions of life in a workhouse in the nineteenth century. In the interpretation, I focused on the topic of shame. I explained how I have begun to rewrite the story of my ancestor Catherine from one of shame to one of heroism in a cruel and unjust system. She was someone who did the very best she could and, against all the odds, managed to survive and keep herself and her sons alive. I shared experiences and insights I gained from visits to London and Northern Ireland as I responded to Catherine's request to 'take me home'. I reflected on Catherine as the unknown ancestor, silenced through shame for almost one hundred and fifty years. I ended this chapter by sharing the shamanic processes of ceremony, soul retrieval and soul exchange and the therapeutic process of Embodied Relational Therapy as ways in which I have honoured and moved through the ancestral grief that lay deep within me.

In the final chapter of Catherine's story in Chapter 5, I focused on her legacy: the life of her second son George Riley, my great-great-grandfather who spent his childhood in an industrial school. I shared an emerging theme that has played out in my life, which is overwork. I reflected on how I recognise in myself the drive to work excessively, putting this above all else. I explained how the modern-day work ethic arose from the Protestant work ethic during the Industrial Revolution. I introduced the therapeutic process of Wild Therapy and how this has helped me understand that I am enough and there is enough. I then offered an antidote: moving away from materialism, playing, being creative, and holding a different vision of the future. I finished by describing my five steps to finding freedom away from the conventional world and talked about the idea of courageously dreaming a new world into being.

An ancestral healing pathway

We have gone on quite a journey together. I have written this book as a practical guide for readers who are interested in ancestral healing and working with genealogical research to tell their ancestors' stories. So, with this in mind, in this final chapter, I would like to reflect on two aspects of ancestral healing.

The first is around my own ancestral healing journey. I embarked on this process ten years ago, and I have shared much of my story here in these pages. I have found it fascinating that I have continued my ancestral healing process by writing this book. As I approached each chapter, events unfolded in my life to shine further light on the underlying ancestral patterns that have passed down through the ancestral line. Also, through rewriting Catherine's story, I have begun the process to rewrite the core language that I have inherited. I will say more about this process in this chapter.

The second aspect is that I would like to offer a path forward for readers to take and start their own ancestral healing journey. There is a person born into every family who has the job of healing on behalf of the whole family. Perhaps that person is you? Whatever changes we make in ourselves goes up and down the ancestral line. This is important healing work both in this physical reality and in the spirit realm.

I will also explore the theory of epigenetics that I introduced in Chapter 1. I will delve a little deeper into the science that argues human beings are born with the capacity to self-heal and rewrite the genetic codes we have inherited, should we choose to.

My healing journey

I have mentioned previously that each year Jason and I hold Space to Emerge, a micro-festival in a beautiful bluebell woodland running up from the banks of Lake Windemere. Two hundred of us gather at the time of the Celtic fire festival Beltane to celebrate the oncoming spring and welcome into our lives whatever creative inspiration needs to come through in the coming months. Early one morning during our gathering in May 2019, I had an ancestral dream. When I gather with like-minded people for weekends out in the wild, I often receive an insight like this, either through my dreams or when taking part or leading the various workshops that take place throughout the weekend.

In the dream, I was carrying out scientific analysis. I was looking at my family tree and seeing which ancestors were happy and which weren't. At the same time, I was looking down each of their ancestral lines and seeing whether this resulted in happy descendants or unhappy ones. I found a statistical correlation. Happy ancestors make happy descendants. I guess it isn't rocket science when you think about it plainly like this, but it was useful to have it clearly pointed out to me. If happy ancestors make happy descendants, then it stands to reason that unhappy ancestors make unhappy descendants.

Taking insights from this dream, I can see that Catherine was unhappy in her life, and there have been unhelpful traits passed down the family line to me. These traits are fear of lack, shame, and a feeling of not being enough. In these modern times, when it is possible to pick and choose which traits I embody, I have an opportunity to rewrite my story and rewrite my ancestors' stories at the same time. I want to show Catherine as the courageous and resourceful woman she was, to whom life dealt a tough hand. Through bringing this book into the world, I have rewritten my story and changed my core language, from 'I am not enough, and there will never be enough' to 'I am resourceful, and everything I need I can find at the base of my feet'. Through the process of rewriting the story, I have woven together the intertwining threads of genealogical research, shamanic practices, and my own life narrative.

I have had a sense that I couldn't move on until I had shared Catherine's story since I first found out about her. This book has been growing inside me for several years and I have put up all kinds of blocks to talk myself out of writing it. I've said to myself: I am no expert, what do I know anyway? There are others who know far more than me. I don't know enough about Irish history. I don't know where we were from in Ireland. I might get things wrong. This was the core language playing, which essentially said 'I am not enough'.

I have done several things to move through this. I have followed what intrigued me, putting aside the notion that I would ever write about it. I simply followed what I loved and the thread of fascination. All I had to do was begin with the vision that I wanted to research my family tree and find my Irish roots. This was the starting point and everything followed from that. This was a bone that I could not put down. All the things I was drawn to doing, unbeknown to me at the time, ended up being research for this book. This included the visits I made to museums and the trips to Ireland and Northern

Ireland, as well as my ancestor-honouring trip to London. Over this period, I have sought out and read historical accounts and first-hand, eyewitness writing of the period. I have been drawn to visiting specific locations and noted down the thoughts that pop into my head and the feelings I experience while I am there. Throughout this time, I have written in my journal and recorded my dreams to take to my supervisor, noticing the core material that was coming up and processing this. None of these actions were carried out in order to write the book, but rather I undertook them to understand Catherine and her life more deeply. However, they all led to me writing this book and shaped what to include.

I have called upon guides in both this world and the Otherworld to come and help me. My ancestor ally in the Lowerworld has been a constant source of support and inspiration. In this physical world, during a ceremony honouring the ancestors at Samhain, I put my intention out to the universe that I was going to write a book. By the Winter Solstice a writing mentor had made contact with me. Up until Sally-Shakti contacted me, I didn't even realise that writing mentors existed. I have also sought support from my supervisor, psychotherapist and shamanic teacher Jayne, as well as from Liz before she retired. During my supervision sessions, I asked for help processing what had arisen. We have dissected dreams and the thought patterns that have arisen whilst out on my ancestral land visits. I wouldn't have been able to do this without the support of my allies in all of the worlds.

The writing process

A fascinating aspect of writing this book has been that, as I wrote about each theme, that theme played out in me. For example, as I wrote about privilege and power in Chapter 2, a confrontation happened between me and my neighbours concerning land. They are owners of the local manor house, and Jason and I live in one of the old workers' cottages that used to be part of their land. This gave me first-hand insight into the dynamics between landowners, the privileged, and the landless. When it came to writing Chapter 4 and the topic of shame, I couldn't catch the words. They kept slipping away from me like mercury. As I wrote about overworking in Chapter 5, I realised that there was no way I would be able to write it if I threw all my energy at it. I needed to spend a fair amount of time being creative and at play while writing that chapter, and so I rewrote my own story as a result and took up an art project to get me through. I played around with drawing and exploring a new strand of creativity that I didn't realise I had in me: cartoons.

There were also interesting synchronicities with the timings during the writing process. When it came to writing Catherine's story, I realised I was writing about the final years of her life as I approached the anniversary of her death date. I finished that chapter one hundred and forty-four years to the day that she passed away, which was a big moment for me. That afternoon I walked up to the place where I first set the intention to write her story at the time of the Summer Solstice two years before. As I approached the moor, I noticed the smell of burnt peat leftover from a moorland fire several weeks earlier. It took me right back to the smell inside the cottages in Ireland at the folk museums I had visited. This was another coming home for Catherine, as the retelling of her story was complete. I chose the exact spot where I received the inspiration to tell her story as the third place to lay a mandala of ferns and heather. I believe the universe operates in synchronicities, and it is instances like this that assure me I am on the right path.

The numbers 1 and 2 have been popping up everywhere since I embarked on writing Catherine's story. This came to my attention initially during my first trip to Belfast. When I arrived at a destination such as a museum or a graveyard, my satnav displayed the time 11:11 am or 11:12 am. A Google search informed me that the number 1111 is often referred to as a wake-up call: a signal that an energy gateway has opened and there is an opportunity for healing. The number 1 by itself signifies independence, self-sufficiency and self-deter-mination. The number 12 signifies completion, perfection, harmony, motivation and achievement and the opportunity to turn over a new leaf. This insight has had great meaning for me in my ancestral healing journey. Also, 12 x 12 equals 144, which is the number of years between Catherine passing away and me bringing her story into the world. This numerology feels significant, as by telling her story through this book it feels like there is a completion, an ending, and she can finally lay to rest, having been seen and heard for the remarkable woman that she was.

When I was in Northern Ireland, I felt that this was the place I needed to be to help Catherine carry out a soul exchange between her and William. I completed the journey at 11:21 am. I journeyed to my ancestral guide Elder, to get advice to begin the process and took Catherine to a circle of stones in Ireland. There across the other side of the circle, she saw her husband William, her sons William and George as grown men, and her daughters Catherine, Mary and Charlotte. I felt a piece come back in the soul exchange into Catherine. Then the whole family went into the centre of the circle and celebrated like any bustling family does when they get together. I thought of how this was missing from Catherine's life, as everyone she loved was taken from her, one by one. I reflected on how different it would have been if Catherine and William had been able to stay living together in Ireland in their home, just as their parents had, and their parents before them, right back up the ancestral line. I thought to myself how nice a woman Catherine must have been. Every woman I met in Belfast and County Down, across Northern Ireland and into Donegal, had a par-ticular way with them: a softness, a kindness in their voice, a warm presence. I felt that Catherine would have been like this.

I also saw Catherine as a little girl during the journey, sitting in the moorland with her dark hair and dark eyes. She had grubby knees from playing, and as I watched her standing there in her innocence, I thought to myself what a future she had ahead of her. As she was growing up, she would have had no knowledge of what was to become of her, and what fate lay ahead as a destitute widow alone in a foreign country. None of her family had endured what she had to endure, and so she was also alone. Yet she did it, she survived. I felt teary when I saw her with her family, all together. I left them there reuniting and then returned in a separate journey to cross Catherine over as it didn't feel the right time at that moment. I speak more later in this chapter about supporting a soul to cross over to the spirit realm, which is called psycho-pomping and is a core shamanic healing process.

I have learned to trust the process as it emerges. I have read other people's books on ancestral healing, and for a time, I felt I needed to incorporate their methodologies into my process and into this book. Each practitioner has their own approach and I have for the most part explored my own theory, ideas and suggestions around ancestral healing. All methods have their place. This is my methodology for people who, like me, want to find the names of their ancestors through genealogical research, discover their core language and rewrite the stories using the ancient practices of the shamanic toolkit.

I have described in Chapter 2 how I align my life with the Wheel of the Year, and I have worked with the energy of the seasons in order to write this book. Setting my intention at Samhain, I went into the winter with the goal of emerging on the other side with the makings of a book. At Imbolc, I walked a labyrinth at Clitheroe Castle, holding the intention that I wanted to bring my book into the world and honour the new shoots emerging in the early stages of the writing process. By the Spring Equinox, I had created a basis for the main part by completing the first chapter and the penultimate chapter. This left me drawing on the heightened spring energies to write the creative content and the main content. I stormed through to the Summer Solstice, and as nature swelled to fruition at Lammas I completed the first draft. I then used the period of harvest time to finish the book and prepare it for its initial proofread. During the winter months, I carried out the edits to produce a final draft, completing this by Beltane and the beginning of summer. The final proofread was completed at the Summer Solstice, exactly three years to the day when I first wrote my initial thoughts down in my journal up on the moorland. The last stages of bringing the book to fruition could then happen during the warmer months, ready to begin the publishing process at harvest time in the autumn.

Early on, when I had discovered Catherine's story, I was feeling very emotional about what I had discovered: I felt some of her pain in me. I walked the labyrinth at Gorton Monastery in Manchester. This was the same labyrinth that brought me to my first psychotherapist, Liz, all those years ago. In the centre, I cried for Catherine. I wept for her in that sacred space. I heard the message spoken in me, to tell her story but focus on the emotion. Genealogy as data does not convey the depth of a story through dates, names and places. But feelings – now this is what people respond to.

I held back from writing about Catherine's story for a long time as I was hung up on not knowing all the facts. I didn't want to make assumptions about someone's life. However, I learned over time to trust the notion that what I couldn't find out in archival documents, I would find out through shamanic journeying, dreamwork and by listening to my body. It had to be this way, otherwise her story would never be told. I felt my way into her story and wove together the threads to build a picture of her life. Invoking my inner storyteller, I went boldly to places I didn't think I would be able to reach, such as conveying her life in rural Ireland and living in the slums of Victorian London. I drew conclusions about pivotal moments in Catherine's life, such as when she became pregnant with both of her sons out of wedlock. I came to this place through years of research, questioning and delving into archival documents. I combined concrete genealogical data with social history research, and I followed my dreams as well as visiting the Otherworld through shamanic journeying. I noticed how Catherine's story was playing out in my life – which themes were arising in me – and I reflected on how I could heal from this through my own actions.

I have incorporated into Catherine's story experiences I had while visiting the places where my ancestors lived. For example, that moment I was walking past the gates of Buckingham Palace and I was stopped by the military parade, or when I was on the ship leaving Belfast, and I looked back to the land that disappeared into the horizon. I have visited the buildings or the locations where the buildings once stood in London, following addresses I found on the censuses and baptism records. I often had to look at old maps in the archives to find these, as building and street names change.

I walked the streets as Catherine would have walked them and have had encounters that I would never normally have experienced, such as staying in a youth hostel. This helped me to imagine her experience, or at least allow me to get a glimpse of what it might have been like sleeping in a room with so many strangers. For example, the argument that erupted in my room in the middle of the night, and how I felt vulnerable sleeping in a room with so many people I didn't know. These experiences had an impact on me and triggered thoughts and feelings that I could incorporate into Catherine's story that I would not have necessarily thought of otherwise. Walking around London helped me get a good geographical picture of Catherine's world and helped me see the shift from the wealth of Kensington as I passed Harrods and walked past Buckingham Palace through to the narrow streets of Soho. I would have missed this if I had taken the tube, as I normally would have done. Following my gut and travelling to London with very little money changed my world and allowed me to enter a little more into hers.

I saw many of the scenes of Catherine's life in my shamanic journeys, which informed me of what I needed to write about. For example, one image of Catherine living in her cottage in Ireland with William and walking along the paths. I noticed in my journey that the tracks had become overgrown through the lack of people using them, as they had all moved away. One time, my ancestor ally, Elder, told me to write about the monotony of life in the workhouse, and of how far Catherine's life was from the tribal way of life, which is the life that humans are designed to live. In this journey, I saw how a broken way of life leads to broken people.

I gained a lot of inspiration through reading first-hand accounts of living in London in that period. Rather than read books written by people in modern times about that period, I was primarily drawn to books that had been written in the period or the following few decades. I took inspiration from the exact words that they used to describe the conditions and people. For example, when describing the workhouse, I incorporated the phrase 'even the very sparrows avoided the place'.[97] I read novels about this time too, like *Oliver Twist* by Charles Dickens[98] and *A Child of the Jago* by Arthur Morrison.[99] I took the descriptions of slum areas and inside the workhouse from such stories, which were written by people who saw this first-hand. This helped to portray what life was like in these places for Catherine.

I spent a lot of time in museums. I would spend hours and hours, in some instances, from opening to closing time, and I would wait for people to leave the rooms and then experience what it was like in there on my own. I did this in the dormitory of the Southwell Workhouse Museum so I could feel what it might have been like to live in that place rather than simply walk in and observe it. I went on all the tours I could and hung out for extended periods of time with the museum staff, who were often dressed in period costume, which helped fuel my imagination. I asked them so many questions that on two occasions the members of staff decided they'd had enough of me, making their excuses to leave the room. I wrote down everything that I was told. I also wrote down my reflections of being in these places as I was there. I described what I was seeing with my own eyes. These were very useful to come back to, to help me write the creative content for Catherine's story.

There is a museum in Leeds called Thackray Medical Museum, where there is a replica slum. I went there one day and spent a good few hours in amongst the buildings taking it all in. I sat on the steps of a slum alehouse called The Black Dog, unintentionally scaring the odd visitor. I had spent many years trying to imagine what it was like to live in a slum. I had been on a shamanic journey to a slum several years before, and the first thing I noticed was the unexpected noise. When I arrived at this museum, it was just as I had envisioned it: dark and oppressive with narrow lanes, buildings tightly packed in and smoke-filled skies. What surprised me during the visit was the smell. It was hard to stand by the mock-up slaughterhouse and take it all in. I incorporated this experience into my writing when I mentioned the slaughterhouses as Catherine arrived and made her way to Falconberg Court in Chapter 3. I had read that there were three slaughterhouses in that area of Soho at the time.

While I was standing in the museum exhibit, I thought of all my ancestors who had lived in slums like this and remembered their names. I remembered how they had come to these places after losing their land, becoming slaves to the Industrial Revolution. I was reminded how life is so very different for me now, and how many choices I have available to me that they were denied. Also, how I am not going to let opportunities slip by. Spending time here flagged up my underlying fear of what might happen if I stopped working. For these people, it was certain death, and so they needed to work sixteen-hour days, six days a week in order to survive.

When I did finally come to the point of writing Catherine's story, I first went on a shamanic journey to my ancestor ally guide, Elder, and asked her what I should write about that day. I would begin my writing by describing what I was told or had seen in my journey, and then follow this with whatever popped into my head. As much as I could, I stepped to one side and took myself out of the picture, and let the words flow. This was during the initial lockdown at the start of the Covid-19 pandemic in 2020. It was a difficult time for everyone. At The Way of the Buzzard, Jason and I had to cancel a year's worth of events, so it was stressful. I was not allowed out in my little red van, one of my favourite writing places. It was not clear whether I was even allowed out into the countryside to write. This unique scenario mirrored the story of restriction and control both in Catherine's life and earlier years in my own life. Determined to stick to my goal of creating the bulk of the content between the Spring Equinox and the Summer Solstice, I developed new ways to focus. I commissioned a necklace to be made: an amulet made of hazel and sodalite. Hazel is the tree used for dowsing for water and can bring the unconscious up to the conscious. Sodalite is a blue crystal known as the 'stone of the poets' and supports my creativity. When I struggle, I take my awareness to the amulet and find the words flow once again.

There were hard questions about Catherine's life that I would never find concrete answers to. There were also themes that had come to me that I was still addressing, some that had only just risen to my consciousness, such as shame. It has taken time to integrate some of these themes and respond to them. The retrieval and integration of this information deep in my psyche was part of the healing process.

I never started out researching my family tree for my own healing. I began this because I had a nagging urge to do it that had lasted many years. I just decided to start building my family tree one day, and it has been an incredibly important part of my spiritual journey. From my experience, I have been able to change the way I look at the whole picture of my family line. From my old position, when I was looking close up, I could not see the bigger picture. But when I look at my ancestral stories now, I can see why things have panned out the way they have. I can see the underlying reasons behind why people are the way they are. I can see the whole picture: the bird's eye view. This has helped me in my healing process as I have discovered the underlying reasons for certain behaviours within me that I wanted to change. These include behaviours such as my drive to put work above my relationships and my health. I have also seen how powerless my ancestors were in making choices that would improve their lives. Seeing this has helped inspire me to use my power to change aspects of my own life that have led me to a greater sense of freedom and enjoyment.

In Catherine's story, I can see how the dynamic of power and powerlessness was playing out then, and this has helped me see how it is still playing out now in the twenty-first century. In Chapter 1, I shared a quote from the Dalai Lama, which was his response when asked his opinion on the most powerful meditation that we can do to help heal the world. He said:

> Critical thinking followed by action. Discern what your world is. Know the plot, the scenario of this human drama. Then figure out where your talents might fit into making a better world.[100]

I feel strongly that if I am to understand my life now, and understand the world that I have been born into and how I can make a difference to create a better world, I need to look into the past. I need to look back several generations and understand what happened then, what decisions were made, what kinds of lives my ancestors had and why this was. This is because what happened then is still having an impact on me now. By understanding my past, I can heal the underlying wounds that have been passed down my ancestral line, and move into the future, having rewritten my core language. I can step forward and live my life more in line with what my soul would like.

The story I have shared in this book is a part of a history that does not get taught at school, or at least I wasn't ever taught about it. My ancestors were forced to leave their culture, their land, plants, the people they loved, and everything they knew, to close that door for several generations. My father was the first generation in our family line to own land, and I was the first to enjoy a particular level of freedom. With the awareness that my ancestors were forced to leave their land, it led me to ask what goes on inside a person when this happens. What happens to someone when they have to leave their land and can no longer grow their own food? What happens when they leave their community and the people they love? What happens when they lose their connection with nature as they move to an inner city? Through Catherine's story, and my story, I have gone some way to answer these questions. If a person cannot feed themselves anymore, then they are reliant on someone else. They lose their autonomy, and they lose their power. If they are divorced from nature, they lose their connection with the Earth, the seasons, the plants and animals that have been a part of their life and their ancestors' lives throughout the history of humankind.

A pathway for readers

People who are interested in my approach to ancestral healing often ask me how to go about healing their own ancestral lines.

The key thing is to follow a line of enquiry. Start with a question about your family and follow the breadcrumb trail. This might be a fragment of an interesting fact. For example, my question was: 'Where did my Irish ancestors come from in Ireland and why did they emigrate to England?' I have heard of many other loose ends people have wanted to tie up, such as 'I know a lot about my mother's side but hardly anything about my father's side' or 'my great-grandmother suffered from mental illness and I want to find out more' or 'the story goes we are descended from royalty'. All of these niggles, these hunches, these longings, have an energy behind them that, experience tells me, will reveal something of significance for your healing journey. Often, they are secrets or unsolved mysteries, and as I have said already, it is the secrets that have the loudest voice of all. There is the intrigue that surrounds them, as it seems secrets get passed down the family line with more consistency than many other stories.

So, my advice is to follow what interests you but at the same time be prepared to be patient. You might not find what you are looking for straight away. Start by finding out everything you can about your ancestors here in this physical world. Here in the UK, going back around two hundred years, our ancestors have left a paper trail that is easily accessible to you just sitting on your sofa at home. If you haven't already done this, it is time to research your family tree. Decades ago, this used to be a very involved process, but nowadays it is incredibly easy and doesn't cost very much. I learnt intuitively by subscribing to one of the main genealogy databases. If this sounds a little daunting, you could sign up for a course to help get you started. These can be found online or perhaps close to where you live through your library or local family history group.

There are three main genealogy websites you can join in order to build your tree. They are Ancestry, Findmypast or The Genealogist. Ancestry has the largest number of users, and this is the one I chose. Each website's database holds census records that have been collected every ten years since 1801 (1821 for Ireland). However, to search on a national level, the records from 1841 offer the most detail as this was the first census to list the names of every individual. Census records are closed for one hundred years, so the most recent records available for public viewing are the 1921 records. These records hold a wealth of information, including the names, birth dates and locations, and occupations of all family members, the address where they lived. Within these databases you will also find marriage certificates, death certificates and parish records, as well as all kinds of other documents from military records to newspaper articles, wills to Poor Law records.

Your task is to research and delve into these records to help build a picture of your ancestors' lives. By doing this, you can discover the names of your ancestors, where they lived and what they did for a living. It is important to remember that this is not simply a data-gathering exercise. Behind each of these names on the chart is a person with a story and feelings, experiences, love, disappointment, joy, and trauma. As you build your family tree, particular individuals will stand out, and certain lines will be more intriguing. It is likely that the ancestral healing you seek lies here in the branches of the tree you are most drawn to. As I have said already, secrets are the most prominent of all. They are lost records, broken links in a chain.

After finding a person who intrigues you, spend time getting to know what their life was like. Write out their biography, describing where they were born and into what family, where they grew up, who they married, where they moved to, what they did for a living, how many children they had, how old they were when they died and what they died from. I have completed this activity for many of my ancestors now, and it helped me formulate the bones of their stories in my mind, and the themes that arose. These are themes of poverty, loss of power, lack of choice, hard work and being just inches away from downfall – these themes run from generation to generation. This led me to discover the core language I have inherited that I would like to rewrite, which is that I need to work hard to survive and that there will never be enough.

I would also like to offer these tips when undertaking genealogy research. The first is to never rely on someone else's research unless you know and trust them. It is possible to view other people's research online, and this is helpful in one sense, but to put it plainly, there is some real nonsense out there, and it is too important to get wrong. Always back up your research with the documentation to prove your findings, in particular with regards to marriage certificates. These prove women's maiden names in your family tree.

Another tip is that when you hit a brick wall, don't give up. The information may have been lost forever, but it is also possible that it is hidden, and you need to up your genealogy skills. Catherine was lost to me for so many years. The person I began this whole process for was the very person I couldn't find. Looking back now I can see that I wasn't ready to uncover the information. If I had found out her story all those years ago, it wouldn't have touched me as it has now, and I wouldn't have had the time to let it seep into me and see its magic unfold.

Every dead end is an opportunity to explore another avenue. I ordered lots of birth certificates when I was trying to locate the birth certificate for Catherine's son, George Riley, and none of them was the correct one. They were each for a different George Riley, born in London around the same time as my great-great-grandfather. Each one closed off a door rather than opened it, but it meant that I could draw a line under that and move on to a different way of searching. If you hit a brick wall with one ancestor or ancestral line, then pick up another. There will likely be a similar story to uncover up another line in your family tree. For example, Catherine's story was hidden from me, but by exploring other lines, I discovered the theme of my ancestors losing their lands and moving into the cities to work in the factories and live in the slums. The awareness I developed over the years prepared me for the time when I finally did find Catherine.

It will mean that you will most probably need to go beyond the basic genealogy searches to gather the stories. There are lots of records beyond the census and birth, death and marriage certificate records. Seek out people to speak to who are authorities on the topics that interest you. Family history societies are incredibly helpful, as are people who are employed in the archives and museums, as well as stallholders at family history conferences. These people all have an interest like you in understanding the lives of their ancestors, so go and find them. Online forums can also be helpful.

If you come to a dead end while searching for documents, remember that many of these records aren't online yet. More are being added every year, and so if there is currently no record available, this situation may well change in the future. Alternatively, take a trip to the local archives of the area you are interested in. When I first discovered the Admissions and Discharge records for St James Workhouse, they weren't online, nor were the records for Battersea Industrial School. I found them by visiting the Westminster Archives. Different genealogy websites hold different records, and so, if you subscribe to Ancestry, you might need to consider taking out a temporary subscription to Findmypast or The Genealogist to gain access to the documents you need.

The question you might be asking at this stage is: 'Is it necessary for me to build my family tree in this way?' There are other ways of doing this without carrying out genealogical research. You can tune in with your ancestors energetically and visualise them, and ask Spirit for their names. Some practitioners use this method. This is not my approach. I feel there is something about stepping up, making the effort and putting in the time to find out who your ancestors were, to look into the records and find out their names. Not only is it possible, if you have access to the internet, but it is also easy to do without even leaving your home: so why not do it? We like it when people remember our names, and so do our ancestors. You can also draw on the research a family member has undertaken. Often, a person in the family has already done this, so if you aren't up for doing it yourself, you can seek them out. Remember to be careful about trusting their methods and if something doesn't stack up, then do look into this yourself.

Once you know who your ancestors are, where they lived and what they did for a living, you can build on this story. You can watch documentaries and visit museums like I did; visit the places where they lived, and read social history books and novels set in that period.

I have mentioned that going through this process helped me realise a trend. Here in the UK, my ancestors moved away from their communities, but only after a certain date. Before the turn of the nineteenth century, people generally stayed where their families had always lived, but there was a lot of movement after this date. When I noticed this, it made me want to know why. This led me to research the social and political context of that time. It led me to find out about the Enclosure Act of 1801 and the impact on so many of my ancestors of removing communities from the land.

Shamanic journeying

The other aspect of pursuing a line of enquiry into ancestral research is to begin meeting one's ancestors in the spirit realm. This is where the shamanic practices are necessary in enabling you to have a foot in both worlds, the physical world and the spiritual world. It is about bringing through the stories of your ancestors from the Otherworld into this physical reality. It is about weaving magic into our lives. So, at the same time as you are researching your family tree, work on your shamanic journeying skills. Shamanic journeying is the easiest way to connect with your spirit guides for a two-way dialogue. Go on a shamanic journey to meet and build your relationship with your ancestor ally. Physiologically, everyone's brain can shift consciousness and go on a shamanic journey, so if to begin with it doesn't come naturally to you, it is well worth persevering. Once you have cracked it, this is a time-efficient practice that you will gain great rewards from. The more time you invest in this, the better.

At The Way of the Buzzard, we teach shamanic journeying in The Mystery School. If you aren't already a member, come and join us. As well as our Foundation in Shamanic Journeying and other programmes that incorporate journeying, we have regular online live gatherings to help you progress your practice.

When it comes to healing ancestral trauma and guiding you through the processes I have shared in this book, I have an online Ancestral Healing Masterclass. If this sounds like something you might be interested in, you can find out more about this via our The Way of the Buzzard website.

Intention is everything, and if you are being pulled towards healing your ancestral lines, then put the intention out there that you are going to do this. Create a ceremony and align yourself to the Wheel of the Year as you progress through each of the stages. I revisit my ancestral healing process and journey to my ancestor ally every Samhain in order to ask what I need to look at next, and what rituals or ceremonies I should undertake. I then tune in with each of the Celtic Sabbats to shift old patterns. For example, with a tendency towards overworking, I drop into the energy of balance and shedding to recalibrate at each Equinox and particularly the Autumn Equinox.

I have found it very empowering to learn how to carry out my own ceremonies. For example, I held little ceremonies at each of the places where I laid the fern and heather mandalas. These were held at the place where Catherine died; in consecrated ground in Northern Ireland, and up on the moorland where I first got the idea to tell her story. Again, this is something we teach in The Mystery School.

As you progress on your ancestral healing journey, the themes that arise might be similar to mine, or they may be different. Whatever they are, they are unique for you. This is your story to rewrite. I have undertaken shamanic healing sessions with people who have descended from slavery and from royalty, as well as people who have been born to a parent who didn't accept their sexuality, and a family who had been cursed because of forbidden love. These stories are there to find, unravel, and re-weave into a silk cloth, soft and pliable, fit for the emerging new world.

Healing ancestral wounds

Once you have found out about your ancestors' lives in this reality and begun to make contact in the spiritual realm, you are ready to begin the process of healing your ancestral wounds by essentially rewriting the story.

In healing the wounds, you need to bridge the two worlds: the physical world and the spirit realm. A useful practice is to visit your ancestral lands. This is common with people interested in genealogy as they are often drawn to visiting the places where their ancestors lived. There is great healing and power in visiting our ancestral lands. The Native Americans believe that the land where our ancestors lived holds their memories, and it is these memories that you can tap into when you visit the places where your ancestors lived. But what do you do when you get there? Well, you can visit as a tourist, or you can visit with intention.

People interested in just genealogy visit as a tourist, but people interested in healing ancestral patterns have a different mindset when they arrive on ancestral land. As you build your family tree and research into the lives of your ancestors, you become a story carrier. Take your ancestor's story with you when you visit the places where your ancestors lived. After all, it is already in your genes, so take it in your mind too. Spend time here, walking through the streets and footpaths through the surrounding countryside. Stand on the ground ancestors would have stood on and sit by the rivers they would have sat next to. Notice the mature trees and reflect on whether these would have been alive at the time when your ancestors lived here. Visit the church, stand by the font where your ancestors baptised their babies, and search out family graves. If it still exists, stand in front of the home where they lived.

Now here is the trick. As you do this, pay attention to your thoughts and notice any behavioural patterns that are old acquaintances. This will reveal more about the core language that you are looking to rewrite. Also, in the run-up to the visit, pay attention to your dreams. When you visit the cities, towns and villages where your ancestors lived, try to arrange to sleep overnight there and pay attention to your dreams. Through doing this, you are bringing forward what lies in your unconscious. Make sure you journal all thoughts, feelings, ideas and dreams that come to you, no matter how random they seem. This is where having a psychotherapist could be helpful as you can take what arises to them to process. I will say more about that later.

Let me give you an example. I mentioned that I had the idea to sleep in all the places where my ancestors lived, and I decided to extend this back to seven generations. I contemplated how I would do this and decided the most practical way was to buy a small van, one that wasn't too noticeable as a campervan, as I would be sleeping out in residential streets. I found the perfect vehicle as soon as I began to search online for one, my little red van, and within a few days I had bought it and picked it up. As I began my ancestral sleepover project, I went through a process of resistance as I prepared to visit each place. I felt as if it was more important to stay at home to work. When I was at each location, I felt that I needed to move on. I couldn't stay in one place and really absorb it, as I described in Chapter 5. There was always something else I should be doing. Just by visiting these places my core language had come more prominently to the surface: 'I must work. I must keep busy doing something productive.' It played out time after time, and it got a little louder and clearer each time. It informs me of the patterns I have inherited that I wanted to change. This became stronger in my conscious mind, and I started to notice patterns in my decision-making. This awareness helped me to seek ways of doing things differently.

I have noticed that just by visiting these places, circumstances occur that give me more information about my ancestors' stories. On one solo trip to Ireland my van broke down, and immediately I shifted from feeling confident and independent to having to rely on other people to ensure I could carry on with my trip. I felt helpless and vulnerable, and it drew my attention to feelings that Catherine must have felt throughout her life. On another occasion, on my way to Ireland, I ended up getting rerouted by my satnav to go through an impoverished area close to the docklands. My van was approached by three men walking across the road, or at least it seemed like that. This brought to my attention how Catherine might have felt arriving at the docklands of a strange new country, and how she would have been the target of people looking to take advantage of poor immigrants such as herself.

My dreams have been particularly revealing throughout this process of gathering the stories of my ancestors. Sometimes I dreamt of my former employer when I was working within the corporations. Other times I dreamt of my ancestors themselves. As you know, I have even dreamt of where Catherine lived in Northern Ireland. The significance of these messages does not pass me by.

My experience in gathering the stories of my ancestors has shown me that important things are happening within me when I simply visit my ancestral lands with intention. Yet, I have found I can add gravitas to this visit in several ways to help me shift even further from being a tourist, to being a visitor with intention. What I am doing when I bring forward my thoughts and dreams during my visits to ancestral lands is weaving together the physical world and the spiritual world through my being. I am the interface between the two worlds, and I am the conduit for the healing to come through.

Now it is possible to take this a step further by carrying out particular activities when standing on the ancestral ground, and when it comes to deciding what to do during the visit, this is where the ancestor ally comes in. Before I leave for a trip, I go on a shamanic journey to ask what it is that I should do and am prepared to hear things that surprise me, and that don't always gel. Over time they usually make sense, but not always. However, I just trust and do them anyway.

Another practice I have been guided to do several times is to lay out a mandala with stones or leaves as a pattern on the ground. I did this in preparation for reading some words aloud to my ancestors during a visit to Tadcaster in North Yorkshire. Once I had laid it out something remarkable happened. A dog came running to me and its owners called it back. The dog was called Annie, the same name as my ancestor who I was preparing to honour in the ceremony. These synchronicities mean so much to me.

Most recently, I have been guided to sleep overnight where each of the places my seventh-generation ancestors lived and observe my dreams, and to collect some soil from these locations. In the case of my paternal line for example, this would be Catherine's parents. Although I am unable to trace back to where Catherine's parents lived, I can for almost all of my other great-great-great-great-grandparents. I don't fully know why I am drawn to embarking on this process yet. I am just sleeping in the locations, writing down my dreams and collecting the soil for now and waiting to be shown the next step.

Stories rewritten

Through visiting ancestral lands with intention, and carrying out ceremonies to honour the ancestors, stories are brought back into being. Words are given to our ancestors' experiences, and through our imagination, our ancestors are given life once again. With these stories alive once more, we can rewrite them with a different emphasis: one that brings us the healing that we need and provides healing for our ancestors.

Let's take Catherine's story as an example to illustrate this, using details I've written about previously in the book. Here is someone who was a victim of an oppressive class system. Catherine was born in a country that was in the midst of being overthrown. The English used the opportunity of the failure of the potato harvest to clear people from their ancestral lands. These indigenous people were left with two choices: stay and starve or emigrate to another country. Catherine emigrated to England and had the misfortune of ending up in one of the worst slum areas of Victorian Britain. When Catherine arrived in London in 1848, there had been a huge influx of Irish immigrants that continued for the next two decades. The slums swelled and inhabitants doubled in number in just a matter of years. It would be almost thirty years before any kind of understanding or aid would become available. Catherine was alive at an incredibly difficult time in history. Had it been several decades later, the plight of the poor was beginning to be better understood, and small improvements were being made to the workhouses and the lives of the inmates who lived there.

Had her husband William lived, Catherine would have been assured of a different life. She would still have been poor, but she would have been able to live with William and raise their children. Using the census records, I have followed the lives of another Catherine and William Riley, who had eight children, moved out into the suburbs of London and enjoyed life together until this Catherine died at an old age with her daughter at her side. My family's Catherine Riley was dealt a different hand, and as a single parent on the streets with a newborn child and no opportunity to work, she was left with only two options. She could pay for Charlotte to live in a baby farm, where she had almost no chance of surviving, or take her to the workhouse.

Over the following years, Catherine descended to the bottom of the social ladder. As I have mentioned already, being Irish was low, being an Irish woman even lower, but having an illegitimate child – two illegitimate children – was something else. There would have been so much shame surrounding Catherine, which was carried through to the next generation, with her son, my great-great-grandfather George, growing up in an orphanage. There would have been a huge stigma for him around his illegitimacy. In the industrial school, he was taught that the way out of this was to work. From the age of three years old, he was instructed to work his way out of the bottom of the pit and assured that this was the only way he was going to be accepted in society after such a shameful beginning in life.

So, this is one version of Catherine's story: Catherine's story told through a Victorian lens and value system. It has triggered a story that has been passed down in my genes that I am still shifting. Yet there is another story, and another way of looking at this. There is the story of a woman who was born into unmitigated circumstances. Given the options she had, she made decisions that were best for her survival and for the long-term future of her family.

She could have taken her chances in the slums, but the following generations would most likely have remained there. The old slum areas of Irish immigrants in Liverpool, Glasgow and the East End of London are still impoverished and have a lower life expectancy even now in the twenty-first century.[101] Catherine's sacrifice led to the creation of a successful family line.

She was a hard worker and she did her best. She didn't turn to crime, and she didn't turn to prostitution. Yes, she turned to drink, and this was perhaps her downfall, but given what had happened to her in her life, who wouldn't turn to the bottle and find some happiness there?

She was a fighter and she was strong. She had strength and courage and I cannot imagine how she maintained this. How did she manage to cope, a stranger in a new land without her husband? How did she manage to survive in the slums of London for so many years? She spent longer out of the workhouse than she did in it, so how did she manage to feed, clothe and house herself for almost half of her time in London? How did she cope day in day out in the workhouse, doing the same monotonous, mind-numbing task every day? Catherine managed to look after her two sons in impoverished London until the youngest was six months old. When the opportunity presented itself, she rose up the ladder. She became a nurse in the workhouse, which would have put her into a position of trust. She became a housekeeper in a middle-class house in Kensington and so she must have been able to turn her hand to many different things.

Knowing all of this, it is clear to me that this feeling of shame can be replaced with heroism: a determination to survive against the odds. This version of Catherine's story shifts something inside me when it comes to rewriting my core language. Instead of 'I need to work hard to survive as there will never be enough', I can replace this with 'I am highly resourceful and can achieve the impossible when I put my mind to it'. That is quite something, isn't it? I think it is incredible to rewrite a story in this way that has such a significant impact on my core language and my core beliefs of who I am in the world and what I can achieve.

Psycho-pomping

In Chapter 4, I shared two practices from Core Shamanism that can help in the healing of both our own wounds, wounds we have inherited from our ancestors, and our ancestors' wounds that they still hold onto within the spirit realm. These practices are soul retrieval and soul exchange. There is a third practice that I would like to explain, which is very relevant for the healing of our ancestors in the spiritual realm. This is called psycho-pomping.

One of the things that is important to indigenous people is to ensure that when a person dies, their soul moves across to the other side. As the soul leaves a body, a tunnel of light appears that the soul is naturally drawn to and guided through to the other side. The light emits an incredible energy of love, and there is a feeling of coming home, of ultimate belonging. Often, but not always, the soul is met by loved ones whom this person knows, and they lead them over.

This is a well-documented phenomenon spoken about by people who have had a near-death experience. However, if the soul fails to see the tunnel, then it can become trapped between the physical world and the spiritual world. The process of psycho-pomping is to journey to meet with trapped souls and guide them towards the light.

This isn't something that is on our radar in Western society, and this is an oversight. In Western culture, when people die, they might not want to move across to the other side for all kinds of reasons. So, there is a likelihood that ancestors may well be trapped between the worlds.

There are a number of reasons I have come across as to why a trapped soul hasn't moved across to the other side. One issue is that they might not have found the light because they believed in the Christian teachings of Heaven and Hell. When they died, they were afraid that they were going to go to Hell, so they remained in limbo, not believing that they had died. Another common reason is that a soul has an attachment to this physical reality. They may have a loved one who is dependent on them and so they don't want to leave. Another reason is that they don't realise that they are dead. They have died in a traumatic event that was very sudden, and the immediacy of death has meant that they didn't realise they were dying.

There are other reasons, but these are the main ones in my experience. Part of the process of healing the ancestral line is to help the trapped ancestors cross over to the other side; otherwise, they are caught in limbo, in a non-space between the worlds. This is not a great place to be as they can't continue their soul journey. I am a believer in the idea that I have come to this physical world to progress my soul's development, and when I die, I will go back to the other side, where I came from, to reflect on the lessons I learned during that lifetime and decide when and who to reincarnate as next time, so that I progress. If I don't cross over to the other side when I die, I can't continue with my ongoing soul progression.

If a person interested in healing the ancestral lines meets an ancestor who hasn't crossed over, they can help them do this. This isn't something that I recommend doing alone. This should be carried out with the help of a shamanic practitioner, either as something they do for you, or in a three-way spoken relationship between the client, the practitioner and the ancestor.

I held within me for several years the knowledge that I would need to cross Catherine over. Then, at the time of Samhain, I felt it was time. I returned to Catherine during a shamanic journey with the specific intention of crossing her over. I first journeyed to the Lowerworld and met with my ancestor ally, Elder, to check that it was the right time to carry out this final step. As I approached the house where I met with Elder, I noticed children playing in the centre of the village. I reflected on how Catherine missed out on seeing her children play like this. I asked Elder if it was time, and she said yes. My tawny owl appeared – the animal spirit guide that supports me when I undertake core shamanic healing work.

I met with Catherine in the same place where I had left her when I carried out the soul exchange work, which I describe earlier in this chapter. She showed me a scene in her cottage in Ireland with William. There was a bonfire outside, and they were apple bobbing with the children. There was laughter and play. She told me: 'I never had this. Make sure you do.' I then saw the beam of light appear from above us, and I received a sense of intense love. This is the feeling I always experience when I carry out psycho-pomping work. I then felt the contrast in feeling in the workhouse, which was symbolic of the oppression in the world. I reflected on how far apart these two opposite worlds are from each other. I watched Catherine walk up to the light. She turned to me and spoke the words: 'It is all done. All is forgiven. It doesn't matter anymore.' I felt a release. From her perspective, looking back from the afterlife, all the trauma has melted away.

Healing on behalf of all ancestors

Often there is a soul exchange to be carried out before a trapped soul can cross over, and sometimes a soul retrieval is necessary as well. I find it doesn't always all happen in the same session, although it can do. In the past, I have preferred to do this over several sessions. It is good to let things settle so more realisations can happen with your own thinking and your own story before your ancestor is finally ready to cross over.

One question that often arises when people begin the process to heal their ancestral line, is: 'Do I need to carry this out for every ancestor?' The answer is no. You can carry out healing with one ancestor on behalf of everyone in your family tree that has this issue. Ancestors who are asking for healing will come forward in your research and in your consciousness. Presumably, once you have completed this process for all the ancestors who need help, they will stop coming forward. I haven't found this yet myself, but in time I do think it will happen.

You may end up carrying out this healing process with one ancestor and feel it is enough; that the issue passed down your family line, which was causing you problems in your life, has been resolved and you are able to move on. But many people find they want to continue this process, as it is something that intrigues them, and like me, they just can't put it down. Either way is fine; it is whatever you are called to do.

Self-healing capacity

Now we are approaching the end of this book, I want to go full circle and return to the science of epigenetics that I introduced right at the beginning. Epigenetics is the science that explains why it is possible to rewrite our inherited core language and rewrite our story. Humans have a huge capacity to self-heal and I find this very empowering.

In Chapter 1, I spoke of the make-up of our DNA. I explained how just 2 per cent of a person's DNA is responsible for their physical attributes. The remaining 98 per cent is now known to hold genetic memory about inherited emotional, behavioural and personality traits. When someone experiences a traumatic event, and they don't process this trauma, there is every chance that their traumatic experience is coded into their DNA. Future generations then inherit this coded DNA. However, it stands to reason that if DNA can be programmed in one way, it can then be programmed again to reverse the code. As I have mentioned, the writing of this book has become part of this process for me.

Gregg Braden is a widely published American author bridging the gap between science and spirituality and many of his views are controversial. I am drawn to his writing around the science of epigenetics, which he addresses in the book *The Science of Self-Empowerment: Awakening the New Human Story.*[102] Braden explains that human beings have the capacity for self-regulated healing.

We are not at the mercy of our ancestors' legacy: we can change our DNA through epigenetics and rewrite what we have inherited. He explains how identical cells express themselves in many ways when they are placed in different environments. For example, Braden argues that if DNA is put into an environment with alcoholism and addiction, it will express itself in a certain way. He highlights that this is not common knowledge, even though it has been supported through scientific evidence.

In an interview during the online Ancestral Healing Summit in 2019, Braden said this in relation to the topic:

> When we take responsibility for our lives in this moment ... we do not have to be confined by the conditions that we come from. Our history worked well enough to bring us to this point now, however we do not have to have our future defined by the conditions of our past. We may, if we choose to, be a victim. But this is where our greatest levels of mastery come from as we become aware of the potential that we have for this genetic plasticity, as we begin to shift our perspectives. Perception changes the chemistry and the DNA in the body.[103]

The words 'we do not have to have our future defined by the conditions of our past' stand out in particular to me. My ancestors had to survive through terribly difficult conditions. Through the discovery of Catherine's story, I saw she suffered trauma after trauma throughout the second half of her life, spanning three decades. Her son, George, grew up within the confines of an institution without the love of a mother or father. These traumatic experiences are imprinted in their DNA, which I have inherited through the ancestral line. However, it doesn't need to stay that way. I can shift my perspective and, through doing this, recode this DNA. I can respond to my life differently. I am fortunate that I live in a time when it is possible for me to do this.

Braden then went on to speak of the work of the late Dr Candace Pert, who was the first person to identify that the emotions in our body have a chemical equivalent. She published her research findings through her book *Molecules of Emotion.*[104] Through her research, Pert discovered that every emotion creates a neuropeptide. At one end of the scale, there is the greatest joy and ecstasy experienced, with trauma at the other end of the scale. We all have trauma in our lives, some experienced consciously and some unconsciously. If we resolve the trauma when it occurs, then the neuropeptide is metabolised by the body, and the trauma is no longer a problem. However, if we don't resolve the trauma, our bodies store neuropeptides in the tissue in an organ where they will be held indefinitely. They are stored there as a survival mechanism at the time of the trauma and we aren't aware of it, maybe right through to adulthood. If that trauma isn't resolved in some way, it is common for the tissue to flag up the message that this needs to be addressed, which it does through disease.

Braden suggests this is a very different way of thinking about disease, where a medical doctor would bombard the tissue with a chemical or remove it altogether from the body. The resolution of the trauma is what frees that chemical or neuropeptide, allowing it to move through the blood and be metabolised, and become free from the tissue. This is what is called healing. Braden suggests that one of the ways that we can arrive at that healing is through what he calls heart-brain coherence: looking at the experience that formed the neuropeptide.

This is something one can do when looking at the trauma experienced both in our own lives and in our ancestors' lives. We have the ability to transcend our own hurts as well as not to be defined by our ancestors' wounds. By finding the stories, the origins of the trauma and bringing them to the light, we can free up the neuropeptides within our bodies and release them. This is the ancestral healing process that I am advocating: bringing through the stories of the forgotten ones. By doing this we forge the path to forgotten freedom.

COMING HOME

When Jason and I run our weekend retreat at the windswept peninsula of Humphrey Head, the place where the last wolf of England drew her final breath, we hold ceremony to her on the rocky outcrop that forms the edge of the headland. In doing this, we honour that wild part within us that is yearning to come back home. During the most recent retreat there, I felt inspired after the ceremony to weave together dreams, stories and windswept inspirations and create a poem called Wolf Time. This is my response to one of my favourite poems called Sometimes A Wild God by Tom Hirons.[105]

Wolf Time

We have left the door ajar,
And set a place at our table
For the wild god.
You are welcome here,
With your companion of gibbons,
And lance of gazelles.

We have taken away your chair,
In fact, we have taken away all the chairs.
We have no need for them now.
We burned the table days ago
And instead, eat from the floor.

We have no need for cutlery.
After we have torn the flesh from the carcass of civilisation
With our teeth,
And sucked the marrow from its bones,
We lie collapsed on the cool earth.

That cool dark enveloping earth,
Which has been hiding all these years
Beneath the dusty floorboards.

We ripped those up hours ago,
You can see them leaning against the shed,
Through the hole where the window once was.

The wind is blowing now inside,
Howling, tussling with our unbridled hair.
The storm drenching our threadbare clothes,
Stained with our hysterical tears,
As we raise our glasses to our new-found
debauchery.

The time has come for a different way of living,
Raw, with our old scabs, picked so they bleed.
A time where three drops of the blood
From those old wounds
Fall on a once-white handkerchief,
So we, at last, remember who we once were.

We remember our home.
That long-forgotten world,
Where the wolf's howl carries across frozen valleys,
And the echo rises up to the mountain tops.

We remember the peace of the dark wood,
Where old women walk out of trees, heads bobbing,
And princesses hide in the branches,
Birds nesting in their hair.

We remember a world where spiders do dream.
Oh yes, they dream,
And as they dream
They spin a new world into being,
With their fine webs of silver thread.

We remember a world where we can stand in the
oven
And tell our stories to the ashes.
Where the old kings listen
And the forgotten parts of us are found.

Where we can sit out under the twisted hawthorn
And the only questions we hear are those of our
own minds.

A world where we sing with the skylark unbounded.
Where we can conjure up rainbows on demand.
Where we run with those gibbons,
Our arses baring recklessly towards the sun,
Tails pointing upwards in honour of those gods.

Gods who throw parties in return.
Where they see our truth,
Our wild, unabridged, shenanigan-filled lives.

Yes, now is the time for something different.
As we welcome the wild god into our home
And welcome the wild wolf into our hearts.
Where we close the door on the circus
And enter that aftermath of deep peace.
Now is that time: wild god time, wolf time.

Following a path of ancestral healing is, for me, a process of coming home. Something important was lost when my ancestors were removed from their land to live a life of servitude. My healing journey is about claiming this back. My healing journey is about finding my way back home and reacquainting myself with my inner wild twin.

Bending my ear

Something is stirring in us. We are awakening to a different way of living. All that we were taught is falling away. This awareness came to me as I reached an unhappiness with my life. When I learnt to bend my ear to hear the quiet voices, I heard that there was a different way to live: a way to live that is based on connection with the Earth, connected with the wisdom from the Otherworld, that feeds my soul. I found my guidance hidden in the place I could only access when I was ready to. It was inside my own mind. We were born to be free, and now is our time to live freely, just as our distant ancestors once did.

With the emergence of the new, there is an inevitable falling away of the old. I needed to look at what it was that I needed to leave behind. I needed to find inspiration as to where the path in front of me was. I needed to find my courage, strength and resilience. I needed to find my softness and willingness to change. Sometimes the road was a bumpy one. I learned to quiet myself, so I could hear the messages spoken to me. I found my place of stillness in the eye of the storm that is modern-day life.

I used the shamanic toolkit to help me awaken to a different way of living: a life of freedom away from the constrictions of a full-time job working to deliver someone else's goals. I called on the very same ancient tools our most distant ancestors used before they were forced to succumb to the controlling forces of those people who exert their power over the powerless. I found myself in the place between stories, as one story fell away and a new one had yet to emerge. I learned how to settle myself in a place of darkness and know which way to turn, so I could see the glimmer of light guiding me out.

Ancestral grief

My ancestors were faced with terrible decisions. Decisions that meant they left their homeland and lived in atrocious conditions in the slums of Victorian Britain. Decisions that led to them being refugees, working in sweatshops, factories, and in service, up to sixteen hours a day, six days a week. If they hadn't made this sacrifice, I wouldn't exist. It is a sobering realisation. Every day they would have had the real threat of losing their job and being destitute with no place to go. If they were to speak up for themselves, they would have lived with the fear of being branded a troublemaker and getting blacklisted from other work. They would have been fearful of getting sick and not being able to work, and carried a fear of not having enough money to support their family and ending up in the workhouse. Some of my ancestors did live in the workhouse: some grew up there and some died there, alone.

It is this fear ingrained into my psyche, built into my DNA in every cell of my body, that I have spent many years unravelling in order to re-find my freedom: to rekindle that freedom my ancestors enjoyed before the Industrial Revolution, over two centuries ago. I am learning to decondition my mind, to remember who I am, to get my own life back and, in the process, to heal my family line.

Spiritual wounding happens when our interconnectedness is severely disrupted: when a piece of our soul is lost or taken. There is so much about our history that hasn't been processed: so much that has happened that hasn't been grieved. Deep healing is needed so that we do not recreate what has been done to us.

Francis Weller speaks of this grief that has not been processed in his book *The Wild Edge of Sorrow*, where he says: 'This is the grief we carry in our bodies from sorrows experienced by our ancestors. Much of this grief lingers in a layer of silence, unacknowledged'.[106]

Some of us will have ancestors who left Ireland. It is estimated that there are more than 80 million people in the world with Irish ancestry.[107] Many people in England are descended from ancestors who were forced off their land through the Enclosure Acts and ended up working as the powerhouse of the Industrial Revolution. Generations of people survived without living on their own land and the knowledge of the old ways. Weller goes on to say:

> The traditions that had nourished and held the people
> for hundreds, if not thousands of years were no longer
> sustained. They lived between the Old and the New
> Worlds, attempting to create something that would
> enable them to endure. Without the protective shelter

of the village, they often coped in ways that created
a secondary layer of suffering: alcoholism, isolation,
rage and a restrictive silence that cut them off from the
loving support of others. There was a gap in the dream
of what it meant to be human. The rich and nuanced
patterns of culture that had evolved over time were
replaced with strategies designed simply to help them
survive. Gone were the patterns that held myth, song,
ritual and the poetic imagination as the heartbeat of
the people. So many of us hold this ancestral grief in
our beings, even after many generations of living in the
new land. This sorrow becomes concentrated over time,
gathering grief unto itself, and is carried in our psyches
unconsciously as a diminished inheritance. The psychic
inheritance from our ancestors was meant to be a blessing, but instead it is a layer of heaviness. The enduring
façade and behaviours of these generations left behind a
legacy of unattended pain.[108]

Weller sums up for me the consequences when our ancestors left their homes, communities and traditions. The grief
they experienced hasn't gone away. Instead, it has been passed
down from generation to generation, and I believe it underpins
many of our troubles.

I reflect back on my dream when I was told that everything
we needed was at our feet: that the Earth would provide. This
was not the case for Catherine once she had left her country
and made her way to England. This belief that there will never
be enough and that I am not enough is a construct of the paradigm of power and powerlessness that has been passed down
in my DNA. It is my task to rewrite this story and recode my
DNA. What I have learned from working for myself is that
there is enough. I have learned that I am enough.

I get a feeling of completeness when I go out into wild
places. I feel complete when I watch nature; when I sit in my
tent and look out at the sun setting over Ingleborough mountain; when I sit around a campfire and listen to the old stories,

and when we gather in our The Way of the Buzzard community and drum and sing together.

Over the years, I have come to the same conclusion. I see the privileged few making decisions that affect the under-privileged or the poor and marginalised. I see the pattern of power and powerlessness being played out time and time again. Whether it be the atrocities of the Great Famine in Ireland, or the Scottish Clearances, or the three hundred years of legislation passed between 1604 and 1914 to enclose the land in England. What brings it all to life with my Irish ancestry is that this was relatively recent. The heart was ripped out of Ireland and the people still talk of it to this day. During our stay with farmer Pat Noon on his farm in Galway, he talked about the famine several times to us. It is in their bone memory. If it is in the bone memory of the people who stayed in Ireland, then it stands to reason that it is also in the bone memory of the people who fled from Ireland.

Here in England, if anyone knows about the Enclosure Acts, it is taught that we benefited from it as a necessary efficiency. The Great Famine of Ireland is known to people as the Potato Famine, and many people believe people starved because the potato crop failed. There is so much more behind the story of the Enclosure Acts in England and the Great Famine of Ireland that isn't common knowledge. Many people don't know about what happened in our collective past. They do not know the plot, the scenario of this human drama, as the Dalai Lama calls it. This information is not part of our conscious story, but it is very much residing in the unconscious of people who have ancestors who were forcibly removed from their land.

What we are taught at school comes from the victorious. I was told that changes were made in land policy to make efficiencies so that our country and the people could prosper. I was taught that the Industrial Revolution led us to become civilised and wealthy. Go back even further, and I was taught that William the Conqueror brought order and prosperity to Britain, as the Romans were said to have done one thousand years earlier. This is one side of the story. It is the side of the story written by those who have power. It is the story told by the privileged. Through Catherine, I have shared another version of the story, and through my experiences in life, I have shone a light on how this trauma has been passed down and is still very much alive today, driving the things I think and the actions I take.

One of my favourite places to write is sitting in amongst those old ruins of the farmsteads on Anglezarke moors that I mentioned right at the start of this book. The people who lived in these homes were forced off their land during the Anglezarke Clearances and took up jobs in the local mills and factories. Some chose suicide rather than leave their land.

This story is close to my heart, not just because the moorland behind our home has claimed me, but also because it was Jason's ancestors who lived in these farmsteads. I have a connection with these people through Jason. It makes me wonder about the ruined homes of my ancestors: homes that shielded them from the cold winter and the summer storms. Homes they built with their hands, gathered within, and listened to stories. One thing that has been with me for many years is this relationship to place. I only feel it when I am in wild places.

My own battle with work is doing things that I think I should be doing. It feels urgent that I need to do this and that, and if I don't then everything will fall apart. It is absolutely an irrational fear. It might have had some weight in the corporate world as there were objectives and a contract to complete, and if I didn't do these things then I would risk losing my job. But when I started working for myself this threat was removed to a certain degree. Yes, there are things that I need to do to make money and keep everything turning, but the pressure I feel and the daily urgency is different. Things are far more in my control.

Honouring the ancestors

My inner process is not to let the past weigh me down. The woes of the old ones belong with them. They lived in a different time: a time where their choices were sorrowfully limited. I want to take hold of the opportunities that surround me, and with both hands, lift myself out of the sinking sand onto firmer ground. I want to shake off the shackles that bind me to emotions that aren't even mine. I will let the wind from the east bring with it a new dawn, a softer light on the horizon, and walk firmly towards that glow. I want to warm my skin under the sun's gaze and lose myself in the gentle arms of the Earth. The echoes of the ancestors grow fainter as the knots are unravelled, and the healing completes.

Through all of this, I want to honour my ancestors. I want to see their lives and the choices they made from a different perspective now, generations on. To see from this the position that nothing was their fault: they were doing the best they could. There is much healing in the act of grieving for our ancestors. There is much healing in the tears that we shed for them. It is important to allow space for this to happen, to give them time and take the time to find their stories and give ourselves space to allow sadness to move through us.

As Mayan Shaman, Martin Prechtel says: 'We are surrounded by the ghosts of unwept ancestors.'[109] I believe now is the time to weep for our ancestors. It is time to address historical trauma: trauma that hasn't had a voice, a space to move through. Let it move through us, our bodies and our psyches. Let us witness it and then release it. It is our ancestor's grief that we carry in our bodies. It is our ancestor's sorrows that hold us down. Now is the time to bear witness, to acknowledge their grief and to shed our tears. Through this act, we can individually and collectively move on. This is sacred.

Out on the wild peninsular of Humphrey Head, the voice of the wolf spoke to me through my aching bones. I saw her final moments here on English soil as she lay on the strandline of high tide. Just hours before, her final howl had haunted the valley, as the trees held a knowing of her imminent fate. The moonlight kissed the limestone rock where she stood, her heart aching for all that she had already lost, and what was going to be taken that day. It was a melancholy sunrise that dawn. Every day since, the sun has searched for her. Now, one hundred thousand sunrises later, her cubs awaken and push through the shadows into the soft light.

Resources

The Way of the Buzzard and The Mystery School

To find out about The Way of the Buzzard including our Mystery School membership site, retreats, masterclasses and sacred tool shop, visit our website at: www.thewayofthebuzzard.co.uk

Our Ancestral Healing Masterclass is a natural progression for readers who have enjoyed this book and wish to embark on a similar ancestral healing journey themselves. It is called Ancestral Echoes: The complete, step-by-step approach to tracing your ancestors, healing unhelpful ancestral patterns and rewriting the story.

The Westcountry School of Myth

The Westcountry School of Myth is run by Dr Martin Shaw. The two programmes I have referenced here are the wilderness vigil Wolf Milk and the five-weekend immersion programme Stalking the Rebel Soul. Their website is: https://schoolofmyth.com

Indie Shaman

Indie Shaman is a resource centre for Shamanism and animism. On their website, they hold a shamanic practitioner register which is a good place to start if you are looking for one-to-one support in healing your ancestral line. Their website is: https://indieshaman.co.uk

Embodied Relational Therapy

Embodied Relational Therapy is an initiative based in the UK offering relational body psychotherapy workshops, relational body psychotherapy training, individual therapy and supervision. Their website holds a list of certified ERT Practitioners: https://erthworks.co.uk

Acknowledgements

First and foremost, I would like to thank my husband, Jason, for his unwavering support in anything I turn my hand to, and for helping me to build a firm ground on which I can stand strong. I would like to express my deep-felt thanks to the following:

My Elders: Elizabeth Clarke and Jayne Johnson, who have sat by my side and gently guided and supported me to understand my inner workings and heal those parts that needed some tender loving care.

My Spirit guides and helpers in all of the worlds: my team of allies who give me support and guide my hand, who are tuned in with the bigger picture of the Earth story and beyond.

My Family and friends: who each give me strength and bring so much richness to my life.

My Teachers at The Westcountry School of Myth: myth-teller Dr Martin Shaw, and wilderness vigil leaders Tina Burchill, Tim Russell and Dave Stevenson for all their knowledge and support through what were incredibly transformational experiences.

The Leaders of the Embodied Relational Therapy and Wild Therapy training programmes: Nick Totton, Jayne Johnson, Stephen Tame and Allison Priestman and my fellow course participants for the healing journey that those three years presented.

Glennie Kindred and Annie Keeling for all of the insights they shared with me on how to work with ceremony and the Wheel of the Year and align my life with the natural cycles of the Earth, and also to Glennie for all of the continuous inspirations I draw from her books.

My writing mentor Sally-Shakti Willow, without whom I may well never have written this book, and who has consistently given me patience and care throughout the process.

Dee Lister and Anne Gillion for their unwavering attention to detail and thoroughness whilst proofreading that I never dreamt of or knew were possible.

The Way of the Buzzard community, without whom the life I live now wouldn't be possible. Community is everything and there is a special magic that unfolds when like-minded fellow seekers come together to laugh and weep, reflect and dance in the woods and on the moorland edges.

My ancestors who stand in a long line behind me: those whose names and stories I have uncovered and those who are unknown to me. My life is possible because of their sacrifices and struggles, carrying the weight on their shoulders in many instances in a world far harder to live in than the one I have been born into.

Most of all, I would like to thank Catherine for her story. She has been my inspiration for this book. When I uncovered her sad tale in those dusty archival records, my life changed at that moment. At the time I had no idea how learning about the hidden ancestor, the one no one spoke of, would impact on my life. It has been a journey of self-discovery, with unexpected twists and turns; not least that her story has led me to writing my first book.

APPENDICES

APPENDIX A: TIMELINE OF FACTS

This table includes a timeline of factual events I have identified through historical records of Catherine Riley's life and her three children who were born in London: Emily Charlotte, William John and George Nobel.

Following on from the table below, I have written a description of which parts of Catherine's story are based on research, imagination and my creative licence as opposed to facts, why this is, and the approach I took.

	Date	Event	
1849	22 January	Charlotte Riley born to parents William & Catherine Riley. Also known as Emily Charlotte Riley.	A
1849	12 February	Baptism of Charlotte Riley. Baptism record notes the address of the parents and child as Falconberg Court.	A
1849	7 April	Catherine Riley (age 30) and Charlotte Riley (age 10 weeks) admitted to St James Workhouse. Reason of admission: destitute.	B

1850	5 April	Emily Charlotte Riley, daughter of Catherine Riley dies aged 15 months having had whooping cough for 8 months. Location of death: Poland Street Workhouse (St James Workhouse).	B, C
1850	9 April	Catherine Riley discharges herself from the workhouse. In the remarks column, she is 'reputed to be on intimate terms with Henry Chard'.	B
1850	9 April	Emily Charlotte Riley from the 'workhouse' is buried, aged 15 months. Cost 3/6.	D, E
1851	30 March	Catherine Riley (age 32 years) was employed as a house servant at 2 York Cottages, Brompton, Kensington. She was widowed. She was born in Ireland. John Hickson, aged 26, Barrister at Law (not practicing), born in Ireland, was staying as a visitor in the house.	F
1851	11 June	William John Riley, son of Catherine Riley was born. *Missing Baptism Record.*	G
1853	13 May	Catherine Riley (age 32) and her son William (age 2) were admitted to St James Workhouse due to 'Distress'. Occupation: Charwoman.	B
1853	16 May	Catherine Riley discharges herself from the workhouse with her son William.	B
1853	2 November	Catherine Riley and her son William (age 2) were admitted to St James Workhouse due to 'Distress (financial)'. Occupation: Servant.	B
1854	29 or 31 October	George Nobel Riley son of Catherine Riley was born [recorded date as 29 October on Battersea School Admissions Register and 31 October on baptism record].	G, H
1855	15 February	Catherine Riley (35) with her two bastard children William (aged 4) and George (aged 3 months) are admitted into St James Workhouse. Reason: distress.	B
1855	22 April	George Riley was baptised in St James's Church, Piccadilly.	H

1855	19 May	William Riley (age 4) is sent to Battersea Industrial School.	G
1855	10 July	William Riley (age 4) is readmitted to St James Workhouse.	G
1855	22 August	William Riley is sent to Battersea Industrial School.	B, G
1856	22 March	William Riley returns from Industrial School to St James Workhouse.	B, G
1856	6 June	William Riley is sent back to Battersea Industrial School.	B, G
1858	29 March	George Riley is sent to Battersea Industrial School where he was to stay until he was 16 years old. Remarks: bastard, mother in workhouse.	B, G
1859	16 June	Catherine Riley is sent to St George Hanover Square Workhouse.	B
1859	9 August	Catherine Riley is readmitted to St James Workhouse from being absent without leave.	B
1859	6 Sept	Catherine Riley is readmitted from being absent without leave.	B
1860	9 October	Catherine Riley left St James Workhouse without permission: 'Absent without leave'.	B
1860	13 October	Catherine Riley was admitted to St James Workhouse. Reason: from being absent without leave.	B
1860	25 October	Catherine Riley left St James Workhouse without permission. 'Absent without leave'.	B
1860	20 November	Catherine Riley is admitted to St James Workhouse.	B
1860	23 November	Catherine Riley leaves St James Workhouse without permission. 'Absent without leave'.	B
1860	27 November	Catherine Riley (40) is admitted to St James Workhouse. Reason of admission: Ill from the drink and absent without leave.	B

1861	7 April	Potential Census record for Catherine Catherine Riley is a lodger at 47 Carnaby Street, Westminster. Widow. Occupation Needlewoman. Born in Ireland. She is lodging with Eliza Jess (aged 30) who is working as a Charwoman, and her son Benjamin Jess (aged 12). The discrepancy is that this record is for Catherine Riley aged 26 years old, not 41 years old as Catherine would have been on that date.	I
1861	20 September	Catherine Riley left St James Workhouse without permission 'absent without leave'.	B
1861	21 September	Catherine Riley (40) admitted into St James Workhouse. Reason for admission: Cut wrist and arm.	B
1866	30 April	Catherine Riley discharges herself from St James Workhouse. Occupation: Nurse.	B
1868	September	William Riley leaves Battersea Industrial School and returns to St James Workhouse.	G
1871	2 April	Catherine Riley (age 52, born in Ireland) is an inmate in St James Workhouse. Occupation: Domestic Servant. She must have been admitted at some point between 30 April 1866 when she discharged herself and this day, 2 April 1871.	J
1873	9 September or December	Catherine Riley is admitted to St James Workhouse. Occupation: Charwoman. Religious persuasion: Church of England.	B
1876	12 June	Catherine Riley (age 60, widow of _ Riley) dies of Pneumonic Phthisis, a respiratory disease of the lungs. Location: St Marys Hospital in Kensington. Profession: Laundress. Signature, Description and Residence of Informant: James Lloyd Date death registered: 13 June 1876.	K

| 1876 | 21 October | George Riley (22, carpenter) marries Mary Ann Dupoy (20) in the Parish Church in St Giles, Cripplegate. George's residence at time of marriage: 39 Mount Ash Road, Sydenham. George's father's name: Late William John Riley, occupation: Publican. Mary Ann's residence at time of marriage: 7 Earl Road. Mary Ann's father's name: Late William John Dupoy, occupation: Painter. In the presence of witnesses William Charles Dupoy & Anne Dupoy. | M |
| 1881 | 3 April | George Riley (age 26) and Mary Ann Dupoy (age 24) are living at 21 Wroxton Road, Camberwell, Peckham. George's occupation is Journeyman Carpenter. They have three daughters: Rosina (age 3), Mary Ann Catherine (age 2) and Emily (age 2 weeks). | N |

Source references:

A: Baptism Register for Parish of St Anne, Westminster, Middlesex, Westminster Parish Records

B: St James Workhouse, Piccadilly, Admission & Discharge Register

C: Charlotte Riley Death Certificate: Registration Quarter April-May-Jun, Volume 1, Page 70

D: Charlotte Riley Burial Record

E: Charlotte Riley Poor Burial Account

F: 1851 Census record H.O. 107/1469

G: St James Westminster Register of Children in the Parochial Juvenile Establishment, 1855, 1859, 1860, 1861, 1862, 1863, 1864, 1865, 1868

H: George Riley Baptism record, St James's Church, Piccadilly, Westminster Parish Records

I: 1861 census record RG09, Piece Number 62, Page 30

J: 1871 census record R.G. 10 139

K: Catherine Riley Death Certificate Quarter 2, Volume 1A, Page 50

M: George Riley and Mary Ann Dupoy Marriage Certificate, Quarter 4, Volume 1C, Page 98

N: 1881 Census, Ward 5, Camberwell, Lambeth, Peckham, page 41

APPENDIX B: FICTION AND EVIDENCE

In the writing of Catherine's story, it was important to me to base as much of it as I could on factual evidence. I have mentioned already how lucky I was to find so many records for her life. This gave me an extraordinary level of insight into her life. However, there are extended periods of her life for which I have no information. I also do not have information as to the reasons for her decisions when she lived in London. Here in these following pages, I set out which parts of Catherine's story are fact, and which are fiction.

Chapter 2: Leaving the Ancestral Lands

There is so little I can find out about Catherine before she came to England. This is common for people who are researching their Irish ancestry because of the limitations around available records. Birth, death, marriage and census records for England, Scotland and Wales are well preserved and widely available online. This isn't the case for records of the Republic of Ireland and Northern Ireland. There are a number of reasons for this. Firstly, the vast majority of Ireland's nineteenth-century census records were destroyed during the civil war in a fire at the Public Records Office of Ireland in 1922. Only fragments survive. Secondly, civil registration only began in 1845 for non-Catholic marriages, and 1864 for Catholic marriages and births. Thirdly, although there are parish records that exist for births, deaths and marriages, many have not been digitised, and so in order to locate the records you are looking for, you need to visit the archives in Belfast or Dublin and search through the microfilms. If you do not know the townland, or even the county, then this is a virtually impossible task. Also, in the case of Church of Ireland records, only 50 per cent of the parish records survived the 1922 fire.

It is possible that Catherine's religion wasn't, in fact, the Church of Ireland. The name Riley does suggest that she might have been Catholic. Riley is derived from O'Reilly, an Irish name originating in County Cavan. Sometimes Irish Catholics would record their religion on documentation in England as Protestant so that they might be more accepted. I have come to the conclusion that this is unlikely the case with Catherine, as she chose to have Charlotte baptised in a Church of England church before entering the workhouse. For the purposes of my story, I have decided that William was Catholic and Catherine was Protestant. I got this idea from a conversation I had with one of the museum staff at Ulster Folk Museum in County Down. I asked him how my ancestor could be Protestant but have an Irish name, when the majority of the Irish were Catholic. He responded immediately with the idea that this could have been through a mixed marriage with a Catholic marrying a Protestant. There is another possible theory as to why Catherine was a Protestant with an Irish name. During the Great Famine, Protestant Bible societies set up soup kitchens. They dispensed soup to starving Catholics on the condition that they received religious instruction at the same time, converting to Protestantism. This was known as 'taking the soup' or 'souperism'. I considered this as one of the possible reasons for Catherine and William converting to become Protestants. I also considered the idea that William and Catherine converted to Protestantism so that they could own land. Having considered all these possible theories, I chose to take the narrative of a mixed marriage.

In writing Catherine's story, I needed to choose a location in Ireland from where to base the first half of her life. I have chosen to set this story in County Down in Northern Ireland, east of Belfast. Although I am not able to find out where in Ireland Catherine came from, I know she was from the Church of Ireland, and so there is around a 95 per cent chance she came from one of the Ulster counties. There were Protestants living elsewhere in Ireland, but they only made up a very small minority, and so there was a much greater chance

Catherine came from the Ulster region. County Down was one of the more affluent counties of Ireland. This may go part way to explaining how she could raise money for the boat fare across the Irish Sea. Also, there was considerable emigration from County Down in the period that Catherine left in 1848, whereas in many other parts of Ireland, by this time, the famine was over.

I know Catherine worked in service in Ireland as she took a job in service when she came to London. She would not have had this opportunity had she not worked in service before she left Ireland.

When she was living in London Catherine worked as a needlewoman. I have included this as a skill she learned whilst she was in Ireland.

I don't know if she was born into a weaver's family, but it is possible as she most likely came from Northern Ireland. This could be how she managed to find money to make the trip over to London so late in the famine years, from 1845 to 1849, with the peak in many areas of Ireland in 1847.

I also know that Catherine's husband was called William and that she travelled to England when she was pregnant. Catherine was in her late twenties when she gave birth to this child, which was very late for someone to have their first child back then. Also, it is normal to call the first child after the parent; so the fact that Emily Charlotte was called Emily Charlotte and not Catherine suggests there was a daughter born before her. Therefore, I have built into the story that, earlier, she had children who didn't survive, which is very likely and happened a lot in Ireland.

Chapter 3: City Life

Once Catherine arrived in London, her life became more documented and therefore easier to trace. Because Catherine went into the workhouse, there are records detailing every time she was admitted and discharged. These records include comments written as to the reason she was admitted and what her last job was before she was admitted. This has enabled me to create a more detailed narrative of her life compared with some of my other ancestors.

The first record I have of Catherine is when her daughter was baptised. William is listed as the father in the church baptism register, and yet just weeks later, Catherine and Charlotte were admitted into the workhouse. The most logical explanation is that William died soon after Charlotte's baptism; however, there is no record of his death being registered. This has led me to the conclusion that he died before he arrived in London, either while travelling through England or perhaps back in Ireland. However, I don't think Catherine would have left Ireland on her own without travelling with someone, especially considering she was pregnant, so I have incorporated into the story that Catherine and William left Ireland together, but that William died in England on their way to London. This was common for the Irish immigrants as they were so weak from the famine and would be exposed to all manner of illnesses in the lodging houses. In a baptism record, both parents can be listed even if just one parent is present. I believe William was no longer alive when he was named as Charlotte's father in her baptism record.

I don't know why Catherine chose to come to London. The Irish came to England rather than America for two reasons, so I based details around this in Catherine's story in the book. One reason was that they had family who had left Ireland earlier and settled in England. The other reason was that it was a lot cheaper to travel to England than it was to America. I have used creative licence in bringing her brother into the story, as it was usual for one family member to emigrate and then be joined by subsequent family members later on. Relatives sometimes didn't manage to find each other. I have read a first-hand account of an Irish street seller who came to

London to find her brother and was left on her own when she couldn't locate him. I drew inspiration from this story.

The facts around the dates and locations of the events taking place in London during Catherine's life are accurate. For example, I know Catherine lived at Falconberg Court when she arrived in London, as this is included in Charlotte's baptism record. I know when Charlotte was born, when she died, what she died of and where she was buried, as this information is recorded in the workhouse records. I know Catherine worked as a house servant in Kensington to the three children and their governess, as this information is documented in the 1851 census. I also know from that census record that at the time Catherine got pregnant, there was a visitor called John Hickson living there who was a barrister of law.

When it comes to writing about the circumstances where Catherine fell pregnant, again I have used some creative licence, but it is based on solid evidence. Fallen women would often include the name of the father of their illegitimate child as the child's middle name, so that the child had some link back to their father. William's middle name is John, which is the same name as the barrister John Hickson. Catherine would have had little opportunity to leave the house being the only house servant, and it was well known that the gentry would take advantage of women in service. With John Hickson being Irish they could well have struck up a relationship. I have no record of Catherine having to leave her employment when she was seen to be pregnant, but this was typical of what would have happened.

Chapter 4: Inside the Workhouse

George is recorded as illegitimate in his baptism record. I do not know the circumstances that led Catherine to fall pregnant with George, but I know that Catherine hadn't remarried. I do not know for certain what his father's occupation was, however under 'Profession of Father' in his marriage certificate, George wrote 'Publican'. I have included this detail within Catherine's story as in my research I have found references to women being taken advantage of by publicans sexually. This is only a theory as to the circumstances leading to Catherine's pregnancy, and I cannot back it up with any further evidence. I do not know George's father's name. It is possible that George's fathers first name could have been Nobel, as this is George's middle name recorded in his baptism record. I do not know George's father's surname. In his marriage certificate, George gave his brother's name instead of his father's name. This practice was commonplace for people who wanted to keep their illegitimacy hidden from both family members and the authorities.

I know that Catherine became a charwoman and a needle-woman as this is included in St James Workhouse Admission and Discharge Register. Catherine entered and departed from the workhouse many times, exceeding double figures. In a number of these instances, there is a note in the 'remarks' column that helped to build a picture of what was happening to her. For example, she was admitted into the workhouse once 'ill from the drink' and another time with 'a cut wrist and arm'. It was common for the Irish to drink: alcohol and poverty went hand in hand.

The moment of George's baptism is an important one, as it is this baptism record that led me to find out Catherine's name, and that George was illegitimate. For almost a decade, I was hunting for George's birth certificate. However, I found that Catherine didn't register George's birth. It struck me one day I could search for his baptism record instead and I booked a trip to the Westminster Archives to track it down.

Once I had George's baptism record, I knew that he and his mother lived at St James Workhouse. I was able to look them up in the St James Workhouse Admission and Discharge Register and gather all the information together. It is unusual for these registers to still exist as most were destroyed.

I know that Catherine struggled with her two sons being sent off to industrial school because she was registered 'absent without leave' several times in the years immediately following her separation from George. When her son William was sent away, he returned several times in the following months. This happened when there were problems with the child settling in. I expect when her second son George was sent away, she had concerns about his well-being and how he coped, given William's experiences a few years earlier.

All of the occupations I described are jobs that Catherine carried out in her life. They are all noted at one stage or another in the St James Workhouse Admission and Discharge Register, or in the census records.

I do not know whether her sons George and William ever met with Catherine once they were released from the industrial school. I expect they did, but I can't see there was ever a relationship there as they would have been brought up to think of her shamefully. I cannot know for sure what they thought of their mother, but they may well have resented her for the childhood they endured and the stigma of being brought up in a workhouse. The stories that were passed down our family line had no mention of her, only going back as far as her son George.

The details of Catherine's death are correct. The only fact I cannot confirm is whether George or William saw her towards the end of her life or whether they attended her funeral. It is unlikely, as they lived in a different part of London. I can't see how they would have found out about her death as they had very separate lives. George lived some distance away from Catherine in another part of London.

Chapter 5: The Next Generation

The annual register of pauper children in Battersea Industrial School still exists, and I have records of George staying at the school right up until just before his sixteenth birthday. The first document I have after this is his marriage certificate which states his occupation as 'carpenter'. This leads me to think that he got an apprenticeship as a carpenter once he left the industrial school.

I haven't found any first-hand accounts of what it was like at the Battersea Industrial School. Some of these schools were very poorly run, and others seemed to have been a lot better. There are some terrible stories associated with some of these schools. I have opted for the middle ground.

There was a story that was passed down the family line via my paternal grandfather, which was that George Riley was a short Irishman. All the Rileys in my family are tall, and we are known for our height. This suggests that George was poorly fed as a child, akin to the Oliver Twist story that was set only thirty years before George's time.

I do not know how George Riley and Mary Ann Dupoy met as they were living in different parts of London. The fact that they moved to a respectable suburb of London is true.

It is encouraging to see they named their second daughter after Catherine and that she went by this name, which was her middle name, throughout her life. It shows that George still remembered his mother, despite everything. The synchronicity of the dates of Mary Ann Catherine's birth and Charlotte's baptism being exactly thirty years apart is true and an interesting coincidence.

APPENDIX C: INSPIRATIONAL MUSEUMS

Doagh Famine Village, County Donegal, Ireland, website: www.doaghfaminevillage.com

Ripon Workhouse Museum, Ripon, West Yorkshire, England, website: https://riponmuseums.co.uk/workhouse-museum-garden/

The Workhouse, Southwell, Nottinghamshire, England, website: https://www.nationaltrust.org.uk/the-workhouse-southwell

Ulster American Folk Park, Omagh, Northern Ireland, website:https://www.nmni.com/our-museums/ulster-american-folk-park/Home.aspx

Ulster Folk Museum, Cultra, Belfast, County Down, Northern Ireland, website: https://www.nmni.com/our-museums/Ulster-Folk-Museum/Home.aspx

Victorian Slum Exhibit, Thackray Medical Museum, Leeds, West Yorkshire, England, website: https://thackraymuseum.co.uk/

References

Chapter 1

[1] FOOR, D, 2017, *Ancestral medicine: Rituals for Personal and Family Healing*, Bear & Company, Rochester, Vermont.

[2] FURLONG, D, 2014, *Healing Your Ancestral Patterns: How to access the past to heal the present*, Atlanta Books, Worcestershire.

[3] WOLYNN, M, 2016, *It Didn't Start with You: How Inherited Family Trauma Shapes Who We Are and How to End the Cycle*, Viking, New York.

[4] O'SULLIVAN, N, and GRAYDON, N, 2013, Ancestral Continuum: Unlock the Secrets of Who You Really Are, Simon & Schuster UK, London.

[5] *I Am*, directed by Tom Shadyac (Shady Acres Entertainment, 2011).

[6] WOLYNN, M, 2016, *It Didn't Start with You: How Inherited Family Trauma Shapes Who We Are and How to End the Cycle*, Viking, New York.

[7] Ibid., p36.

[8] Seventh Generation Foundation, *7th Generation Principle*, viewed 15.06.21, https://www.7genfoundation.org/7th-generation/

[9] WCED, 1987, *Our Common Future*, Oxford University Press.

[10] WOLYNN, M, 2016, *It Didn't Start with You: How Inherited Family Trauma Shapes Who We Are and How to End the Cycle*, Viking, New York.

[11] SMALLEY, A.J and SMALLEY, N, 2018, The Mystery School, https://thewayofthebuzzard.co.uk/the-mystery-school/.

Chapter 2

[12] LECKY, W.E.H, [1892] 1972, A History of Ireland in the Eighteenth Century, The University of Chicago Press, Chicago & London.

[13] DORNEY, J, 2019, 'Hugh O'Neill and Nine Years War, 1594-1603, The Irish Story', 10.01.2019, https://www.theirishstory.com/2019/01/10/hugh-oneill-and-nine-years-war-1594-1603/#.YdmPkC-l30p

[14] MULRANEY, F, 2020, Oliver Cromwell's war crimes, the Massacre of Drogheda in 1649, Irish Central, 11.09.20, https://www.irishcentral.com/roots/history/oliver-cromwells-massacre-of-drogheda-1649

[15] Ibid., p65.

[16] PÓIRTÉIR, C, (editor), 1995, The Great Irish Famine, Mercier Press, Cork.

[17] DAVIS, G, 1991, The Irish in Britain, 1815–1914, Gill & Macmillan Ltd, Dublin, p35.

[18] KINEALY, C, 2006, This Great Calamity (2nd Edition), Gill Books, Dublin.

[19] PÓIRTÉIR, C, 1995, Introduction, in PÓIRTÉIR, C, ed. The Great Irish Famine, Mercier Press, Cork, p9.

[20] PHOENIX, E, 2015, 'Irish Famine: How Ulster was devastated by its impact', BBC News, 26.09.2015, https://www.bbc.co.uk/news/uk-northern-ireland-34369080.

[21] WHELAN, K, 'Pre and Post-Famine Landscape Change' (p19) in PÓIRTÉIR, C, (editor), 1995, The Great Irish Famine, Mercier Press, Cork.

[22] CHARLTON, J, 1997, The Chartists: The First National Workers' Movement, Pluto Press, London.

[23] THOMPSON, D, [1984] 2013, The Chartists: Popular Politics in the Industrial Revolution, Breviary Stuff Publications, London. First published 1984 by Pantheon.

[24] Corn Laws, Wikipedia, viewed 05.03.2021, https://en.wikipedia.org/wiki/Corn_Laws.

[25] QUINN, D, 2009, Ishmael: A Novel, Bantam, New York. First published 1992 by Bantam.

[26] Ibid., p126.

[27] GOLDSMITH, O, (1770) 'The Deserted Village', *Poetry Foundation*, viewed 03.05.2021, https://www.poetryfoundation. org/poems/44292/the-deserted-village.

[28] WELLER, F, 2015, *The Wild Edge of Sorrow: Rituals of Renewal and the Sacred Work of Grief*, North Atlantic Books, Berkeley, California, p63.

[29] EISENSTEIN, C, 2020, 'Lights Out: The Space Between Stories', *BBC SOUNDS*, 16.03.2020, https://www.bbc.co.uk/ sounds/play/m000gcx5?fbclid=IwAR2mzwYGIcPkIGPi1P XbQ-bPYPzKwpx2N4SeMY-VVyPIQBsnRvqM_H12dZ0.

[30] LOUV, R, 2009, *Last Child in the Woods: Saving Our Children from Nature-Deficit Disorder*. Published 2005, 2008 by Algonquin Books, North Carolina.

[31] CARRELL, S, 2018, Scottish GPs to begin prescribing rambling and birdwatching, *The Guardian*, 05.10.2018, https://www.theguardian.com/uk-news/2018/oct/05/ scottish-gps-nhs-begin-prescribing-rambling-birdwatching.

[32] EINSTEIN, A, 1951, *Memorable Albert Einstein Quotes*, A.S.L & Associates, viewed 06.05.21 https://www.asl-associates.com/ einsteinquotes.htm.

[33] KINDRED, G, 2019, *Walking with Trees*, Permanent Publications, East Meon, Hampshire

  KINDRED, G, 1999, *The Tree Ogham*, Glennie Kindred, Derbyshire.

[34] SWAN, J.A, 1993, *The Power of Place: Sacred Ground in Natural and Human Environments*, Gateway, Bath.

[35] TRANSITION TOWNS, https://en.wikipedia.org/wiki/ Transition_town.

[36] QUINN, D, 1999, *Beyond Civilization: Humanity's Next Great Adventure*, Three Rivers Press, New York. Member of the Crown Publishing Group.

[37] MCINTOSH, A, 2001, *Soil and Soul: People Versus Corporate Power*, Aurum Press, London.

[38] TIMMINS, B, 2017, 'Scientist reveals why it's important to let your kids be exposed to germs', The Independent, 18.07.2017, https://www.independent.co.uk/life-style/health-and-families/ health-news/why-its-important-to-expose-kids-to-germs-scientist-explains-jack-gilbert-children-babies-immune-a7845031.html.

Chapter 3

[39] RICE-OXLEY, M, 2018, 'Grenfell: the 72 victims, their lives, loves and losses', The Guardian, 14.05.2018, https://www.theguardian.com/uk-news/2018/may/14/grenfell-the-71-victims-their-lives-loves-and-losses.

[40] DAVIS, G, 1991, The Irish in Britain, 1815–1914, Gill & Macmillan Ltd, Dublin, p107

[41] GOV.UK, *Employing someone to work in your home*, viewed 26.07.21, https://www.gov.uk/au-pairs-employment-law/au-pairs.

[42] TAYLOR, S, 2005, *The Fall: The Insanity of the Ego in Human History and the Dawning of a New Era*, Iff Books, UK.

[43] SHELLEY, P.B, 1822, *To Jane: The Invitation*, The Poetry Foundation, viewed 06.05.21, https://www.poetryfoundation.org/poems/50260/to-jane-the-invitation.

[44] QUINN, D, 1999, *Beyond Civilization: Humanity's Next Great Adventure*, Three Rivers Press, New York. Member of the Crown Publishing Group.

[45] Ibid.

[46] KINGSNORTH, P, 2015, *The Wake*, Unbound, London.

[47] CARTWRIGHT, M, 2019, 'William the Conqueror's Harrying of the North', *Ancient History Encyclopaedia*, viewed 26.07.21, https://www.ancient.eu/article/1319/william-the-conquerors-harrying-of-the-north/.

[48] The Royal Household, *Kings & Queens from 1066*, viewed 31.07.20, https://www.royal.uk/kings-and-queens-1066.

[49] EVANS, R, 2019, 'Half of England is owned by less than 1% of the population', *The Guardian*, 17.04.2019, https://www.theguardian.com/money/2019/apr/17/who-owns-england-thousand-secret-landowners-author.

[50] 'Lone Marcher Tracks Down MP', The Guardian, 29.05.1981, excerpt taken from SHOARD, M, 1997, 'This Land is Our Land – The Struggle for Britain's Countryside', Gaia Books Ltd, London.

[51] HAYES, N, 2020, *The Book of Trespass: Crossing the Lines that Divide Us*, Bloomsbury Publishing, London

[52] SHAW, M. 2014, Snowy Tower: Parzival and the Wet Black Branch of Language, White Cloud Press, Oregon.

Chapter 4

[53] WORTH, J, 2012, Call the Midwife: A Memoir of Birth, Joy and Hard Times, Penguin Books, London.

[54] DAVIS, G, 1991, *The Irish in Britain 1815–1914*, Gill and Macmillan Ltd, Dublin, p57.

[55] Celtic Thunder, 2009, *Take Me home*, Celtic Thunder: Take Me Home, [CD], New York, UMG Recordings Inc.

[56] Stalking the Rebel Soul is run by Dr Martin Shaw at The Westcountry School of Myth, https://schoolofmyth.com/five-weekend-programme/

[57] FULL FACT, *Claim about UK wealth and poverty is flawed*, viewed 06.05.21, https://fullfact.org/economy/uk-sixth-or-ninth-richest-country/.

[58] ONS, 2018, Wealth in Great Britain Wave 5: 2014 to 2016, viewed 06.05.21, https://www.ons.gov.uk/peoplepopulationandcommunity/personalandhouseholdfinances/incomeandwealth/bulletins/wealthingreatbritainwave5/2014to2016.

[59] WELLER, F, 2015, *The Wild Edge of Sorrow: Rituals of Renewal and the Sacred Work of Grief*, North Atlantic Books, Berkeley, California.

[60] Ibid., p68.

[61] Recommended books for readers who would like to explore Embodied Relational Therapy further: TOTTEN, N, 2018, *Embodied Relating: The Ground of Psychotherapy*, Routledge, Abingdon (First published 2015 by Karnac Books Ltd), and KAMALAMANI, 2012, *Meditating with Character*, O Books, Alresford. For readers who would like to find an ERT Practitioner, visit Embodied Relational, Therapy, 2020, *ERT Practitioners*, Embodied Relational Therapy, viewed 06.09.20, https://erthworks.co.uk/members/.

[62] Recommended books to read more of Michael Harner's work: HARNER, M, 1992, *The Way of the Shaman*, HarperSanFrancisco and HARNER, M, 2013, *Cave and Cosmos: Shamanic Encounters with Spirits and Heavens*, North Atlantic Books, Berkeley, California.

[63] INGERMAN, S, 2010, *Soul Retrieval: Mending the Fragmented Self*, HarperOne, San Francisco.

[64] Indie Shaman, 2020, Shamanic Practitioners Register, Indie Shaman, viewed 06.09.20, https://indieshaman.co.uk/community-resources/shamanic-practitioners/.

[65] QUINN, D, 1999, Beyond Civilization: Humanity's Next Great Adventure, Three Rivers Press, New York. Member of the Crown Publishing Group.

Chapter 5

[66] DUFFELL, N.D and BASSET, T, 2016, Trauma, Abandonment and Privilege: A guide to therapeutic work with boarding school survivors, Routledge, Abingdon.

[67] Ibid., p63.

[68] *Tribe: Complete BBC Series 1–3*, 2007, DVD, Bruce Parry, BBC, 2entertain, London.

[69] SHAW, M, 2020, *Courting the Wild Twin*, Chelsea Green Publishing, London.

[70] HODGKINSON, T, 2007, *How to be Idle*, 2nd Edition, Penguin Books, London.

[71] THOMPSON, E.P, 1963, *The Making of the English Working Class*, Penguin Books, London.

[72] WEBER, M, 2011, *The Protestant Ethic and the Spirit of Capitalism*, Revised 1920 Edition, Oxford University Press, New York.

[73] URE, A, 1835, *Philosophy of Manufacturers*, Routledge, Abingdon.

[74] Ibid.

[75] THOMPSON, E.P, 1963, *The Making of the English Working Class*, Penguin Books, London.

[76] Happy Planet Index, 2020, *Happy Planet Index*, NEF, viewed 30.07.20, https://happyplanetindex.org/what-happened-in-2020/

[77] JHA, A, 2010, 'Happiness doesn't increase with growing wealth of nations, study finds', *The Guardian*, 13.12.2010, https://www.theguardian.com/science/2010/dec/13/happiness-growing-wealth-nations-study.

[78] Happy Planet Index, viewed 10.02.22, https://happyplanetindex.org/countries/

[79] *HUMAN the movie*, 2015, directed by Yann Arthur-Bertrand (Humankind Production), viewed 26.07.20, https://www.youtube.com/watch?v=fC5qucSk18w.

[80] HODGKINSON, T, 2007, *How to be Idle*, 2nd Edition, Penguin, p26.

[81] WILDE, O, 1895, The importance of Being Earnest, Act 1: p16.

[82] *Born Free*, 1966, [DVD], James Hill, United Kingdom, Shepperton Studios.

[83] HODGKINSON, T, 2007, *How to be Idle*, 2nd Edition, Penguin, p34.

[84] GILBERT, E, 2016, *Big Magic: How to Live a Creative Life, and Let Go of Your Fear*, Bloomsbury Paperbacks, London.

[85] DAVIS, R, 2010, *The Gift of Dyslexia: Why Some of the Brightest People Can't Read and How they Can Learn*, 3rd Edition, Souvenir Press, London.

[86] TOESLAND, F, 2019, *Dyslexic CEOs are behind some of the most successful companies*, The CEO Magazine, 10.09.19, viewed 06.05.21, https://www.theceomagazine.com/business/management-leadership/dyslexic-ceos/.

[87] EISENSTEIN, C, 2020, *Charles Eisenstein live with Time of the Sixth Sun*, streamed 18.05.2020: https://www.youtube.com/watch?v=XpRYNobFiCU.

[88] VILLOLDO, A, 2008, *Courageous Dreaming: How shamans dream the world into being*, Hay House Inc, New York.

[89] GRANT, A, 2017, Originals: *How Non-conformists Change the World*, WH Allen, London.

[90] Ibid., p12.

[91] Ibid., p12.

[92] Ibid., p11.

[93] EISENSTEIN, C, *Space Between Stories*, Charles Eisenstein, viewed 06.05.21, https://charleseisenstein.org/courses/space-between-stories/.

[94] RUMI, *300 Rumi quotes that will expand your mind*, Wisdom Quotes, viewed 06.05.21, https://wisdomquotes.com/rumi-quotes/.

[95] HODGKINSON, T, 2007, *How to be Idle*, 2nd Edition, Penguin Books, London, p193.

[96] EINSTEIN, A, Albert Einstein Quotes, BrainyQuote, viewed 06.05.21, https://www.brainyquote.com/quotes/albert_einstein_121993.

Chapter 6

[97] HIGGINBOTHAM, P, 2013, Preface and images in ANONYMOUS [1885] 2013, Indoor Paupers: Life inside a London Workhouse by 'One of Them', CreateSpace Independent Publishing Platform, California, p33.

[98] DICKENS, C, [1837] 2014, *Oliver Twist*, Scholastic Fiction, New York.

[99] MORRISON, A, 1995, *A Child of the Jago: a novel set in the London slums in the 1890s*, Academy Chicago Publishers, Chicago.

[100] *I Am*, directed by Tom Shadyac (Shady Acres Entertainment, 2011).

[101] KENTISH, B, 2016, 'People expected to die 10 years earlier in poorer parts of UK, new figures reveal', *The Independent*, 29.11.16, https://www.independent.co.uk/news/uk/home-news/life-expectancy-britain-london-liverool-scotland-ten-years-a7445726.html.

[102] BRADEN, G, 2019, *The Science of Self-Empowerment: Awakening the New Human Story*, Hay House Inc, USA.

[103] BRADEN, G, 2019, Healing DNA and Ancestral Healing, in *The Ancestral Healing Summit 2019: Connect with Your Ancestors to Heal Your Lineages & Transform Your Life*, The Shift Network, viewed 31.07.20, https://www.facebook.com/watch/?v=1992453090866169.

[104] PERT, C.B, [1997] 2010, *Molecules of Emotion: Why You Feel The Way You Feel*, Scribner, New York. Original paper: PERT, C.B. *et al* 1985, *Neuropeptides and their receptors: a psychosomatic network*, National Library of Medicine, viewed 06.05.21, https://pubmed.ncbi.nlm.nih.gov/2989371/.

[105] HIRONS, T, *Sometimes a Wild God*, viewed 03.05.21, https://tomhirons.com/poetry/sometimes-a-wild-god.

[106] WELLER, F, 2015, *The Wild Edge of Sorrow: Rituals of Renewal and the Sacred Work of Grief*, North Atlantic Books, Berkeley, California, p63.

[107] MULRANEY, F, 2018, 'How many Irish people around the world are there?' *Irish Central*, https://www.irishcentral.com/culture/craic/how-many-irish-people, 30.05.2018.

[108] WELLER, F, 2015, *The Wild Edge of Sorrow: Rituals of Renewal and the Sacred Work of Grief*, North Atlantic Books, Berkeley, California, p63–4.

[109] Referenced in WELLER, footnote 50, Martin Prechtel explores these themes on his CD 'Grief and Praise', www.floweringmountain.com/CATALOG.html.

BIBLIOGRAPHY

BARRATT, N, 2008, Who Do You Think You Are? *Encyclopaedia of Genealogy: The definitive guide to tracing your family history*, Harper Collins Publishers, London.

BEBBINGTON, D, and SWIFT, R, 2000, *Gladstone Centenary Essays*, Liverpool University Press, Liverpool.

BRADEN, G, 2019, *The Science of Self-Empowerment: Awakening the New Human Story*, Hay House Inc, USA.

CHARLTON, J, 1997, *The Chartists: The First National Workers' Movement*, Pluto Press, London.

COELHO, P, 1995, *The Alchemist: A Fable About Following Your Dream*, Harper Collins, New York.

CRACE, J, 2013, *Harvest*, Picador, London.

CRAWFORD, E.M, (editor), 1997, *The Hungry Stream: Essays on Emigration and Famine*, Institute of Irish Studies, Northern Ireland.

DAVIS, G, 1991, The Irish in Britain, 1815–1914, Gill & Macmillan Ltd, Dublin.

DAVIS, R, 2010, *The Gift of Dyslexia: Why Some of the Brightest People Can't Read and How they Can Learn*, 3rd Edition, Souvenir Press, London.

DICKENS, C, [1837] 2014, *Oliver Twist*, Scholastic Fiction, New York.

DUFFELL, N.D, and BASSET, T, 2016, *Trauma, Abandonment and Privilege: A guide to therapeutic work with boarding school survivors*, Routledge, Abingdon.

EISENSTEIN, C, 2018, *Climate: A New Story*, North Atlantic Books, Berkeley, California.

FARMER, S.D, 2014, *Healing Ancestral Karma: Free Yourself from Unhealthy Family Patterns*, Hierophant Publishing, San Antonio.

FOOR, D, 2017, *Ancestral medicine: Rituals for Personal and Family Healing*, Bear & Company, Rochester, Vermont.

FURLONG, D, 2014, *Healing Your Ancestral Patterns: How to access the past to heal the present*, Atlanta Books, Worcestershire.

GILBERT, E., 2016, *Big Magic: How to live a creative life and let go of your fear*, Bloomsbury Paperbacks, London.

GRANT, A, 2017, Originals: *How Non-conformists Change the World*, WH Allen, London

HARNER, M, 1992, *The Way of the Shaman*, HarperSanFrancisco, New York.

HARNER, M, 2013, *Cave and Cosmos: Shamanic Encounters with Spirits and Heavens,* North Atlantic Books, Berkeley, California.

HAYES, N, 2020, *The Book of Trespass: Crossing the Lines that Divide Us*, Bloomsbury Publishing, London.

HERITAGE, C, 2013, *Tracing your Ancestors through Death Records: A Guide for Family Historians,* Pen & Sword Books Ltd, Barnsley.

HINTZE, R. L, 2006, *Healing Your Family History*, Hay House Inc, California.

HIGGINBOTHAM, P, 2013, Preface and images in ANONYMOUS [1885] 2013, *Indoor Paupers: Life inside a London Workhouse by 'One of Them'*, CreateSpace Independent Publishing Platform, California.

HIGGINBOTHAM, P, 2012, *The Workhouse Encyclopedia*, The History Press, Stroud. Reprint 2014.

HIGGINBOTHAM, P, 2012, *Voices from the Workhouse*, The History Press, Stroud. Reprint 2014.

HIGGINBOTHAM, P, 2017, *Children's Homes: A History of Institutional Care for Britain's Young*, Pen & Sword History, Barnsley.

HODGKINSON, T, 2007, *How to be Idle*, 2nd Edition, Penguin Books, London.

INGERMAN, S, 2010, *Soul Retrieval: Mending the Fragmented Self*, HarperOne, San Francisco

JORDAN, D, and WALSH, M, 2008, *White Cargo: The Forgotten History of Britain's White Slaves in America*, New York University Press, New York.

KAMALAMANI, 2012, *Meditating with Character*, O Books, Alresford.

KELLY, J.K, 2012, *The Graves Are Walking: The History of the Great Irish Famine*, Henry Holt & Company, New York.

KELLY, M.A, 2009, *Galway Bay*, Grand Central Publishing, New York.

KINDRED, G, 1999, *The Tree Ogham*, Glennie Kindred, Derbyshire.

KINDRED, G, 2014, *Sacred Earth Celebrations*, Permanent Publications, East Meon, Hampshire.

KINDRED, G, 2019, *Walking with Trees*, Permanent Publications, East Meon, Hampshire

KINEALY, C, 2006, *This Great Calamity* (2nd Edition), Gill Books, Dublin.

KINGSNORTH, P, 2015, *The Wake*, Unbound, London.

LECKY, W.E.H, [1892] 1972, A History of Ireland in the Eighteenth Century, The University of Chicago Press, Chicago & London.

LONDON, J, [1903] 2014, *The People of the Abyss*, Heritage Illustrated Publishing

LOUV, R, 2009, *Last Child in the Woods: Saving Our Children from Nature-Deficit Disorder*, Atlantic Books, London. Published 2005, 2008 by Algonquin Books, North Carolina.

LUPTON, H, 2010, *The Ballad of John Clare*, Dedalus Ltd, Sawtry.

MAYHEW, H, and GREENWOOD, J, 2013, *Tales from Victorian London*.

MCINTOSH, A, 2001, *Soil and Soul: People Versus Corporate Power*, Aurum Press, London.

MORRISON, A, 1995, *A Child of the Jago: a novel set in the London slums in the 1890s*, Academy Chicago Publishers, Chicago.

O'SULLIVAN, N, & GRAYDON, N, 2013, *The Ancestral Continuum: Unlock the secrets of who you really are*, Simon & Schuster UK, New York.

PALEY, R, 2004, *My Ancestor was a Bastard: A guide to sources for illegitimacy in England and Wales*, Society of Genealogists Enterprises Limited, London.

PERT, C, 1997, *Molecules of Emotion: Why You Feel the Way You Feel*, Scribner, New York.

PHOENIX, E, 2015, 'Irish Famine: How Ulster was devastated by its impact', *BBC News*, 26.09.2015.

PLOTKIN, B, 2010, *Soulcraft: Crossing into the Mysteries of Nature and Psyche,* New World Library.

PÓIRTÉIR, C, (editor), 1995, *The Great Irish Famine*, Mercier Press, Cork.

PRECHTEL, M, 2015, *The Smell of Rain on Dust: Grief & Praise,* North Atlantic Books, Berkeley, California.

QUINN, D, 2000, *Beyond Civilization: Humanity's Next Great Adventure,* Three Rivers Press, New York.

QUINN, D, 2009, *Ishmael: A Novel, Bantam,* New York. First published 1992 by Bantam.

RICE-OXLEY, M, 2018, 'Grenfell: the 72 victims, their lives, loves and losses', *The Guardian*, 14.05.2018.

SCALLY, R.J, 1995, *The End of Hidden Ireland: Rebellion, Famine and Emigration*, Oxford University Press, New York.

SHARKEY, O, 2000, *Ways of Old: Traditional Life in Ireland*, The O'Brien Press Ltd, Dublin.

SHAW, M, 2011, *A Branch from the Lightning Tree: Ecstatic Myth and the Grace in Wilderness*, White Cloud Press, Oregon, United States.

SHAW, M. 2014, *Snowy Tower: Parzival and the Wet Black Branch of Language*, White Cloud Press, Oregon.

SHAW, M, 2020, *Courting the Wild Twin*, Chelsea Green Publishing, London.

SHOARD, M, 1997, 'This Land is Our Land – The Struggle for Britain's Countryside', Gaia Books Ltd, London.

SMITH, P, (editor) 2008, *Henry Mayhew's London: London Labour and the London Poor*, Wordsworth Editions Ltd, London.

STEWART, A, 2015, *My Ancestor was Irish: A guide to sources for family historians*, 2nd edition, Society of Genealogists Enterprises Limited, London.

SWAN, J.A, 1993, *The Power of Place: Sacred Ground in Natural and Human Environments*, Gateway, Bath.

TAYLOR, S, 2005, *The Fall: The Insanity of the Ego in Human History and the Dawning of A New Era,* Iff Books, UK.

THOMPSON, E.P, 1963, *The Making of the English Working Class,* Penguin Books, London

TOTTEN, N, 2018, *Embodied Relating: The Ground of Psychotherapy,* Routledge, Abingdon. First published 2015 by Karnac Books Ltd.

TREE, I, 2018, *Wilding,* Picador, London.

URE, A, 1835, *Philosophy of Manufacturers,* Routledge, Abingdon.

VILLOLDO, A, 2008, *Courageous Dreaming: How shamans dream the world into being,* Hay House Inc, New York.

WALLER, I.H, 2010, *My Ancestor was an Agricultural Labourer: A guide to resources for family historians,* revised edition, Society of Genealogists Enterprises Limited, London.

WCED, 1987, *Our Common Future,* Oxford University Press, Oxford.

WEBB, C, 2010, *My Ancestors were Londoners: A guide to London sources for family historians,* 6th edition, Society of Genealogists Enterprises Limited, London.

WEBER, M, 2011, *The Protestant Ethic and the Spirit of Capitalism:* The Revised 1920 Edition, Oxford University Press, New York.

WELLER, F, 2015, *The Wild Edge of Sorrow: Rituals of Renewal and the Sacred Work of Grief,* North Atlantic Books, Berkeley, California.

WOLYNN, M, 2016, *It Didn't Start with You: How Inherited Family Trauma Shapes Who We Are and How to End the Cycle,* Viking, New York.

WORTH, J, 2009, *Shadows of the Workhouse: The Drama of Life in Postwar London,* W&N, London.

WORTH, J, 2012, Call the Midwife: A Memoir of Birth, Joy and Hard Times, Penguin Books, London.

INDEX

pre-famine life 26–31, 101
religion 27–8, 47, 52, 170–1, 296–8
retracing ancestral footprints
    168–72, 174, 209–10, 248–9, 250–2,
    262, 265
see also Great Irish Famine

Jenkins, M.-A. 162–3
Johnson, J. 60, 75, 97, 125, 128, 186,
    246

Keeling, A. 120
Kensington Workhouse 154, 159–60,
    294
Kindred, G. 69, 120
Kinealy, C. 51
King, Martin Luther Jr. 226
Kingsnorth, P. 108

labyrinths 116, 249, 250
Lammas
  aligning life with 78, 79
  celebration time 77
  as festival in Wheel of the Year 75–6
  and writing project 80, 250
land
  account of impossibility of owning
      110–11
  Catherine's family's ownership and
      use of 26–8, 33, 297
  confrontation over 246–7
  finite amount of 57
  following end of Nine Years War 47
  government taking away right to 18
  grazing sheep and cattle on 39
  and Gregory Clause 49–50
  and identity 62–5
  impact of Enclosures 44–5, 282
  memories held in 263
  people forced from 2, 41–2, 44, 47–8,
      61, 100, 175, 241, 256, 280
  reconnecting with 66–83, 232
  returning to 40–1, 65

rich removing people from 51–6, 58
school teachings on 282
suicide versus leaving 283
Takers of 58–9
and William the Conqueror 108, 109
landless 18–19, 61, 110, 247
landlords 39, 43, 47–8, 49–50, 52, 100,
    175
landowners 45, 47, 49, 55–6, 59, 110,
    175, 246–7
last of the free folk 107–11
Laws of Life 57, 59, 64
Leavers 59
Lecky, W.E.H. 46–7
Louv, R. 66–7
Lowerworld 132, 191, 246, 271

Massacre of Drogheda 47
Mayan civilisation 106
McIntosh, A. 82
McKenna, T. 221
mental health 113–18
mice, experiment on 16–17
Middleworld 132
Morrison, A. 252
Mujica, J. 217–18
museums 247, 252–3, 260, 297, 304
The Mystery School 21, 191, 233, 262,
    287

Native Americans 17, 59, 263
nature
  author's connection with 40–1, 43,
      66, 71, 118, 281
  Catherine's entwinement with 31, 38
  disconnect from 71, 102, 256
  rewilding 210–12
  seeking guidance from 231
  Shelley's poem 104
  transformational energies 235
  and Way of the Buzzard 21
  see also healing through nature
nature-time 66–7